# Unsettling Narratives
Postcolonial Readings of
Children's Literature

Clare Bradford

Wilfrid Laurier University Press
WLU

We acknowledge the financial support of the Government of Canada through the Book Publishing Industry Development Program for our publishing activities.

Library and Archives Canada Cataloguing in Publication

Bradford, Clare
    Unsettling narratives : postcolonial readings of children's literature / Clare Bradford.

Includes bibliographical references and index.

ISBN 978-0-88920-507-9

    1. Children's literature — History and criticism.  2. Children — Books and reading. 3. Postcolonialism in literature.  I. Title.

PN1009.5.H57B73  2007             809'.89282             C2007-901767-3

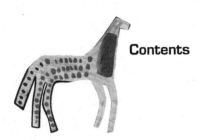

# Contents

## List of Illustrations

## 6   Borders, Journeys, and Liminality

## 7   Politics and Place

## 8   Allegories of Place and Race

## Acknowledgements

I have been greatly assisted in the writing of this book by many people who have provided suggestions, advice, and information, especially Rod McGillis, Debra Dudek, Emma LaRocque, Ron Jobe, Don Long, Cynthia Leitich Smith, Nicholas Ostler (who helped me with information on North American languages), Margaret Aitken, Elizabeth Braithwaite, Gavin Bishop, Trish Brooking, Eleanor McIntyre, Bill Nagelkerke, and Juliet O'Conor. Thank you to the Canadian team with whom I worked on the SSHRC-funded project "In Their Place: The Discourse of Home and the Study of Canadian Children's Literature." The members of this group—Mavis Reimer, Andrew O'Malley, Anne Rusnak, Danielle Thaler, Deborah Schnitzer, Louise Saldanha, Paul DePasquale, Perry Nodelman, Doris Wolf, Margaret Mackey, and Neil Besner—provided me with many insights about Canadianness and Canadian children's literature. I learned a great deal from the Indigenous publishers who discussed their policies and publishing practices with me: Greg Young-Ing from Theytus; Kateri Akiwenzie-Damm from Kegedonce Press; Audreen Hourie, then at Pemmican; Ruth Gilbert and Rachel Bin Salleh at Magabala; and Robin Bargh and Brian Bargh at Huia. Many thanks to Beverly Slapin at Oyate, for an informative and helpful visit. I thank Theytus Books Ltd. and Jeannette Armstrong for permission to use the poem "Threads of Memory," from *Breathtracks*; and I thank Annick Press for permission to use *Northern Lights: The Soccer Trails* (1993), by Michael Avaarluk Kusugak and Vladyana Krykorka. Closer to home, my friends and colleagues Kerry Mallan, John Stephens, and Liz Parsons have been unfailingly supportive; and the Faculty of Arts at Deakin University has provided me with the resources and time to see the project to completion. Finally, thanks to my family, Alan, Alice, Maggie, and Phil, for their constant encouragement.

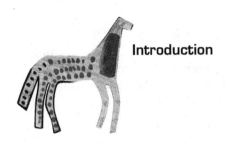

# Introduction

When I travel from Australia to America, I frequently find myself, marooned between flights, perusing the shelves of airport bookshops. As all travellers know, such outlets cater to buyers seeking last-minute gifts, or distraction from the tedium of waiting, or lightweight reading for long flights. In airport book displays during 2002, I noticed an unusual phenomenon, in that a picture book for children claimed the kind of prominent position (at the front of shops, directly facing customers as they entered) usually allocated to bestsellers for adults. The book was Lynne Cheney and Robin Preiss Glasser's *America: A Patriotic Primer*. The political agendas of this book are very obvious: to promote patriotism and nationalism, and specifically, in the wake of September 11, to reassure young readers and the adults who mediate texts to them that America has a glorious history and a commanding future.

The book works its way through the alphabet, its key terms referring to abstractions, historical events, or famous Americans, as follows—America, birthday, constitution, declaration, equality, freedom, God, heroes, ideals, Jefferson, King (that is, Martin Luther King), Lincoln, Madison—until the text reaches the letter N, which refers to "Native Americans, who came here first."[1] The verb "came," rather than "were," denotes travel and arrival, and constructs Native Americans as one group among the many immigrants who, on the page for "O" (which faces "N is for Native Americans") are said to take the Oath of Citizenship. What is occluded by "came" is reference to the fact that the autochthonous inhabitants who occupied the land prior to white settlement hold a unique position in the history of America as a colonized people displaced by waves of settlers from the late sixteenth century.

Notes to Introduction on pages 229–31.

The *Patriotic Primer*'s representation of Native Americans as merely another group of new arrivals constructs America as a nation of migrants rather than as a settler society. The book's peritextual notes include the information that "early *migrants* to North America began to come across the Bering land bridge from Asia at least 15,000 years ago."[2] More than this, the "N is for Native Americans" page manages to avoid any reference to the conflict and loss of life that marked the colonial period. The colonial figures it names—Pocahontas, Sequoyah, Tecumseh, and Sacajawea—are described in the following terms:

> Pocahontas, daughter of Powhatan, helped the colonists at Jamestown.
> Sequoyah, a Cherokee, created an alphabet for his people.
> Tecumseh, a Shawnee leader, with his brother the Prophet, organized
>    Native American nations into a confederation.
> Sacajawea, a Shoshone woman, guided and translated for Lewis and
>    Clark as they explored the West.[3]

These lame and one-dimensional sketches produce a version of American history in which Native Americans are cast as friends and helpers to colonists, or (in the cases of Sequoyah and Tecumseh) as endowing their people with benefits (the alphabet, a confederation) that mirror practices in the colonizing culture. The issue here is not how these descriptions distort history, but rather how they contribute to the myth of "this greatest of countries"[4] whose racialized others merely valorize the superiority of the European cultures dominant in Cheney and Glasser's construction of America.[5] While "came here first" echoes the title of the important anthropological and historical study *They Came Here First: An Epic of the American Indian* (1949) by the Cree/Salish author D'Arcy McNickle, the *Patriotic Primer*'s construction of Native American history inverts McNickle's approach, since whereas *They Came Here First* argues that "American" values of energy and resourcefulness are founded in Indian history prior to colonization, the *Patriotic Primer* reduces Native American identities to an assimilated, docile presence within the nation.[6]

In her discussion of settler colonization in the United States, Dolores Janiewski points out that "although an emphasis upon 'American exceptionalism' has led many American scholars to avoid consideration of the United States as a 'settler society,' it can, nonetheless, be usefully compared to other examples of settler colonialism."[7] Again, Peter Hulme argues in his essay "Including America" that to regard the United States as a postcolonial culture is to enable a "nineteenth-and twentieth-century imperial and colonial history that helps in the understanding of its current stance within the world."[8] The strategies of elision and romanticization evident in the *Patriotic Primer* are visible as well in contemporary texts from New Zealand, Canada, and Australia, which similarly enact a repression of memory concerning colonization, a manifestation of what Freud and Lacan describe as *Verdrängung*, the process of censoring and so forgetting a painful past redolent with violence and conflict.[9]

The term "settler society" seems to derive from the component "settle" a certain staidness, as though the hostile encounters occasioned by colonization have been consigned to a past time discontinuous with a modernity marked by stable, "settled" national and individual identities. Rather, I want to suggest, first, that many children's texts produced in the former settler colonies of New Zealand, Australia, Canada, and the United States evidence varying degrees of unease, a sense of being un-settled or de-settled; and second, that postcolonial theory affords a set of reading strategies capable of scrutinizing the varied and often conflicting discourses of the settler cultures in which contemporary texts are produced, and in which colonial and assimilationist ideologies are liable to jostle against anti-racist and anti-colonial agendas. Children's texts reinvoke and rehearse colonialism in a variety of ways: for instance, through narratives that engage with history in realistic or fantastic modes; through sequences involving encounters between Indigenous and non-Indigenous characters; through representations of characters of mixed ancestry; and through metaphorical and symbolic treatments of colonization. As Graham Huggan notes, it is not the case that "all post-colonial writing is 'about' colonialism"; rather, "writers from formerly colonized countries are sensitive to the largely unwanted legacy of their colonial past."[10]

The example of *America: A Patriotic Primer* demonstrates that the intentions of authors and illustrators are never sufficient as a means of understanding texts. Cheney's aim, "because I want my grandchildren to understand how blessed we [Americans] are,"[11] constructs the implied author as a proud American, a parent, and a grandparent; however, the text does not exist merely as a bundle of meanings transferred from Lynne Cheney to her readers, but also as a proposal about how to read "America," a set of terms and modes of discourse that position readers as admiring and patriotic Americans.

Within the discourses and practices of postcolonial studies as they have developed over the last two decades, settler societies have often been yoked together with nations whose colonial histories took quite different turns, such as India, where Britain exercised colonial power through the establishment of administrative, juridical, and educational systems implemented by a "thin white line" of imperial men; or the West Indies, where the Indigenous people, the Caribs, Arawaks, and Ciboney, were effectively wiped out, displaced by European invaders who imported Africans as slave labour in the sugar plantations established in the seventeenth century. In a reaction to the homogenizing tendencies of early versions of postcolonial theory, more recent studies drawing on the disciplinary fields of literary and cultural studies, history, anthropology, ecology, and economics have focused on the common characteristics of settler societies and on the differentials of power relations and representation within this category of nations.[12] For the purposes of this study, I define settler societies as those where colonization took the form of invasion by a European power, where colonizers (settlers) exercised racial domination over the autochthonous inhabitants of the lands they invaded, and where Indigenous peoples continue to seek recognition, compensation, and self-determination. While many European nations, including Spain, France, and the Netherlands, established colonies and maintained colonial rule, my focus is on settler societies that were the products of British imperial expansion.

In his discussion of Bligh's voyage in the *Bounty*, the historian Greg Dening says this about the initial encounter between European explorers and natives in Tahiti: "There is now no Native past without the Stranger, no Stranger without the Native. No one can hope to be mediator or interlocutor in that opposition of Native and Stranger, because no one is gazing at it untouched by the power that is in it. Nor can anyone speak just for the one, just for the other. There is no escape from the politics of our knowledge, but that politics is not in the past. That politics is in the present."[13] This book arises from my conviction that indeed "there is no escape" from the colonial past, that the past enters the present in the form of relations of power, systems of government, modes of representation, and myths of national identity. This is not to say that settler societies are condemned to perpetuate the cultural imbalances produced by colonial encounters; rather, what Dening calls "the politics of our knowledge" exist "in the present," where there is scope for those processes of change that effect decolonization.

My aim is to show how "politics of knowledge" about colonization, relations between Indigenous and non-Indigenous people, and the projected futures of postcolonial societies inform contemporary children's books, keeping in mind that the enmeshing of Indigenous and European histories renders it impossible, as Dening says, for anyone to speak "just for the one, just for the other." I focus on texts produced in English from the 1980s until the present, a period during which Indigenous peoples have increasingly turned to the production of children's texts to address the multiple legacies of colonialism. This is most strikingly demonstrated by the institution and development of Indigenous publishers during the last two decades: in Canada, Pemmican and Theytus; in Australia, Magabala Books and IAD (Institute of Aboriginal Development); in New Zealand, Huia Publishers; and in the United

States, Oyate, which also acts as a distribution point for texts. While most of these publishers produce fiction and non-fiction texts for adults and children, they recognize the crucial importance of children's texts within processes of socialization, and their cultural and political agendas to a large extent distinguish them from mainstream publishers.

I am well aware that there exist deep differences across the settler societies on which I focus, in regard to colonial histories, relations between Indigenous and non-Indigenous people, and cultural values. Each settler nation developed its own myths of foundation: in the United States, the doctrine of manifest destiny; in Canada, a conviction that its dealings with Indigenous people were benign and fair (especially in comparison with the violent appropriation of land that occurred in the United States); in Australia, the concept of *terra nullius*; in New Zealand, the sense that the land and the Maori people were to be subdued and domesticated by British rule. These self-promoting fictions, which occluded or disguised the fact that British imperialism was propelled by the desire for land, play out in contrasts between contemporary settler society texts.

Given the dangers of universalizing readings that forget the local and the particular in their desire for order and consistency, my approach is to attempt what Robert Wilson describes as "seeing with a fly's eye,"[14] considering texts in relation to the politics of production and reception that inform them, even as I look for features that they share. Crucially, the United States gained political independence well before the other three societies whose literatures I discuss, so that American myths of origin derive from an early separation from Britain and a rejection of British institutions, whereas Canada, New Zealand, and Australia all experienced lengthy periods as "dominions" of Britain before gaining independence. The following table, adapted from William H. New's essay "Colonial Literatures,"[15] shows when former British colonies became independent states:

1776  the 13 American colonies
1867  Canada (federating the colonies of Upper and Lower Canada, Nova Scotia, and New Brunswick; other colonies—including Prince Edward Island, British Columbia, and Newfoundland—joined between 1870 and 1949)
1901  Australia (federating Queensland, New South Wales, Victoria, South Australia, Tasmania, and Western Australia, with the Northern Territory transferred to the country in 1911)
1907  New Zealand

In line with its status as the first British colony to achieve independence, the United States occupies a special place in literary history as the first nation to develop a national literature that both drew on British models and traditions, and produced texts that reflected and formed an emerging national culture.

A ready marker of the difficulties involved in discussing settler societies as a category is the matter of how colonized peoples are to be named. So as to avoid the longueurs of lists such as "Maori, Aborigines, Native Americans, First Nations," I have chosen the term "Indigenous" when referring in general to colonized peoples. I might have used "Aborigine," except that this is not a word generally used of Maori; or "Native," except that this term is not used of Aborigines in contemporary Australia, being associated with its pejorative deployment in colonial texts. My use of upper case for "Indigenous" is consistent with the use of upper case for "Native," "Maori," and "Aborigine" in North American, New Zealand, and Australian usage, respectively. When I discuss individual texts and settler societies, I will adopt the terms used in texts and appropriate to particular cultures and groups or nations within them. Here again, I have often struggled to decide. "Maori" is a relatively clear-cut case, because it has been the accepted term for the Indigenous people of New Zealand since colonization, when it was used to distinguish the people of the land (*tangata whenua*) from white strangers (Pakeha). The word "Aborigine" is more problematic, because as a term applied to the Indigenous people of Australia it omits reference to the inhabitants of the Torres Strait Islands to the north of the Australian continent; and as it is used in Canada it includes three groups: North American Indians, Métis, and Inuit.[16] My dilemmas concerning naming reflect the freight carried by words, the fact that even when Indigenous people resignify terms, such as has occurred in some North American usages of "Indian," and claim positive instead of negative meanings, the echoes and associations of those older meanings nevertheless hover about them.[17]

Language is the primary mode through which colonizers and colonized encountered one another, and it is the principal means whereby relations of power are challenged and altered. The language of children's books performs and embodies ideologies of all kinds, since children's texts purposively intervene in children's lives to propose ways of being in the world. Settler society texts for children thus constitute an important and influential body of postcolonial works that construct ideas and values about colonization, about postcolonial cultures, and about individual and national identities; yet apart from examinations of imperial systems of education such as Gauri Viswanathan's *Masks of Conquest: Literary Study and British Rule in India*, the field of postcolonial studies has ignored texts for children.

More surprisingly, from the publication of Edward Said's *Orientalism* in 1978, generally regarded as marking the beginnings of postcolonial studies, it took more than a decade for scholarship in children's literature to begin to engage with postcolonial theory and its potential for informing critical work. It is worth pausing to consider Perry Nodelman's 1992 article "The Other: Orientalism, Colonialism and Children's Literature," because this article has had far-reaching effects in its application of Said's theory to child readers rather than to colonized peoples and cultures as they are represented in children's books. Nodelman proposed what has come to be accepted almost as a given in children's literature criticism: that children constitute a colonized group *spoken for* by adults just as Orientals are *spoken for* by Orientalists. Nodelman's mobilization of Said's work converts an analogy into a model of child-adult relations, constructing "children" as a dehistoricized and homogenized category. I would argue that children stand in a quite different relationship to adults than do Orientals to Orientalists, since children are always seen as occupying a state or stage that will lead to adulthood, whereas Orientals never transmute into Orientalists and are thus always and inescapably inferior. Most importantly, Nodelman's use of postcolonial theory sidesteps the question of race, which is central to the binary distinctions between "civilized" and "primitive" on which colonialism and colonial relations were built.

Only over the last few years have writers on children's literature begun to deploy postcolonial theory in order to inform discussions of colonial and postcolonial texts, as can be shown by a cluster of publications: the themed issue of *Ariel*, "Postcolonial / Postindependence Perspectives: Children's and Young Adult Literature," edited by Roderick McGillis and Meena Khorana in 1997; Roderick McGillis's *Voices of the Other: Children's Literature and the Postcolonial Context*; Meena Khorana's edited collection *Critical Perspectives on Postcolonial African Children's and Young Adult Literature*; my own monograph, *Reading Race: Aboriginality in Australian Children's Literature*; and a cluster of individual essays.[18] However, in many of these publications postcolonial theory is more often than not invoked by way of textual citations rather than through the systematic application of key ideas and analytical strategies. Interrogations of postcolonial theory itself as it applies to readings of children's literature are almost absent from critical discourses.

One reason for the relative neglect of postcolonial studies in children's literature lies in the continuing dominance, both in children's books and critical discourses, of liberal humanist modes of thought, which foreground the concept of self-determining individuals engaged in processes of self-actualization and emphasize what humans have in common across time and space, a paradigm that leaves little space for more historicized and politicized readings. Another reason, connected with the emphasis on the transmission of traditional narratives to child readers, is the influence of Jungian interpretations that identify common patterns of symbolism and meaning in stories from different cultures. In contrast, postcolonial literary studies consider how texts inscribe the shifting relations of power and knowledge evident in colonial and postcolonial societies, and in their discussions of traditional narratives, postcolonial literary studies resist universalizing interpretations, preferring to focus on the local and the particular.

The dominance of British and American scholarship in the development of critical studies of children's literature has also contributed to the under-use of postcolonial literary theory. American work on race in children's books has generally drawn on civil rights paradigms, historicist forms of analysis that focus on the "historical accuracy" of representations of the past, and African American studies rather than postcolonial studies. While African American studies have in common with Native American studies an emphasis on the lasting effects of racialized discrimination, they have taken different directions from postcolonial studies, notably in their engagement with the political struggles of diasporic African cultures.[19] British scholarly texts on children's literature, from Bob Dixon's discussions of race in the 1970s to studies of texts of empire such as Kathryn Castle's *Britannia's Children* and Jeffrey Richards' collection of essays, *Imperialism and Juvenile Literature*, have relied on empiricist and reader-response models of analysis, which go only so far in theorizing matters of race and colonialism.[20]

Postcolonial studies developed, as Bill Ashcroft notes, "as a way of addressing the cultural production of those societies affected by the historical phenomenon of colonialism."[21] As a field of theory and critical practice, it bifurcates into two modes of thought and expression. The first is an optimistic and even celebratory view of postcolonial societies emphasizing the transformative effects of hybridity and transculturation, as proposed by theorists such as Homi Bhabha and James Clifford, and in texts such as *The Empire Writes Back* and Mary Louise Pratt's *Imperial Eyes: Travel Writing and Transculturation.* The other direction taken by postcolonial studies is the more agonistic and skeptical line exemplified, for instance, by Gayatri Chakravorty Spivak's famous essay "Can the Subaltern Speak?" which claims that the voices of subaltern people are lost in the noise of Western theorists as they talk *about* the colonized, and by Dipesh Chakrabarty's argument that postcolonial historiography is always incorporated into a Eurocentric historical master narrative.[22]

A frequent objection to postcolonial theory and critical practice relates to the "post" of "postcolonialism," which to some critics seems to suggest a linear progression from colonialism to the time succeeding it, or even to a time free from the ruptures and violence of the colonial era;[23] but as Dening says, "There is now no Native past without the Stranger, no Stranger without the

Native," and so neither the past nor the present can be imagined without reference to the other, just as the terms "Indigenous" and "non-Indigenous" always shadow and imply each other. Like Ashcroft, I see "postcolonial" as referring to "a *form of talk* rather than a *form of experience*,"[24] a form of talk which enables investigation of how children's texts represent the experience of colonialism in the past and its effects in the present, and offers an array of concepts and critical strategies that enables nuanced and thorough discussions of individual texts and supports comparisons across national literatures.

It is no part of my argument that the term "postcolonial" implies that decolonization has already occurred in settler societies. On the contrary, the trauma and disruption of colonization continue to impact on the material conditions of colonized peoples, and are evident in markers of disadvantage that include high rates of youth suicide, levels of incarceration out of all proportion to Indigenous populations, higher infant mortality statistics than those for the general population, and so on. The sociologist Augie Fleras summarizes as follows the colonizing processes that have produced these effects:

> destruction of indigenous culture and society; colonisation of its inhabitants; forced compliance with dominant values; inferiorisation as the "other"; absorption into the mainstream; forcible incorporation into the prevailing political framework; and deference to the State as sovereign source of authority or entitlement. Indigenous peoples have been further marginalised by the combination of occupational segregation, weak involvement in the labour market, restricted promotional opportunities, and inferior educational facilities.[25]

At the same time, it is misleading to construct Indigenous peoples as victim populations, suffering the effects of colonization without agency or capacity for opposition. From the beginnings of colonization the Indigenous peoples of North America, Australia, and New Zealand experienced a variety of encounters with non-Indigenous people and cultures, and despite the imbalance of power that marked colonialism, they engaged in strategies of resistance and negotiation.

Across all the settler societies on which I focus, non-Indigenous rather than Indigenous writers and artists have in the main represented colonized peoples, given that political power, educational achievement, and access to opportunities for publishing have been on the side of the colonizers. This is what the Aboriginal anthropologist Marcia Langton says about representations of Aborigines in Australia: "Textual analysis of the racist stereotypes and mythologies which inform Australian understanding of Aboriginal people is revealing. The most dense relationship is not between actual people, but between white Australians and the symbols created by their predecessors. Australians do not know and relate to Aboriginal people. They relate to stories told by former colonists."[26] Similarly, Daniel Francis's study *The Imaginary Indian* points out that, beginning with Christopher Columbus's misnomer for the Indigenous inhabitants of North America, "The Indian began as a White man's mistake, and became a White man's fantasy. Through the prism of White hopes, fears and prejudices, indigenous Americans would be seen to have lost contact with reality and to have become 'Indians'; that is, anything non-Natives wanted them to be."[27] Judging from census figures for Australia, Canada, and the United States, Langton's claim that "Australians do not know and relate to Aboriginal people" can be broadened to apply in material terms to the experience of non-Indigenous people in these nations, since even if we take into account the uneven distribution of Indigenous populations across different geographical areas, many non-Indigenous Canadians, Americans, and Australians rarely encounter Indigenous people, who comprise around 2.8 per cent of the total population in Canada; around 0.9 per cent in the United States, and around 2.0 per cent in Australia. The situation in New Zealand is quite different, since there the Maori population comprises 14.4 per cent of the total population; moreover, Maori people are far more urbanized than are Indigenous people in Australia, Canada, or the United States. Nevertheless, the higher proportion of Maori in the population of New Zealand does not necessarily result in children's texts that offer more enlightened and diverse representations of Maori culture, at least as far as mainstream texts are concerned.

The fact that non-Indigenous people learn about Indigenous people largely through representations produced, in Langton's phrase, through "stories told by former colonists" means that Indigenous cultures and people are generally the objects of discourse and not their subjects. In the field of children's literature, one of the most important consequences is that Indigenous children rarely encounter texts produced within their own cultures, so that representations of Indigeneity are filtered through the perspectives of white culture. Nor are worthy intentions any guarantee that texts produced by white authors and illustrators are free of stereotyped or colonial views, since the ideologies of the dominant culture are so often accepted as normal and natural and are thus invisible.

An example of how ideologies of race inform textual production at a level below that of intentionality can be seen in the representations of girls and young women in an American text, Diane Matcheck's *The Sacrifice* (1998).[28] The principle that females are equal to males is a given in contemporary adolescent novels, even if patriarchal gender relations frequently resurface because of the pressures exerted by genre schemata and the expectations they imply for readers.[29] *The Sacrifice* is set in the mid-eighteenth century and is focalized by a fifteen-year-old Crow girl known as "Weak-one" because of her frailness as an infant. Weak-one wishes to be regarded as a warrior and resents her inferior status as a female; she says, for instance, "Just being a girl is nothing ... I could never live like that."[30] The novel assumes that Weak-one is an exceptional female because of her resistance to the gender ideologies of her culture, and while the book's narrative closure depicts her rejecting the warrior's life and returning to her people to become their "Great One,"[31] her acceptance of a patriarchal order is signaled by her resolution that she will go to the chief, Broken Branch, and tell him, "I am ready."[32]

A historicist response to Matcheck's treatment of the oppressed Indigenous woman would produce arguments about female power and agency in Crow culture; indeed, Matcheck seeks to circumvent such criticism in her author's note, where she explains that "Although it was rare for Crow girls to become warriors, it was not forbidden."[33] However, to contend that the novel's representation of females is in error because it does not accord with how Crow culture *really* operated at the time of the narrative's setting is to claim a universal and constant pattern of gender relations, whereas cultures are always engaged in processes of change. More than this, the argument that representations such as occur in *The Sacrifice* are bad because they are not "accurate" is to oversimplify how representation works; for texts never simply mirror a reality that exists in time and space, but embody interpretations and judgements of value. Colonial discourse theory, which draws on Michel Foucault's use of the concept of discourse, focuses on the unspoken but powerful rules governing what can be said about colonized and colonizers. In the case of *The Sacrifice*, Matcheck's representation of the oppressed Indigenous female adheres to discursive traditions that inscribe gender relations in Native American cultures as endemically patriarchal, and hence as inferior to an implied Western norm in which females have (notionally) attained equal status with males. In turn, this comparison between Native American and Western cultures folds into colonial binaries that compare "primitive," "undeveloped" cultures with advanced ones.

It is not the case that texts by Indigenous writers always produce "better" representations of Indigenous peoples and cultures than those by non-Indigenous writers. For one thing, Indigenous people have frequently internalized colonial ideologies as they have been subjected to socializing practices that promote white superiority, so that texts by Indigenous people are not necessarily free of stereotypes and colonial mythologies. More than this, as Langton explains concerning film and video texts by Australian Aborigines, it does not follow that "any Aboriginal film or video producer will necessarily make a 'true' representation of 'Aboriginality,'"[34] because there is no single "correct" mode of being Aboriginal, and because "the assumption ... that all Aborigines are alike and equally understand each other, without regard to cultural variation, history, gender, sexual preference and so on"[35] amounts to a belief in an undifferentiated and homogeneous other.

I would nevertheless argue that Indigenous authors and illustrators, writing out of their experience and cultural knowledge as members of colonized groups, are much less likely than non-Indigenous producers to fall back on the myths and stereotypes that inform Western modes of thought. Texts by Indigenous writers are liable to offer Indigenous children experiences of narrative subjectivity by proceeding from the norms of minority cultures. For non-Indigenous children, the experience of engaging with such narratives can afford an appreciation of cultural difference and a realization that many ideologies that they thought to be natural and universal are culturally constructed.

To return to my earlier example of Diane Matcheck's representation of the Indigenous feminine in *The Sacrifice*, a striking contrast can be seen in *Eagle Song*, a novel for young readers by the Abenaki author Joseph Bruchac. To be sure, in this text (and in many others) Bruchac locates the narrative in a culture not his own—here, in an Iroquois, not Abenaki, family. However, I would argue that *Eagle Song* is informed by Bruchac's sense of what it is to belong to a marginalized group and by his research into Iroquois culture. Danny Bigtree, the narrative's focalizer, has moved with his family from a reservation to live in Brooklyn, and the novel follows his progress as he adjusts to his new environment. An important strand of the narrative is concerned with the relations between Danny and his parents, which are informed by the practices of Iroquois society. Consider the following exchange between Danny and his father:

> "Why don't I belong to your clan?" Danny said. He knew the answer, but he wanted his father to keep talking. It made him feel good to hear his father's voice. Their apartment seemed so empty without it.
>
> "Clan membership always come from the mother. That is the way it always is among our Iroquois people. It goes back a long time that way. The women are the ones who hold our nations together. We have to remember that." Richard Bigtree looked across the room at his wife. "And if we don't remember it, the women make sure to remind us of it!" Danny's mother made a fist and shook it at her husband as he pretended to be afraid. Danny laughed.[36]

That the matrilineal lines of descent in Iroquois culture construct women as "the ones who hold our nations together" is a crucial piece of information interpolated into a represented relationship characterized by playfulness and humour. Here the switch from focalization through Danny ("He knew the answer, but he wanted his father to keep talking") to the narrator-focalized second paragraph allows the narrative to linger on Danny's appreciative recognition of his parents' mutual affection, so that a minority culture is treated as normative in two ways: through the assumptions of the omniscient narrator, and through Danny's perspective as a child situated within Iroquois culture and observing the dominant culture from this vantage point.

Throughout this book, I focus on two broad areas of postcolonial textuality for children: language, and treatments of space and place. These two fields intersect, because a key function of language in colonization is to redefine space through such means as cartography, the renaming of places that were already known and named by Indigenous peoples, and the redesignation of lands for the purposes of colonizers—for instance, as farming land, towns, and harbours. In the settler societies that I discuss, colonization was effected by the English language as it was imposed on colonized peoples. Further, as settler societies achieved independence from Britain, they did so by developing literatures and variant forms of English that distinguished them both from the imperial centre and from one another. Equally, however, resistance was conducted through English as Indigenous people mobilized the language of the invaders, frequently deploying what Richard Terdiman calls "counter-discourse," through which colonial ideologies were resisted and subverted. In contemporary children's texts, strategies of counter-discourse are evident in works such as *A Coyote Columbus Story*, by Thomas King and William Kent Monkman, which contests and parodies the discourses of heroic endeavour endemic in standard accounts of Christopher Columbus's "discovery" of the New World. While oppositional strategies are evident in many children's texts, I argue that colonial discourses persist in the signifying systems of language and pictures.

The imperial project was justified by the claim that it brought civilization and Christianity to savages and pagans. In truth, however, it was built on the desire for land and for the resources (minerals, timber, soil for farming) that derived from the appropriation of territory. Ideas of space and of place taken for granted in Western culture include the notions that space is empty when it is uninhabited; that land is a commodity to be bought and sold; that there exists a hierarchy of space, from "waste" or "wild" to "settled"; and that space and time are distinct and separate concepts. These are by no means universal concepts. For instance, the Walmajarri people of the Great Sandy Desert in Western Australia lived in their country[37] for over forty thousand years without imagining it as inferior to places where there was abundant water and game. As the Walmajarri say, "You [Europeans] call it desert—

we used to live there."[38] To be *at home* in the desert is possible only if the desert is seen as an inhabited space full of resources and known sites endowed with meaning.

While tropes of travel and movement across space are endemic in children's literature generally, in postcolonial texts they take on particular inflections, rehearsing colonial journeys involving the dislocation of colonized people from their ancestral homes, alluding to the expeditions of exploration that characterized and symbolized colonialism, and thematizing the many journeys through which individuals and groups of colonizers sought to find or make homes for themselves.[39] One category of contemporary texts by Canadian, American, and Australian authors traces the journeys of Indigenous children forced to travel from their homes to institutional sites (orphanages, residential schools, mission stations) in accordance with assimilationist policies that sought to induct Indigenous children into white culture. These journeys are about traversing the spaces between cultures as much as between places, and in the Canadian text *My Name Is Seepeetza*, by Shirley Sterling, the American picture book *Home to Medicine Mountain*, by Chiori Santiago and Judith Lowry, and the Australian novel *Two Hands Together*, by Diana Kidd, contemporary writers and artists flesh out the connections between journeying and identity-formation for Indigenous child characters.

The approach I have adopted throughout this study is to select texts from the last two decades, chosen from my reading of a large number of works from settler societies, and including fiction by Indigenous and non-Indigenous writers, with a focus on the large body of works that refer to colonialism and to relations between Indigenous and non-Indigenous people. Although the field of postcolonial studies increasingly incorporates discussions of ethnic and racial diversity and of the neocolonial tendencies of globalization, it is beyond the scope of my discussion to engage in more than a passing way with questions of ethnicity and multiculturalism in settler societies. I confine myself, too, to works in English, which means that I do not deal with texts written in the languages of Indigenous peoples (unless these are published as dual language texts), or with Canadian texts written in French.

Discussions of race, class, and gender in children's literature have always evoked heated debate around questions of literary quality and aesthetics. For instance, Donnarae MacCann shows in her introduction to the "Anti-Racism and Children's Literature" issue of *The Lion and the Unicorn* that throughout its history the Council on Interracial Books for Children, instituted in New York in 1965, has been accused of special pleading, left-wing bias, reductionism, tribalism, and political correctness. My position is that there is no such thing as an innocent text, that all texts are informed by ideologies, some overt but others implicit and often invisible to authors and illustrators.[40] It is perfectly possible for texts to be skillfully written and at the same time racist, or classist, or sexist, just as it is possible for readers to admire skillful writing at the same time that they resist the ideologies that inform particular texts. Two examples, which I will return to later in the book, will illustrate this distinction. An Australian example is the Wirrun trilogy by Patricia Wrightson, whose long and successful career as a children's writer has relied on the deployment, in her fantasy novels, of Aboriginal narratives and spirit figures.[41] Wrightson is a fine stylist, particularly adept in the evocation of landscapes. Her work is also deeply appropriating and Eurocentric in its representation of Aboriginality. Another example is Martha Brooks's well-received *Bone Dance* (1997), whose narrative strategy of character focalization powerfully positions readers to identify with the two protagonists, Alex and Lonny, at the same time that the novel reduces and cheapens First Nations traditions in its representations of dreams and visions.

Arguments about aesthetics and sociocultural values often founder on competing conceptualizations of narrative and representation. Older models of literary quality tended to dismember fiction into components such as plot, theme, characterization, and so on, thus detaching aesthetics from content. It is this view of narrative that, for instance, informed Roger Sutton, the editor of *Horn Book*, when he told a Native American reviewer that the term "stereotype" was inappropriate in *Horn Book* reviews because "socio-political commentary... doesn't belong in a literary review of a children's book."[42] In contrast, postcolonial theory argues, to quote Ashcroft, that "the written text is a social situation. That is to say, it has its being in something more than the marks on the page, for it exists in the participations of social beings whom we call writers and readers, and who *constitute* the writing as communication of a particular kind, as 'saying' a certain thing."[43] Ashcroft here argues that, rather than existing as a bundle of meanings and features that are unlocked by reading, a text operates as a site where meaning is negotiated by readers who bring their own cultures and languages to the act of reading. This does not mean that any text can mean anything, but that, in Ashcroft's words, "meaning is achieved constitutively as a product of the dialogic situation of reading."[44] In postcolonial settings, a reader and writer may come from very different linguistic cultures, even if they both speak varieties of English, and such differences will be embodied in how texts are written and read. Thus, a narrowly aesthetic reading such as Roger Sutton proposes for the "literary review" would omit a large part of a text's meaning.

Judgements of quality in children's literature frequently rely on naturalized notions about literariness, such as the convention that well-written realistic novels incorporate rounded rather than flat characters, that they are not overtly didactic, and that their plots are well constructed and their settings convincing. Such ideas are problematic for their inadequate theorizing of how texts relate to the world, but in regard to postcolonial literature they are even more troubling because they rely on a bundle of assumptions derived from Western notions of literary quality and apply them to all texts, whether they have been produced within Western or non-Western cultural contexts. The consequences of this hegemonic view of narrative are most obvious when Indigenous traditional narratives are retold, but they are pervasive in critical discourses and in representations of Indigeneity in children's literature.

Throughout this book, I seek to read texts in relation to the cultures in which they are produced, resisting the literary universality of Eurocentrism and the Orientalist tendency to homogenize colonized peoples. I have often experienced a sense of the opacity of texts not from my own culture; and discussions of Australian texts by non-Australians have sometimes struck me as unaware of textually inscribed values and ideas that are obvious to me. If I am an outsider to non-Australian texts, I am much more an outsider to texts by Indigenous authors and artists, since these proceed from cultures outside the intellectual and linguistic frameworks of Western thought with which I am familiar. In reading Indigenous texts, I have consulted the work of Indigenous and non-Indigenous scholars from the settler societies whose literatures I discuss; but I also accept that I am quite simply unable to access many of the meanings and implications of Indigenous texts. In her essay "Ethical Reading and Resistant Texts," Patricia Linton outlines the dilemma of "cultural outsiders,"[45] noting that the fact that "an ethnic or postcolonial writer hopes to be read by a broad or varied audience does not mean that he or she invites all readers to share the same degree of intimacy."[46] Rather, many Indigenous texts deploy strategic silences and omissions to construct boundaries that remind "cultural outsiders" that they should not seek to understand all that there is to know of the worlds of these texts. In Linton's words, these texts "require a readerly tact that recognizes boundaries and respects them."[47] My readings of Indigenous texts seek to observe such readerly tact, and so to honour difference.

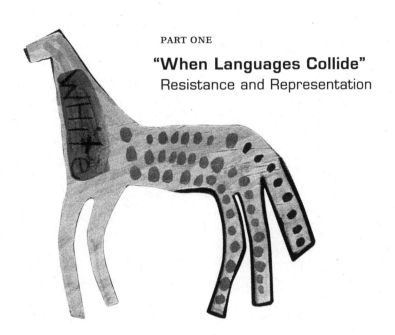

# PART ONE

# "When Languages Collide"
## Resistance and Representation

# 1 Language, Resistance, and Subjectivity

> when languages collide in mid air
> when past and present explose in chaos
> and the imaginings of the past
> rip into the dreams of the future
> —Jeannette Armstrong, "Threads of Old Memory,"
> from *Breath Tracks*

The first encounters between colonists and Indigenous peoples generally involved the exchange of words—the names of people, places, objects—and are emblematic of the central importance of language in colonization. Relations of colonial power were constructed through language. Place names were used to claim ownership, to define, and to make connections between the Old World and the New; language was used to divide tracts of land, producing boundaries between one group of people and another; the language of disciplines such as ethnography and anthropology was used to objectify and classify colonized peoples; and the language of treaties was frequently used to dispossess Indigenous peoples of their lands. Usually colonizers did not learn the languages of Indigenous peoples, but in British settler colonies English (and, in Canada, English and French) were constituted as national languages. As Ngugi wa Thiong'o puts it in *Decolonising the Mind* (1981), "the domination of a people's language by the languages of the colonising nations was crucial to the domination of the mental universe of the colonised."[1]

Nevertheless, it would be a mistake to imagine Indigenous peoples as merely passive and powerless objects of colonial rule, or the imposition of English as a sign of the voicelessness of the colonized. Mary Louise Pratt uses *transculturation*, a term borrowed from ethnography, to refer to the interpenetration of Indigenous and non-Indigenous cultures in what she terms "the contact zone," a social space where "disparate cultures meet, clash and grapple with each other, often in highly asymmetrical relations of dominance and subordination—like colonialism, slavery, or their aftermaths as

Notes to chapter 1 on pages 232–34.

they are lived out across the globe today."[2] Pratt notes that, while colonizing groups are always conscious of the effects of colonization upon the colonized, they are often blind to the extent to which marginalized people influence metropolitan modes of thought and representation; and if Indigenous peoples were obliged to speak the language of the oppressor, they did not necessarily speak as the oppressor spoke but developed strategies of resistance and self-representation whose subversiveness often went unrecognized by colonizers.

A crucial problem in postcolonial theory lies in how resistance is to be understood—as a collision of force and counter-force, as it appears in the lines from Jeannette Armstrong's poem "Threads of Old Memory" that begin this chapter; or as the more dialogical and transformative process suggested in these lines from the same poem:

> ... I glimpse a world
> that cannot be stolen or lost
> only shaped by new words
> joining precisely to form old patterns
> a song of stars
> glittering against an endless silence.[3]

Armstrong's image of "new words / joining precisely to form old patterns" gestures toward the transformative possibilities of language and the capacity of marginalized peoples to use the language of colonizers for their own purposes. In a related manner, Homi Bhabha characterizes colonial mimicry as a mode of covert and subtle resistance where the colonized, in the act of seeming to replicate the speech of the colonizers, produce texts "almost the same but not quite."[4] Bhabha sees this "not quite" quality as metonymic of cultural difference, and as capable of undermining colonial authority through its very ambivalence, which defies hegemonic control. If resistance is theorized as simply a force to counter colonialism, however, the formulation runs the risk of locking resistance into colonial binaries, so that the margins merely replace the centre and thus reinscribe relations between colonized and colonizers as inevitably and always antagonistic. Moreover, such a binary view assumes that cultures and languages are fixed and immutable, whereas all cultures are engaged in constant processes of change as they adapt to circumstances and events.

The difficulties of theorizing resistance according to a binary scheme are evident when we examine a text such as *This Land Is My Land* (1993), a picture book written and illustrated by the Canadian Cree artist George Littlechild. The title of the book refers to Woody Guthrie's Depression-era song "This Land Is Your Land," which is far from an unproblematic expression of patriotic love for country but (especially in its seldom-sung fourth and sixth verses) ironizes the line "This land was made for you and me" by pointing to distinctions between those who have access to the bounty of the land and those who do not. Through his intertextual reference to Woody Guthrie's song, Littlechild acknowledges traditions of resistance in white culture, even as he draws attention to the effects of colonization upon Native Americans. In this way, resistance is freed from a binary us/them, good/bad scheme and inserted into a dialogical relationship with other forms and instances of dissent.

Throughout the book, Littlechild puts to strategic use photographs of two kinds: those of members of his family over several generations back to the 1890s, and colonial photographs such as Edward S. Curtis's famous studies. The family photographs, several of them grainy and indistinct, contradict stereotypes of the homogenized Indian by reclaiming personal and communal histories. As well, these photographs of Littlechild's ancestors produce their own narrative about the survival of one representative American Indian family despite the ravages of colonialism and their consequences over many generations.

Littlechild's deployment of colonial photographs refers to and contests the uses to which such photographs were put in the nineteenth and early twentieth centuries, when they functioned as signifiers of a dying race caught in picturesque splendour on the point of extinction. Photographic studies of Indigenous people constituted symbols of the "primitive" cultures supplanted through colonization and reified people as decorative objects that, as Renato Rosaldo has pointed out, evoked "imperialist nostalgia,"[5] a strategy of memorialization that sanitized the violence of imperialism by celebrating ancient and preferably vanished civilizations. Such strategies effected a disassociation between the photographs and the material conditions of dispossessed Indigenous people, and Littlechild's insistence on the biographies of photographed individuals targets precisely this disassociation to demonstrate the persistence and durability of Indian cultures and the consequences of the past in the present.

In the painting "Red Horse in a Sea of White Horses" (fig. 1), Littlechild places one of Edward Curtis's photographs of "an Indian warrior"[6] astride a red horse, emblematic of Plains Indians. The building at the back of the picture signifies the school to which Littlechild was sent after his parents died; the white horses represent the dominant culture and its purchase on what is normal and correct, suggested by the check marks that appear on each of the white horses—but not on the red horse, which is "always wrong."[7] Curtis identifies the warrior as "Double Runner" and describes him as "an excellent type of the Piegan physiognomy, as well as the ideal North American Indian

FIGURE 1   George Littlechild, "Red Horse in a Sea of White Horses," *This Land Is My Land.* Reprinted with permission of the publisher, Children's Book Press, San Francisco, CA, www.childrensbookpress.org. *This Land Is My Land*, illustration © 1993 by George Littlechild.

as pictured by the average person,"[8] depicting him looking obliquely out of the frame, the object of the viewer's gaze, fixed as though in a moment of melancholic regret. By locating the warrior on the red horse and surrounding this image with signs of whiteness, Littlechild constructs a causal relationship between the warrior's expression and his state of being "not at home in his own territory,"[9] thus resisting Curtis's strategy of treating him as a type, isolated against a shadowy background.[10] The complex processes of transculturation are evident in *This Land Is My Land* through dialogue between colonial representations and their reworking in a postcolonial text.

## Counter-Discourse in Children's Texts

I now turn to Richard Terdiman's study *Discourse/Counter-Discourse* (1985) to inform my discussion of how children's texts propose new and different political and social systems. Although Terdiman's work focuses on French literature of the nineteenth century, his treatment of counter-discourse has been useful to postcolonial theory[11] because it demonstrates both how dominant discourses retain their dominance, and how symbolic resistance occurs. Michel Foucault characterizes discourse as incorporating "relations of power, not relations of meaning,"[12] and the implication of this view of discourse is that language does not merely represent and embody opposing meanings, but that the struggle for power is a struggle *over* language.

In settler societies, two counter-discursive movements coincide. For the Indigenous peoples of these nations, struggle occurs over the clusters of ideologies, beliefs, and practices that maintain the dominance of settler over Indigenous cultures. For colonists, the issue has been how to carve out identities distinguishing them, as individuals and members of nations, from their British origins. The development of literatures and dialects of English in New Zealand, Canada, the United States, and Australia instantiated the shift from dependence upon Britain to political and cultural autonomy.[13] Non-Indigenous as well as Indigenous people in settler societies mobilized counter-discursive strategies to resist the dominance of British rule under colonialism and its continuing power over ideologies and cultural formations following independence. The power of dominant discourses is such that they have often been internalized by Indigenous people. It is thus never safe to assume that, for instance, Indigenous-authored works always resist dominant discourses, or that texts produced by non-Indigenous authors always support them.

The principal characteristic of a dominant discourse is, according to Terdiman, that it should "go without saying," that it should be accepted as the normal or default model: "The dominant is the discourse whose presence is defined by *the social impossibility of its absence.*"[14] In the settler societies whose texts I consider, for instance, it "goes without saying" that Indigenous peoples did not utilize the resources of the land, that such underutilization was addressed through the processes of colonization, and that colonization, even though it involved violence and suffering for Indigenous peoples, was to be equated with progress. To maintain its drive toward what Terdiman calls "automatism," the automatic, general, and ordinary acceptance of its truth, a dominant discourse engages in strategies of totalization. The over-determined representation of Native Americans in *America: A Patriotic Primer*, for instance, relies on claims that what makes "them" Americans is that "they" are in effect exactly like "us."

A dominant discourse is always contingent and constructed, but to defend itself from conscious awareness of its contingency, it deploys what Pierre Bourdieu calls "genesis amnesia,"[15] a strategy by which it forgets instances of conflict or dissent in its formation. Again, *America: A Patriotic Primer* provides a ready example, in the nonchalance with which it names Pocahontas, Sequoyah, and Tecumseh as prominent historical Native Americans while effacing any reference to colonial conflict. Strategies of amnesia never quite succeed in banishing the past, so that, as Terdiman says, dominant discourses "always have a guilty conscience."[16] Settler society children's texts are caught between discursive pressures: the socializing agendas that influence the production of books for children; the dominant discourses that constitute cultural givens; and the counter-discourses that seek to undermine them. In many texts these pressures manifest in ambivalence and ambiguity.

Writers on (and of) children's books often assert, as John Stephens notes, that "young children require (that is, both 'demand' and 'need') certainties about life rather than indeterminacies or uncertainties or unfixed boundaries."[17] Issues around colonialism and its repercussions in contemporary settler societies are, however, far from determined, certain, or fixed. Stephens's observation is made in the context of his discussion of narrative closure, but it applies more broadly to tensions between the desire for positive character models and plot outcomes in fiction for children, and representations of colonialism and relations between Indigenous and non-Indigenous characters, which cannot help but enact postcolonial anxieties of various kinds.

According to Terdiman, the object of counter-discourse is "to represent the world differently," to "detect and map"[18] the naturalized protocols through which dominant discourses maintain their purchase upon power, and in so doing to subvert them. An Australian text that amply demonstrates the workings of counter-discourse is the *Papunya School Book of Country and History* (2001), a picture book that incorporates a rich variety of narrative styles and modes, and whose production, effected through collaboration between Indigenous and non-Indigenous people, can be seen as exemplifying the workings of transculturation.[19] Papunya is a town in the central desert region of Australia, a place where various desert clans, dispossessed of their traditional lands by the incursion of cattle and sheep farmers and by the development of transport and communication systems, were "resettled" during the 1950s, under an assimilationist policy that relocated thousands of Aboriginal people and forced them to live in large settlements. This imposition of Western forms of social organization radically altered cultural systems that had developed over 40,000 years, and that were centred on discrete communities of people who derived their identities from kinship relations and connections with country.

The counter-discursive strategies of the *Papunya Book* rely on a mode of address that accords with Terdiman's description of the most usual tone of counter-discourse, "a corrosive irony concerning the here-and-now."[20] What is at stake is the bundle of paradigms that have dominated historical accounts of discovery and settlement in Australia, especially as they have been promoted to generations of Australian children, Indigenous and non-Indigenous. Such paradigms include the following givens: that the Australian continent comprised an empty and uncharted land; that explorers discovered lands previously unknown; and that settlers opened up the land, mapped the contours of the country, and named its features. The *Papunya Book* writes back to these histories, describing how the Anangu (the collective term for the Aboriginal people of the central desert region) observed the behaviour of these newcomers and how the world of the Anangu was altered by the arrival of the Tjulkura, or white people.[21] The ideologies that have shaped dominant discourses in Australia are active and influential in the "here-and-now" of Anangu people as they deploy the strategies of subversion and self-representation enacted through the *Papunya Book*.

The various narrative modes of the *Papunya Book* maintain an enunciative position at the margins, from which they interrogate colonial discourses. For instance, the *Papunya Book* focuses on how the Anangu perceived the behaviour and activities of the settlers, and strategies of defamiliarization are deployed to position readers as detached observers of the processes of colonization. An exemplary episode is the following description of the building of the overland telegraph line across the country from Adelaide to Darwin: "Every few hundred kilometres there had to be a station with machinery, to push the messages along the wire. One station was built on Arrente land, at a spring of good water named 'Theyeyurre.' This country is Caterpillar Dreaming.... Anangu found the telegraph insulators useful for spear heads and scraping tools, but the Telegraph Line brought more and more Tjulkura into their *ngurra*.[22] This meant less water and less food for Anangu.[23]

Two clusters of terms here construct a dialectical relationship by which a sequence of events is read along different axes of meaning. One cluster comprises signifiers of European progress through the land, as communication systems are established together with their institutional support: station, machinery, Telegraph Line, insulators. The other semantic cluster incorporates key terms of Anangu culture: Arrente, spring, good water, Caterpillar Dreaming. The explanation that "there had to be a station ... to push the messages along the wire" implicitly pits the European regard for progress and for technology against Indigenous systems of relaying messages, such as smoke signals and sign systems; and the sentence "This country is Caterpillar Dreaming" evokes an entire world view based on Aboriginal traditions concerning the Dreaming, the time-space when sacred beings moved about the land creating humans, geographical features, animals, and plants, and establishing the Laws that determine the relationships between humans and other species. To say "This country is Caterpillar Dreaming" is to make an assertion about an epistemological scheme accepted as normal and natural by Anangu, and hence to undermine the epistemologies that inform dominant discourses relating to Western models of knowledge, progress, and technological advances.

The mordant humour that often characterizes counter-discourse serves to destabilize the illusion of certainty that permeates the dominant discourse. Such a strategy occurs in "Anangu found the telegraph insulators useful for spear heads and scraping tools," a statement that wryly comments on the capacity of Anangu to turn the colonial encounter to their advantage. The Anangu practice of appropriating telegraph insulators is a small act of resistance; the larger resistance is the discursive strategy of undermining by mockery, as the *Papunya Book* shows how the Anangu, comprehensively overpowered by the resources of the colonizing power, nevertheless offered a symbolic resistance. Of course the dominant discourse remains dominant—notions of progress remain pre-eminent in standard versions of the "opening up" of the central desert—but the counter-discourse of the *Papunya Book* niggles away at the illusion of certainty by which dominant institutions maintain their purchase on power.

Terdiman's discussion of the counter-discursive uses of caricature in nineteenth-century satirical newspapers may appear to have little application to fiction for children, which generally calls on narrative strategies such as focalization, point of view, plot sequences, and intertextual references to carry out the ideological work of proposing ways of being and acting in the world. Caricature, which relies on exaggeration and burlesque, seeks rather to confront dominant discourses by mockery, provocation, and pointed social critique, often through satirical treatment of the bodies of powerful people. These overtly political strategies are, however, not absent from children's texts, although they are more often deployed in texts directed at dual audiences of children and adults.

Two books by Beverly Slapin and Annie Esposito, *Basic Skills Caucasian Americans Workbook* (1990) and *10 Little Whitepeople* (1995), exemplify a style of satirical representation that relies on an interplay of two elements: aspects of Western consumer capitalism are represented as monolithic and all-encompassing, at the same time that they are shown to be fragmented and unreliable. The title *10 Little Whitepeople* refers to the counting rhyme "One Little Indian," the substitution making strange the objectification of Indians as merely items to be counted off. The life-threatening dangers faced by the ten little whitepeople include losing an ATM card, collapsing while trying to lose weight, being downsized by a corporation, and eating mouldy brie. An understanding of the text presupposes considerable knowledge of institutions and cultural practices, and for this reason *10 Little Whitepeople* is directed not at the young audience implied by the counting rhyme, but at older children, adolescents, and adults. The satiric charge carried by Slapin and Esposito's visual and verbal text has broader implications than those pertaining to race, since it lampoons a world view preoccupied with material possessions, personal appearance, and the accumulation of wealth. It is through its expressive techniques rather than its themes that its satire operates: specifically, through the intertextual reference that activates the echo of "Ten Little Indians," and through its insistence on the conformity of the little Whitepeople to bourgeois socioeconomic systems.

Thomas King and William Kent Monkman's *A Coyote Columbus Story* (1992) targets the ways in which dominant discourses produce normative versions of the past, namely the treatment of Columbus as a heroic figure and his "discovery" of the New World as a triumph for European civilization. Monkman's visual representations are characterized by exaggeration and burlesque. In the illustration where Columbus and his men reach America (fig. 2), the counter-discursive possibilities of caricature are evident: Columbus is depicted in cartoon style, a diminutive figure wearing a ruff, tights, and high-heeled boots, and his associates are shown as shady, cross-dressing adventurers. Monkman deploys a mélange of historical periods and cultural associations, loading this illustration with a ludic excess of details such as the fishnet tights and suspenders worn by the figure at top left, the women's pumps worn by the Elvis look-alike next to him, and Columbus's golf clubs placed at the ready in the boat. The cumulative effect of these details, together with Monkman's palette of lurid, even fluorescent hues, is to construct Columbus and his men as cultural artifacts, inventions of the dominant discourse. The transparent cynicism with which they carry out their roles is

FIGURE 2   Illustration from *A Coyote Columbus Story*, by Thomas King and William Kent Monkman. Illustration copyright © 1992 by William Kent Monkman, reproduced by permission of Douglas & McIntyre.

played as a theatrical double-entendre that shows Columbus simultaneously as a comical and a sinister figure, to be both laughed at and feared.

Despite their capacity to shock readers into realizing the contingency of dominant discourses, counter-discursive textual strategies sometimes traverse a fine line between subversion and an uneasy complicity. Terdiman uses the example of Flaubert's *Voyage en Orient*, in which Flaubert describes his travels through the Middle East, to demonstrate the fragility of counter-discourse. While Flaubert describes in the most loving detail the objects, people, and places he sees, his writing is itself implicated in "the social structures determined by the West's domination of the East."[24] Specifically, his descriptions of places and scenes return again and again to manifestations of European culture—paintings, practices, commerce—in the East, and to his disillusionment with the Orient as contaminated and cheapened by European influences. Terdiman argues that Flaubert's distaste for such signifiers of Occidental exploitation and subjection folds back into something like contempt for an *other* culture "conceived as inferior on account of its very availability for such exploitation."[25] In turn, Flaubert's disdain leads him to a mode of representation that accords with the givens of Orientalism—that he, as a European expert, is obliged to speak for and on behalf of an Orient incapable of representing itself.

A somewhat similar constellation of discursive tensions is apparent in Paul Goble's Iktomi books, a series that began with *Iktomi and the Boulder* (1988) and includes seven titles, the most recent of which is *Iktomi Loses His Eyes* (1999). Goble's picture books, produced over a career of more than three decades, are based in the main on the cultures and traditional stories of the Plains peoples. I will return to a discussion of his work in chapter 3, but for now I want to concentrate on Goble's treatment of Iktomi, the Lakota trickster figure. The Iktomi books have increasingly manifested a narrative mode that deploys postmodernist strategies, such as a pervasive irony, a propensity for self-conscious narrative forms, an emphasis on parody, a tendency for characters to move across and between notional worlds, the use of a confrontational and teasing mode of address.[26]

My focus here is on *Iktomi Loses His Eyes* (1999), in which Iktomi is taken in by a swindler who tricks him into signing his land away in exchange for the ability to order his eyes to fly from his head and back again. When he exceeds the number of times that he is permitted to perform this feat, he loses his eyes, and cannot find his way home. Mouse and Buffalo both give Iktomi an eye, and he eventually reaches his home, where his wife scolds him. The narrative ends when he goes off to find Squirrel, who has hidden Iktomi's eyes in Woodpecker's old nest hole. The peritextual material positions readers as amused observers of Iktomi, whose first-person address includes the following: "Hi kids! I'm Iktomi. This is more lies about me by that white guy, Paul Goble....I've warned you about him before. And he doesn't give me a penny of his royalties. So tell your librarians to ban the books. Huh? You're cool kids. I luv yer!"[27] By establishing Iktomi as an unreliable narrator, Goble undermines his arguments about the appropriation of Indigenous traditions, implying that such concerns are based more on economic than cultural concerns ("he doesn't give me a penny of his royalties"). More than this, Goble's treatment of Iktomi involves a bundle of negative implications concerning Native American culture: he "borrows" grocery money from his wife to go gambling; he gives away his land to the swindler without a second thought; his adherence to traditional modes of dress demonstrates a superficial, New Age belief in "getting in touch with [his] heritage";[28] he is attracted to alcohol; he "never bothers to 'speak proper'";[29] and he blames everyone else for the predicaments in which he finds himself. Parodic treatments of cultural stereotypes are always in danger of seeming to valorize the negative meanings they contest, an effect that applies to Goble's representation of Iktomi.

In the book's defence, it might be said that after all Iktomi is a legendary trickster figure and not a realistically drawn Native American character. Nevertheless, Goble's version of the trickster is a peculiarly narrow one, bereft of the parodic edge with which trickster narratives challenge the dominant culture, so that *Iktomi Loses His Eyes*, like the other Iktomi books, accords exactly with Peter Nabokov's characterization, in *Forest of Time*, of the "legions of non-Indian readers, creative writers and scholars"[30] who "may chortle over Coyote as glutton, thief, clown, and mischief maker and think they know him. But that is because they have not put themselves into those episodes in which he rises to the occasion as their direct antagonist—as the Indian's saboteur, samurai, Zapata, or, better yet, Scarlet Pimpernel, scheming and grinning not to get fed or laid this time, but to ridicule, subvert, and even overthrow everything they represent."[31] What Goble's narrative strategy overlooks is that relations of discursive power are unequal: the authority and influence of the white author is disproportionately greater than the capacity of Native Americans to represent themselves, so that Goble's depiction of Iktomi ignores "the profoundly *directional* nature of the exchange between two unequal societies."[32] Terdiman notes that as Flaubert wrote about the East, despite his intentions of critiquing the operations of imperialist power, "the pages of his *Voyage* appear as the *text of his consumption* of the Orient."[33] The Iktomi books similarly give the impression that Goble's understanding of Native Americans is complete and incontrovertible, and hence that he is in a position to play out the role of defending Plains culture against its own aptitude for being corrupted by dominant discourses.

## Resisting the Canon

In postcolonial literatures generally, one of the most powerful counter-discursive strategies involves writing back to canonical works, since such texts are sites of the received ideas of dominant cultures. Thus, Jean Rhys's *Wide Sargasso Sea* (1966) draws attention to the colonial silences in *Jane Eyre* by telling the story of Bertha Mason, Rochester's first wife, a mixed-race Caribbean woman; and J.M. Coetzee's *Foe* (1988) reworks *Robinson Crusoe*, making the figure of Friday central to a narrative that exposes the imperial and patriarchal ideologies of Defoe's novel. Such postcolonial reversions of canonical texts are uncommon in children's literature, apart from works such as Robert Leeson's *Silver's Revenge* (1978), which rewrites Robert Louis Stevenson's *Treasure Island*, and William Golding's *Lord of the Flies* (1954), a reversion of R.M. Ballantyne's *Coral Island*.[34]

Many settler society texts incorporate another mode of writing back, in which young characters encounter canonical and institutional texts, often within educational contexts, and resist the ideologies of these texts. This strategy sets canonical texts against the lived experience of characters struggling for identity and for legitimacy. In Joseph Bruchac's *The Heart of a Chief* (1998), the Native American protagonist Chris, in his first year attending Rangerville Junior High, discovers that in his Language Arts class the set text is Elizabeth George Speare's *The Sign of the Beaver* (1983), a novel whose canonical status is evident in the awards it received and its high usage in educational settings.[35] His teacher Mr. Dougal "loves the book";[36] indeed, it seems to Chris that Mr. Dougal's admiration for Indians of the past obscures his view of Indians in the contemporary setting of the novel, and especially of his pupils who come from the Penacook reserve. For Chris, in contrast, *The Sign of the Beaver* is "about my people,"[37] and he is keenly conscious that, contrary to the novel's representation of Attean and his people fading into the forest while the settlers establish homes and towns, the Penacook people have stubbornly maintained their connections with the land and the ritual practices that embody these connections.

When Chris objects in class that there is "something wrong"[38] about *The Sign of the Beaver*, Mr. Dougal takes refuge in an articulation of received ideas: "I have been assured that it is an accurate portrayal of the times. It's a balanced view of both the settlers and the Native Americans, wouldn't you agree?"[39] The phrase "wouldn't you agree?" implies, as Chris recognizes, that "a teacher knows more than you do and it is time to shut up."[40] Chris undermines Mr. Dougal's claim to balance and accuracy by pointing to the discrepancy between the closure of *The Sign of the Beaver* and the facts of Penacook survival:

Mr. Dougal has his hand on his chin now as he looks at me. I can't tell what his look means, but it doesn't shut me up.

"*Nda*," I say in Penacook. "No. We did not go away. We're still here."[41]

Bruchac's representation of this moment of resistance incorporates the Penacook word "Nda," which is metonymic of the language and culture to which it gestures, and instantiates their endurance. That Mr. Dougal maintains silence in the face of Chris's intervention signifies his preparedness to rethink his reading of *The Sign of the Beaver*, implying the possibility that dominant discourses are not, after all, impregnable, that canonical texts are not immune from interrogation, and that children can exercise agency through strategic resistance.

In addition to representations of resistance to canonical texts, many autobiographical and fictive works of the last two decades depict Indigenous children who encounter institutional texts, and especially dominant versions of history. In Beatrice Culleton Mosionier's novel *In Search of April Raintree* (1983), two Métis sisters, April and Cheryl, are removed from their parents, who are deemed incapable of caring for them.[42] The two girls differ sharply in the subject positions they adopt: April is co-opted into dominant discourses, while Cheryl aligns herself with Métis traditions and culture. In a crucial series of episodes, Cheryl's development as a Métis subject is plotted in relation to her reading of historical texts. When, at school, she argues against a story read aloud to the class, which tells "how the Indians scalped, tortured, and massacred brave white explorers and missionaries,"[43] she is given the strap for her "disruptive attitude."[44] As an added punishment, her foster mother, Mrs. DeRosier, cuts off her long hair, and when April defends her sister she receives the same penalty, an action that effectively defeminizes the girls and anticipates a scene in which April is accused of promiscuous behaviour. Later, when the sisters are separated, Cheryl sends April a copy of her speech on Métis hunting practices and her essays on Métis resistance to colonial rule.

April's experience of reading these accounts of history merely reinforces her sense that colonial binaries are inescapable: she reflects that "White superiority had conquered in the end."[45] Nonetheless, her sense of the overwhelming power of dominant discourses does not prohibit resistance, but channels it in a direction different from Cheryl's direct assault on white versions of history. When her teacher tells the class about a competition that requires school pupils to write Christmas stories, April submits a story entitled "What I Want for Christmas," which outlines her miserable existence in the DeRosier household and concludes with the words "What I want for Christmas is for somebody to listen to me and to believe in me."[46] In this case,

April's story subverts a genre of autobiographical writing often required of schoolchildren, one that might be expected to include a description of desired Christmas gifts and perhaps a wish for such things as family unity, the health and well-being of family members, or world peace. The effect of April's story is to expose the cruelty of the DeRosiers, so that she is removed from this setting and sent to St. Bernadette's Academy, where she conceals her Métis origins and pretends that her parents have died in a plane crash.

April's strategy of subversion in this episode from *In Search of April Raintree* enables her not to resist dominant discourses but to escape into them, a demonstration of how, in Terdiman's words, tactics of resistance "risk fostering the counter-discourse's own colonization from within, its contamination by the power of the dominant."[47] That this is a false move on April's part, a manifestation of her split consciousness, is clear in the novel's closure, in which, following Cheryl's suicide, April realigns herself with Métis culture.

It is of course the case that dominant discourses pervade cultural formations far beyond institutional settings, and Anita Heiss's historical novel *Who Am I? The Diary of Mary Talence* (2001) traces the connections between identity formation and textuality in relation to an Aboriginal girl removed from her family and sent to live with a white family in the wealthy Sydney suburb of St. Ives in 1937. Mary Talence's account of her new life is studded with references to institutional, popular, and literary texts. At school, she hears accounts of Australian history that assume that Aborigines are a dying race; at the home of her foster family, the Burkes, she is introduced to textual icons of Anglo-Australian popular culture, such as directions for making ANZAC biscuits; and her foster sister Sophie reads canonical works: *The Magic Pudding* and *Snugglepot and Cuddlepie*.[48]

Surrounded as she is by texts of the dominant culture, Mary Talence begins to wish to be "white like everyone else."[49] What sustains her sense of being an Aboriginal subject is her friendship with a young Aboriginal woman, Dot, who works as a domestic servant in the home of a local family. Dot introduces Mary to an alternative system of textuality, comprising stories about the Aboriginal children removed from their families and sent to orphanages, and words from the Wiradjuri language, that of the clan to which both Dot and Mary belong. Mary's resistance, silent and unnoticed by her foster family, is constituted by her refusal to accede to the givens of dominant forms of discourse. She is alert to the operations of discursive power; thus, when her foster mother maintains that she cannot take Mary to see a dramatic production because the performance takes place too late for children, Mary recognizes Mrs. Burke's reluctance to acknowledge that Mary cannot attend because Aboriginal people are not admitted to public performances. Such episodes lay bare the fissures and contradictions of dominant discourses, contradicting their appearance of naturalness.

## Language and Postcolonial Subjectivities

Far from being an unproblematic effect or outcome of individual identities, language is deeply implicated in the production of human subjects. Various theories of subjectivity propose relations between language and subjectivity. Thus, Louis Althusser's concept of interpellation suggests that humans are subjected to the ideologies perpetuated by institutions such as churches and education systems, which interpellate individuals—that is, which determine the ways in which subjects view themselves by situating selfhood within language, codes of behaviour, and organizational structures.[50] Similarly, Lacan's theory of subjectivity is centred on the processes by which subjects are produced through language and shaped by systems of law, conventions, and values, which are constructed by language.[51] A third framework for understanding subjectivity is Michel Foucault's explanation of the ways in which knowledge and power are constructed and circulated through the discourses that determine what can be said in any culture and what is held to be true.[52]

These theories raise significant questions for the study of children's texts from settler societies. Given that subjects are produced through language, the fact that colonizing groups dominate the social and political organization of settler societies would seem to leave little room for agency by Indigenous subjects; in addition, it is not necessarily the case that non-Indigenous subjects locate their identities unproblematically within colonizing cultures. I propose now to consider how four settler society texts construct postcolonial subjects: Cynthia Leitich Smith's *Rain Is Not My Indian Name* (2001), which features Rain Berghoff, a fourteen-year-old girl who is one of a handful of Native Americans in the small Kansas town of Hannesburg; the New Zealand novel *Owl* (2001), by Joanna Orwin, which treats relations between Maori and Pakeha in relation to an ancient story that irrupts into a contemporary setting; Brian Doyle's *Spud Sweetgrass* (1992), in which environmental activism and Aboriginality intersect; and Meme McDonald and Boori Monty Pryor's *Njunjul the Sun*, which traces the progress of the sixteen-year-old protagonist, Njunjul, as he "becomes Aboriginal" in a world of competing and conflicting discourses.[53]

In *Rain Is Not My Indian Name*, the narrative comments sharply on the fact that meaning does not inhere in language but is constructed dialogically within social practice. An instructive example relates to the text's playful interrogation of signifiers of Indigeneity and their shifting frames of reference. Rain Berghoff, invited by her great-aunt Georgia to enroll in the Indian Camp that Georgia is running over the summer holidays, reflects that an Indian Camp sounds like "the kind of thing where a bunch of probably suburban, probably rich, probably white kids tromped around a woodsy park, calling themselves 'princesses,' 'braves,' or 'guides.'"[54] If Rain's skepticism derives from her awareness of the potential for Indian culture to be devalued and trivialized through appropriation, Mrs. Owen, who wishes to block the use of civic funding for the Indian Camp, carefully uses the term "Native American youth program,"[55] to lay claim to respect for Native culture even as she demonstrates her resentment at what she regards as favouritism toward "one small ethnic group."[56]

Rain's light complexion and mixed-race ancestry ("Muscogee Creek–Cherokee and Scots-Irish on Mom's side, Irish-German-Ojibway on Dad's")[57] mean that she is often obliged to field questions such as "What are you?," "How much Indian are you?," and "Are you legally [or a card-carrying] Indian?" as well as comments like "You don't seem Indian to me."[58] By focusing the narrative through Rain's perspective, Smith positions readers to consider the implications of such encounters for what they reveal about the false assumptions common in dominant discourses: for instance, that "Indianness" is largely a question of appearance, and that whiteness is taken for granted as the standard against which difference is defined. Rain agrees to take photographs of the Indian Camp's participants and their activities for the local newspaper, the *Examiner*, working with The Flash, the young intern detailed to prepare a written account of the Camp. The Flash is initially unaware of Rain's ancestry, and when Rain tells him that she knows of nine Indians living in Hannesburg, he offers her the following advice: "They prefer 'Native Americans.'"[59] In addition to his misplaced reliance on the fixedness of signifiers such as "Native American," which he regards as more correct than "Indian," Flash's use of an overdetermined "they" provides a comedic moment in which readers, positioned to align themselves with Rain, enjoy a mild Indian joke at the expense of a white person.

The reflexivity of Rain's narration, and the agility with which she engages in dialogue between Native and mainstream cultures, contradict the tendency toward determinism evident in theories such as Althusser's, which emphasizes the extent to which subjects are interpellated by the ideological and discursive operations of dominant cultures. Rain's passion for photography symbolizes her capacity for meaning-making as she selects images of the Indian Campers and frames them. When she takes the further step of joining the camp as a participant, she does so in part to support Aunt Georgia; but her alignment with the other campers also signals her determination to formalize her connection with Native culture.

Throughout the novel, the narrative traces a number of thematic strands: Rain's shift from depression to an acceptance of the death of her best friend Galen; the events associated with the Indian Camp; her grandfather's romance; her discovery that her brother's partner is pregnant; and her strained relationship with her second-best friend, Queenie. Across these varied experiences of social and interpersonal relations, Rain is shown to be sharply conscious of how she is constructed as a representative Native person, and of the models of subjectivity presented by family members and by the other campers.

In the episode that constitutes the closure of the novel, Rain examines her photographs of Galen for the first time since his death, scans her favourite images, and reconstitutes them in a website. This act of invention is metonymic of Rain's subject-formation, in that processes of self-fashioning incorporate hybrid textual elements. She includes iconic signifiers of middle America: a photograph of Galen and herself at their lemonade stand in third grade; and one of Galen eating popcorn as part of a science project in fifth grade, testing "Which Brand of Popcorn Is the Poppingest?"[60] Alongside these she places a photograph of Galen and herself seated in the bleachers at a powwow to which they were taken by Aunt Georgia. This sampling of images symbolizes a subjectivity formed across and between cultures; at the same time, Rain stakes a claim to agency in her own subject-formation. Just as the website is a project under construction, so Rain's sense of self is incomplete and provisional, constituted by her experience of marginalization as much as by her negotiations with the signifiers and symbols of mainstream culture.

In *Rain Is Not My Indian Name*, the neighbourhoods, shops, and public buildings of Hannesburg are figured in relation to socioeconomic zones, such as the Blue Heaven Trailer Park on the one hand and Mrs. Owen's palatial house on the other; or in reference to discourses and interpersonal relations. Thus, the First Baptist Church represents the sense of order and permanence that Rain experienced as a young child, while the checkout of Hein's Grocery Barn represents the exchange of gossip that accompanies commercial transactions between the store clerk Lorelei and her customers. In Joanna Orwin's *Owl*, in contrast, the novel's setting is a key component in the subject-formation of its adolescent characters. Spirits associated with Maori traditions of narrative and ritual are immanent in the landscape, the mountainous terrain of the South Island. More than this, the farm where the events of the novel occur constitutes a site of struggle in a three-cornered contest between Maori elders who wish to reclaim important ancestral land, the MacIntyre family who own the farm, and outside interests in the form of "an Asian consortium"[61] bent on developing a tourist resort. The novel's treatment of the land as a site of struggle mobilizes ideas of New Zealand nationhood,

since it rehearses the colonial appropriation of land by Pakeha and advocates the restitution of the MacIntyre farm to the Ngati Ruru, the descendants of the Maori tribe that owned this land prior to colonization.[62]

The fact that individual subjectivity is situated within a sociopolitical
context in *Owl* means that the interpersonal relations between the siblings
Hamish, Tod, and Kirsten MacIntyre, and Tama Mitchell, a fifteen-year-old
Maori boy, are imbued with questions about race relations. The focalizer of
the narrative is Hamish MacIntyre, and Maori characters and culture are
represented through his eyes, tracing his shift from apathy about colonial
history to a dawning realization of the consequences of colonization to the
Indigenous inhabitants of New Zealand: "[Hamish] was beginning to see
what it must've felt like. To lose your whole way of life. To have your trust betrayed."[63] Tama, on the run because of conflict with his stepfather, is, like
Rain in the previous novel, not obviously Indigenous: he has yellow hair and
a pale complexion, so that Hamish is obliged to unlearn his preconception
that Maori identity resides in a person's appearance.

When Hamish removes a small, carved stone from a cave high in the
limestone columns that he calls the Seven Sentinels and takes photographs
of the rock paintings he finds, he activates an ancient story, bringing to life a
long-extinct giant eagle, Pouakai, which preys on the sheep in the district, attacks Tama, and kills Storm, Hamish's dog. The postcolonial implications of
the narrative hinge upon the fact that while it is Hamish, a Pakeha boy, who
inadvertently destabilizes the balance between humans and the world of
spiritual beings, it is incumbent upon Tama and Hamish, Maori, and Pakeha,
to act collaboratively to restore order by killing the eagle, its mate, and its
young. Hamish's identity formation is thus woven into a narrative that constructs an ideal young New Zealander, guided by respect for Maori tradition
and knowledge as it is exemplified by the Maori elder Taua Gray. In the process, he has to move beyond his previous reliance on Western epistemologies
(notably those that insist on rationality and scientific explanations), and
must accept that Maori systems of knowledge and valuing are built on modes
of thought and belief quite different from those he has assumed to be universal.

Orwin's construction of Hamish's subjectivity promotes a version of nationhood sharply distinguished from that represented by the local farmers,
who insist on a material and physical explanation for the killing of sheep
and lambs, in the form of a rogue band of wild dogs marauding around the
district. These bluff, action-oriented men fit within a representation of New
Zealanders that constitutes an enduring national stereotype—that of the
tough, unimaginative high-country farmer. In exposing the limitations of
the farmers' strategies for countering the attacks—that is, calling in the army

and spraying the area with bullets—the text undermines an older view of the nation as an outpost of Britishness populated by "real men" who subdue the land through determination and physical toil. The MacIntyre children and Tama are all too aware that the farmers' world view does not allow for reference to a world of ancient beings or the irruption of this world into mundane contemporary existence; Hamish reflects, "What hope did they have of convincing these bullshitting adults of the attacker's identity? No help would come from this lot—they would be laughed out of town. They were on their own."[64] That is, the new subjectivities proposed by the novel are incompatible with older concepts of nation, and the young characters must look to Maori elders and Maori knowledges for guidance.

Despite the novel's advocacy of reciprocity and mutual respect between Indigenous and non-Indigenous New Zealanders, there are moments when Orwin's construction of relations between Maori and Pakeha falls back into quasi-colonial modes of representation. The cave paintings that Hamish discovers at the beginning of the narrative show a sequence of events where Pouakai attacks a yellow-haired figure, who traps and kills the eagle with the assistance of his companions. These paintings, created hundreds of years before the setting of the novel, feature the MacIntyre children and Tama, and thus imply, as Hamish says, that the events of the narrative are "sort of predestined."[65] Such a claim to the incorporation of Pakeha figures into Maori textuality comes uncomfortably close to indigenizing the non-Indigenous, thereby situating imperialism within an amelioristic and deterministic schema.

I began my discussion of *Owl* by noting the significance of place for constructions of identity formation in this novel. In the last few pages, the young characters are shown to speculate about their individual futures, and it is striking that for the three McIntyre children selfhood is bound up with orientations toward the land: Tod plans to undertake a course in adventure tourism; Kirsten proposes to study agriculture as a pathway to a farming career; and Hamish imagines himself as an archaeologist. Tama plans his progress toward becoming Maori in relation to his recovery of family and his acquisition of traditional knowledge and language: "Back home to check my Mum's okay, and the kids. Then, I dunno. Check out some of my background. Learn some stuff."[66] In the exchange that follows, Hamish reminds Tama that the MacIntyre farm is now Ngati Ruru land, and that Tama is thus entitled to undertake a training scheme to become a farmer. For his part, Tama is uncomfortably conscious of the MacIntyres' attachment to their former home. Hamish acknowledges, "It's your place too ... you being Ngati Ruru—you belong here":[67] his words advocate intersubjective relations between Maori and Pakeha that acknowledge both the ancient connections of

Indigenous people to the land and the significance of the land as home for the descendants of settlers.

Like *Rain Is Not My Indian Name*, the Australian novel *Njunjul the Sun* is focalized through the perspective of an Indigenous protagonist whose identity formation is traced across a sequence of significant events. The opening words of *Njunjul the Sun* are "Our home's gone,"[68] a reference in its narrowest sense to the demolition of the house in which Njunjul grew up with his siblings and parents, and from where he moved to live with his Aunty Milly in Happy Valley, an Aboriginal community on the outskirts of a country town. More broadly, the statement refers to Njunjul's sense of displacement as he struggles to forge his identity, with his development as an Aboriginal subject situated against the depiction of an Australia where formulations of nationhood are based on a strategic forgetting of the colonial past.

In the first sequence of the novel, Njunjul travels by bus from Happy Valley to Sydney, the "big smoke,"[69] where he is to live with his Uncle Garth and Emma, Garth's non-Aboriginal partner. Njunjul's family have gathered the funds to support his journey because they are anxious about his well-being: he is, they think, in danger of succumbing to depression following a beating at the hands of the police. Njunjul regards Happy Valley as "Un-happy Valley,"[70] its location next to the town cemetery a reminder that "many of us mob buried over there."[71] The novel's references to the high incidence of youth suicide and incarceration among Aboriginal populations underpin its treatment of Njunjul's fragmented subjectivity, caught in his description of himself as drifting in a world where "my skin don't fit me no more,"[72] where Aboriginal culture is devalued while Njunjul's fantasies of living a glamorous existence as a basketball star offer an illusory escape.

One of the most telling episodes in the novel occurs when Njunjul accompanies Emma to the school where she teaches, in order to enroll as a student. Accustomed to the more ethnically homogeneous setting of a country town, where relations between Anglo-Australians and Aborigines are conducted according to long-observed protocols whereby the two groups "keep to [their] own places,"[73] Njunjul finds himself in a school population that is ethnically diverse and multilingual. His sense of being out of place in this setting is conveyed through his reflections on the welcome sign in the school office, which is written in the many languages of the students:

> Then I'm looking at that sign up above the front desk. I can read "Welcome," that's it, but. I'm trying to get my head around all these other languages written up there. What is this place? The United Nations?
>
> I'm starting to get it. Aunty Em teaches English as a second language. That's 'cause no one talks the same first language. Now I'm wishing I had my language. Mine got taken away, but.[74]

Njunjul's reflection on the punishments meted out to Aboriginal people who spoke their languages during colonial times produces a sharp contrast between the promotion of diversity in the contemporary school setting and the weight of colonial and assimilationist regimes: "Down here ... you can hear these kids talking their different ways all over the place. Even the asphalt looks like it's got its own language. Makes me sad as. Gives me that death feeling like I got nothing of me left."[75] The school setting is here represented as a homologue of the nation, whose multicultural mix conceals its settler origins and its colonial foundations. Caught between his sense of the plenitude of languages spoken by the "kids talking their different ways" and his own lack of a language that articulates his sense of self, Njunjul refuses to attend school, citing his sense of a fractured selfhood, of which part is "back [in Happy Valley] in those broken up pieces," while in his life in the city he is "still travelling, not arrived nowhere."[76]

The point when Njunjul resolves to become an Aboriginal subject is the moment when he asks his uncle to teach him the dances and traditions of the Kunggandji nation to which they both belong. Towards the end of the novel, Njunjul returns to a school setting as his uncle's apprentice in a performance of dance and stories. This episode symbolizes Njunjul's recuperation of Aboriginal traditions and offers a corrective to the earlier representation of the school as a place where Aboriginal culture is invisible. As Njunjul plays out the part of a "binna-gurri [heedless] hard-head boy-with-attitude,"[77] his performance of the role inscribes his growing capacity for reflection, embodied in his sense that he has left behind the "binna-gurri boy" of his former self.

When the schoolchildren, guided by Njunjul and his uncle, participate in a dance honouring totemic figures such as the crocodile, the kangaroo, and the goanna, their bodies enact an exemplum, a model of how non-Aboriginal Australians might learn from Indigenous people and cultures. These children, who have not learned the lessons of racism, represent a version of Australianness that acknowledges the primacy of Aboriginal culture, its powerful presence in the land, and its capacity to inform the lives and value-systems of non-Aboriginal Australians.

Aboriginal traditions of narrative are in many ways quite different from Western practices, and *Njunjul the Sun* exemplifies a feature common in Aboriginal narratives—that is, that characters are viewed within a typology of human and other figures. Thus, the relationship between Njunjul and his Uncle Garth situates Njunjul as an initiate and his uncle as a mentor, and triggers a process whereby Njunjul will be introduced to stories and dances according to ancient economies of knowledge. In contrast, Njunjul's relationship with his neighbour Rhonda is built on her view of him as representing a universalized Aboriginal victimhood, a cipher on which to load her New Age fantasies of primitive environmentalists, and is thus a type of a dysfunctional mode of relations between Aboriginal and non-Aboriginal Australians.

I will argue in chapter 2 that many Indigenous texts are built on narrative and conceptual models quite different from those that prevail in Western culture. This is especially the case in relation to conceptions of subjectivity, and Njunjul's identity formation in *Njunjul the Sun* is built upon a set of principles somewhat different from those privileged in mainstream Western texts. For instance, Njunjul's development as a subject is dependent upon his acceptance of the authority of his uncle, since the relationship between uncle and nephew carries significances connected with protocols governing access to narratives and traditions. Such a formulation of self-actualization, centred on kinship, community, and ritual, constitutes a radical contrast to mainstream young-adult narratives, in which rites of passage to adulthood are commonly represented in narratives featuring individual growth and agency.

Brian Doyle's novel *Spud Sweetgrass* locates Aboriginality in the context of a Canadian national identity characterized by cultural and ethnic diversity: Spud Sweetgrass, the first-person narrator, describes himself as "part Irish and part Abo and part of a whole lot of other things"[78] and his girlfriend Connie Pan as "half Vietnamese and half Chinese," so that "if I married Connie Pan and we had babies, the babies would be part Chinese, part Vietnamese, part Irish, part Abo and part of a whole lot of other things. What a mix-up!"[79] Within this formulation of national identity, it seems that Aboriginality is figured as merely one of the ethnic and cultural minorities that constitute the modern nation of Canada. However, Doyle's narrative seems to privilege Spud's Aboriginal heritage over his Irish ancestry or the other ethnicities that contribute to his construction as a multicultural figure; for the narrative of *Spud Sweetgrass* is framed by a prologue and epilogue that describe Spud's ninth birthday, when his mother and father took him to the bush and left him, with a knife, a fishing line, and one match, to fend for himself for one afternoon and night.

Doyle's strategy of situating the narrative within this frame invests the events of the story with a certain weightiness, as though they are folded into the ritual testing that Spud experienced at the age of nine. Despite this, Aboriginality is figured through a narrow range of representations, one of which is signaled in Spud's description of his encounter with his teacher, Mr. Boyle:

> "Let's go down and see the man downstairs," [Boyle] says, and puts his hand out and grabs my arm.
> I throw his hand off. I'm just as tall as Boyle. Our noses are almost touching. We look like that famous photograph of the soldier and the Mohawk Warrior that was in all the newspapers during the Oka crisis![80]

The intertextual reference evoked here is that of an iconic photograph that came to represent the tense standoff between Mohawks and soldiers in 1990, when conflict arose over a plan by the town of Oka (near Montreal) to enlarge a golf course on land claimed by the Kanesatake Mohawks. This association locates Spud within Aboriginal traditions of dissent and resistance, a strand of signification that permeates the novel's plot, which concerns Spud's attempts to discover who is polluting Westboro Beach by offloading waste oil into the city's sewer system. When Spud's mother discovers the secret he has kept from her, that he has been suspended from Ottawa Tech because of his argument with Mr. Boyle, she warns him that he resembles his dead father: "She's yelling how my father got laid off at the paper mill for mouthing off and how I'm doing the same now and mouthing off."[81] Later, Spud's employer Mr. Fryday makes a direct connection between Spud's environmentalism and his Aboriginal ancestry: "'You're just like your father. You Abos are all the same. Making stuff up about pollution. Your father was kicked out of his job at the paper plant across the river for the same thing! When will you ever learn?'"[82] Another formulation of Aboriginality promoted in *Spud Sweetgrass* involves spiritual beliefs and ritual practices. When Spud seeks help from "Nenaposh the Medicine Man,"[83] an old friend of his father's, Nenaposh asks him to provide tobacco and a gift, which is used when Nenaposh carries out a smoking ceremony on Westboro Beach, a ceremony brought to an end when the police intervene. In producing a formulation of Aboriginality focused around environmental activism, disregard for authority, and ritual practices, the narrative promotes the idea of a pre-existing and fixed Aboriginal subjectivity.

Spud's consciousness of his Aboriginality is mediated through perspectives external to him: the picture of the Mohawk warrior and soldier at Oka, his mother's remark that he "mouths off" just like his father, and Mr. Fryday's reference to his father's activism. The narrative insistence on external verifications of Spud's Aboriginal heritage, together with the framing of the narrative within the ritual testing he experienced as a child, produce a curiously segmented sense of selfhood, as though Spud's subjectivity comprises a cluster of features or traits, some Aboriginal and others not. The implications of this style of representation are, first, that Aboriginality is defined by virtue of its difference from non-Aboriginal Canadian culture; and, second, that if Spud is viewed as a symptomatic Canadian figure, Aboriginality figures as a component of a national identity constructed as a patchwork of historical and cultural traces.

As this chapter demonstrates, representations of subjectivities in settler society texts eloquently attest to the diversity and complexity of cultural discourses in contemporary postcolonial nations. Some texts, such as *Owl* and

*Spud Sweetgrass*, allude to the ways national identities intersect with constructions of Indigeneity; in others, such as *Njunjul the Sun* and *Rain Is Not My Indian Name*, the focus is rather on the identity formation of Aboriginal subjects. To close this chapter with *Spud Sweetgrass* is to gesture toward ambivalence and contradiction; for even as this novel seems to promote a celebratory view of Spud's Aboriginal heritage, whiteness is taken for granted as the standard against which Aboriginality is defined, and Aboriginal identities are restricted to a limited range of representational modes. Toward the end of the novel, Spud learns that a heavy downpour of rain is needed to flush out the grease that has been dumped into the sewers of the city of Ottawa. He reflects, "There's an idea that my father would like. Praying for rain. To God, or the great Spirit of the Abos!"[84] In this moment of textual slippage, the language of the narrative constructs an either/or choice: "God, or the great Spirit of the Abos." Leaving aside the homogenizing and trivializing effect of this phrase, what is also signalled is the sense of a split consciousness, between "us" and "them," with the term "the Abos" suggestive of an identity outside Spud's subjectivity—"God" as the familiar, given, normal term, and "the great Spirit of the Abos" as an exotic, strange, and alien formulation of the sacred.

The texts I discuss in this chapter introduce many of the concepts I explore through this book. A critical aspect of postcolonial textuality is that of representation, which in Bill Ashcroft's words refers both to "both the site of identity formation and the site of the *struggle* over identity formation."[85] In chapter 2 I consider how texts by Indigenous authors and illustrators, produced in the language of the colonizers, both construct Indigenous subjectivities and also thematize the struggles over identity formation that are central to the experience of colonized peoples and their descendants. Chapter 3 focuses on the issues that arise when non-Indigenous authors represent Indigenous cultures: in particular, questions of authority, notions of authenticity, and what constitutes appropriation.

## 2 Indigenous Texts and Publishers

You must not lose, leave your culture behind and story.
You got to hang on and give it behind ... your children.
Keep going.　　　　　—Bill Neidjie, *Story about Feeling*

In *Jingle Dancer* (2000), by Cynthia Leitich Smith, Cornelius Van Wright, and Ying-Hwa Hu, the protagonist Jenna dreams of jingle-dancing like her Grandma Wolfe, but it is too late to mail-order jingles for the coming powwow.[1] She visits her Great-aunt Sis, her friend Mrs. Scott, her cousin Elizabeth, and finally Grandma Wolfe, each of whom provides her with jingles so that she ends up with enough for four rows, which are sewn onto her dress by her grandmother. At the powwow, Jenna dances for each of the women who have helped her, ending with Grandma Wolfe, who "warmed like Sun."[2] The story is shaped by Native American narrative traditions in a number of ways. First, it is organized around the number four: the stages of life represented by the four women, the rows of jingles, the four visits, and the four directions taken by Jenna as she proceeds on her quest. Second, the passage of time is signified by reference to the personified figures of moon and sun ("As Moon kissed Sun good night"; "As Sun arrived at midcircle").[3] Third, when Jenna visits Great-aunt Sis, she is told a Muscogee Creek story about Bat, inserted as an interpolated story within the account of Jenna's progress toward the state of jingle dancer, so alluding to Native American traditions whereby cultural values are transmitted indirectly and through narrative. Crucially, the significances of *Jingle Dancer* are located in Jenna's experience of interdependence and communal endeavour as the four women help her and she in turn honours them by dancing.

What distinguishes *Jingle Dancer* from the vast majority of settler society texts is that it treats as normal and natural Jenna's aspirations and the values of her culture. In this way, it offers Native readers the kind of narrative

Notes to chapter 2 on pages 235–37.

subjectivity taken for granted by the white children who are the implied readers of most children's literature, while positioning non-Indigenous readers as outsiders to a culture that they may imaginatively comprehend but that is marked by difference. In her essay "A Different Drum: Native American Writing," Smith describes the advice given her by an author unsettled by the structure of *Jingle Dancer*: "'It's three,' I was told by a living legend. "Three because that's the tradition. Three pigs, three wishes, three goats. The Father, Son, and the Holy Ghost. It's three, always three, because that's what feels right.'"[4] The conviction of the "living legend" that three is "what feels right" is of course a highly Eurocentric view of what is normal, built on a lifetime of narrative experience incorporating Western folktales ("three pigs, three wishes, three goats") and Christian traditions ("the Father, Son and the Holy Ghost"). The "legend" has internalized these narrative structures so thoroughly that a story based on the number four is literally unthinkable.

In her essay, Smith describes the processes of self-censorship that shaped her writing of a story incorporating "a heavy dose of old-time Indian humor— a slow-boiling, ridiculous situation becoming ever more ridiculous."[5] On the advice of two non-Indian readers, she cut out the joke so that the story would appeal to a mainstream audience; but she was left with questions about her own practices as an author and about diversity in children's literature: "Is there any place in children's books for writing that reflects Native idiosyncrasies? Or rather, if diversity of voice matters at all, does it only apply to diversity that appeals to the mainstream audience?"[6] Many Indigenous authors tell similar stories about the dilemmas they face when writing for mainstream audiences, but aside from self-censorship of the kind Smith describes, systemic forms of intervention occur in mainstream publishing companies as the processes of selection, translation, editing, and marketing typically shape Indigenous texts into mainstream products. In the settler societies I consider, access to publishing houses favours those for whom English (and, in francophone Quebec, French) is their first language, and the minority status of Indigenous readerships ensures that mainstream publishers produce relatively little Indigenous writing except that which can readily be marketed to non-Indigenous readers. There are notable exceptions: in Australia, University of Queensland Press, which publishes Aboriginal work in its well-regarded Black Australian Writers Series; in New Zealand, Reed Publishing, which has produced many Maori works; and in the United States, Children's Book Press, which publishes picture books by Native American authors and illustrators in addition to work by writers from other minority cultures. In general, however, publishing houses in settler societies are dominated by the Eurocentric cultures that maintain their purchase on political power and cultural production.

The words chosen as the epigraph for this chapter, from the poem "One man, that's all," by the Australian Aboriginal author and elder Bill Neidjie, are directed to Aboriginal adults charged with the duty of "hang[ing] on" to culture and story, and "giv[ing] it behind" to young people.[7] Neidjie's description of cultural transmission alludes to the connections between narrative and spatiality in Australian Aboriginal traditions, where to "lose, leave your culture behind and story" instead of passing them on to succeeding generations is to abandon communal and personal identities. In these cultures, custodians—that is, those who are responsible for transmitting knowledge of stories, places, and customary practices to those entitled to access such knowledge—walk before the children of the clan, guiding them in their journey. It is not the case here that traveling through country is merely a metaphor for life; rather, stories are embedded in the land, and to walk in the steps of the ancestors and learn the stories associated with particular places is to live as a member of a language group and clan. While Neidjie's injunction captures the interconnectedness of narratives, kinship, and country particular to Australian Aborigines, his words can be applied more generally to the predicament of Indigenous cultures threatened by the effects of colonialism, the extinction of languages, and the encroachment of Western culture on traditional practices.

The emergence of publishing houses owned and operated by Indigenous peoples has encouraged Indigenous cultural production, and for many such publishers children's texts have been a high priority. In New Zealand, the Maori publishing house, Huia, produces educational as well as trade books for children. In Canada, Theytus Books publishes children's and general texts by First Nations authors, and Pemmican Publications, the only Métis publishing house, specializes in children's texts, mainly by Métis and First Nations authors. In Australia, the two Indigenous publishing houses are Magabala Books and IAD Press, the publishing arm of the Institute for Aboriginal Development. In addition, Aboriginal Studies Press, which publishes broadly in the field of Aboriginal Studies, publishes children's texts by Aboriginal authors and illustrators. In the United States, Oyate in San Francisco acts as an information centre on material by Native and non-Native authors, distributes children's texts produced by Native presses and mainstream publishers, and has itself published several children's texts.

Indigenous authors have worked across the genres of fiction, autobiography, poetry, and drama, with autobiography comprising a prominent mode of production in Australia, Canada, and New Zealand. Through autobiographical writing, Indigenous people have written back to those dominant versions of the past that occlude the appropriation of land, the violence, and the marginalization that characterized colonial and assimilationist regimes, and the effects that persist in contemporary settler societies. Maori author Linda Tuhiwai Smith says, "Imperialism frames the indigenous experience. It is part of our story, our version of modernity. Writing about our experiences under imperialism and its more specific expression of colonialism has become a significant project in the indigenous world."[8] Autobiographical works trace individual and communal histories that construct Indigenous experiences and identities in their variety and complexity, carrying out the counter-discursive task, as Terdiman puts it, of "represent[ing] the world differently"[9] and thus of exposing the strategies of forgetting and totalization by which dominant discourses maintain power.

Indigenous publications for children, including works produced by Indigenous and mainstream publishers, tend to fall into a somewhat different range of genres and text types. A significant proportion of texts across settler cultures comprise retellings of traditional narratives, generally in the form of picture books or illustrated books. In the United States (but less in Canada, Australia, and New Zealand), another prominent category is that of non-fiction texts thematizing aspects of Indigenous cultures, history, and the lives of individuals. The largest category of texts, however, comprises picture books and illustrated books dealing with contemporary characters and settings.[10] The titles that follow are symptomatic of this group: Jordan Wheeler and Bill Cohen's sequence of picture books, published by Theytus, which feature the adventures of Chuck, a young Cree boy; Pemmican titles such as *Flour Sack Flora* (2002), which focus on relationships between Métis children and their grandparents; the Penumbra Press publication *Where Only the Elders Go: Moon Lake Loon Lake* (1994), by Jan Bourdeau Waboose and Halina Below, in which a young Ojibway boy, hearing the call of a loon, recalls the sacred lake where his grandfather went to prepare for death; Michael Arvaarluk Kusugak and Vladyana Krykorka's *Hide and Sneak* (1992), in which an Inuit girl, Allashua, outwits the Ijaraq when it kidnaps her;[11] the Huia publication *Taming the Taniwha* (2001), by Tim Tipene and Henry Campbell, where a young Maori boy "tames" a boy who bullies him at school; from IAD Press in Australia, Yvonne Edwards and Brenda Day's *Going for Kalta* (1997), which traces the progress of a group of contemporary children as they learn to track and cook lizards (*kalta*); and a text from Thursday Island in the Torres Strait, *Betty and Bala and the Proper Big Pumpkin* (1996), by Lorraine Berolah, LilyJane Collins, and Noel Cristaudo, about a runaway pumpkin, two children, and their grandmother. Texts like these, which represent the identity formation of Indigenous children living in contemporary settings, offer a crucial corrective to the many texts by non-Indigenous authors and illustrators that persist in treating Indigenous cultures locked into ancient and unchanging modes of thought and behaviour, or that depict Indigenous adolescents within the shallow paradigms characteristic of "problem" or "issues" novels.

Across settler cultures, the production of Indigenous novels for adolescent and young adult readers has lagged behind publications for younger readers. In New Zealand, although there are many distinguished novels for general audiences by Maori authors such as Witi Ihimaera, Patricia Grace, Keri Hulme, and Alan Duff, adolescent novels by Maori authors are only now emerging, such as Tim Tipene's *Kura Toa: Warrior School* (2004) and Kingi McKinnon's *When the Kehua Calls* (2002). In Australia, Indigenous novels for adolescents are also a recent development; many of the texts have been published by mainstream rather than Indigenous presses from the late 1990s, including Melissa Lucashenko's *Killing Darcy* (1998) and *Too Flash* (2002), Anita Heiss's *Who Am I? The Diary of Mary Talence* (2001), Meme McDonald and Boori Pryor's *My Girragundji* (1998), *The Binna Binna Man* (1999), and *Njunjul the Sun* (2002).[12] In Canada, Maria Campbell's *Halfbreed* (1973) was a pioneer work, followed in the 1980s by Beatrice Culleton Mosionier's *In Search of April Raintree* (1983), Jeannette Armstrong's *Slash* (1985), and Ruby Slipperjack's *Honour the Sun* (1987), all of which trace the formation of Aboriginal subjects and have attracted both adolescent and adult readers. However, there are still relatively few Canadian novels for adolescents by Aboriginal authors, among them Lee Maracle's *Will's Garden* (2002), Diane Silvey's *Raven's Flight* (2000), and Richard Wagamese's *Keeper 'n Me* (1994). In the United States, a small number of Native American authors have published works for adolescents (mainly through mainstream publishing houses), such as Joseph Bruchac's *Skeleton Man* (2001), Craig Kee Strete's *The World in Grandfather's Hands* (1995), Michael Dorris's *The Window* (1999), Louise Erdrich's *The Birchbark House* (1999), and Cynthia Leitich Smith's *Rain Is Not My Indian Name* (2001). Many factors contribute to the patchy production of adolescent fiction by Indigenous authors, among them the limited number of Indigenous relative to non-Indigenous authors, and the fact that mainstream publishers have often been slow to publish Indigenous work.

While Indigenous children's literature in Canada, New Zealand, and Australia focuses principally on the identity formation of contemporary child characters, historical settings, and events are thematized through a small number of realist historical novels, such as Louise Erdrich's *The Birchbark House* (1999); in texts such as *In Search of April Raintree* and Shirley Sperling's *My Name is Seepeetza* (1992), that trace the lives of Indigenous characters displaced from homes and families because of assimilationist policies; and in novels such as Melissa Lucashenko's *Killing Darcy* and Lee Maracle's *Will's Garden*, which treat colonization through narratives involving contemporary characters who uncover information about the lives and experience of their ancestors. As I have said, non-fiction writing by Indigenous authors constitutes a prominent mode of production for children in the United States, including autobiography, biography, and historical accounts of the experience of individuals and communities.

Terdiman's observation that dominant cultures are defined by their reflex acceptance of what "goes without saying"—that is, the ideologies and discourses that underwrite their power—applies especially to the production and reception of texts. There is no reason why Indigenous texts produced within non-Western cultures should accord with the categories of Western literary traditions—why terms such as "fantasy," "realism," "prose," or "poetry" should be regarded as holding universal meanings across cultures. The hegemony of Western discourses plays out in publishing practices and in the conditioned responses of audiences unaware of the extent to which their cumulative experience of narrative patterns, motifs, forms, and genres shape their reading. Nor is such conditioning confined to non-Indigenous readers, as is clear from Cynthia Leitich Smith's account of her act of self-censorship, that demonstrates how difficult it is for authors to resist the tyranny of dominant discourses.

As an instance of an epistemological gap between Indigenous and non-Indigenous traditions of narrative, I want to focus on conceptions of fiction in Australian Aboriginal cultures. In *Gularabulu* (1983), a collection of stories by the Aboriginal storyteller Paddy Roe, Stephen Muecke, who transcribed Roe's stories and wrote a scholarly introduction, describes Roe's categorization of stories as follows: "Paddy Roe distinguishes between three types of story: *trustori* (true stories), *bugaregara* (stories from the dreaming) and *devil stori* (stories about devils, spirits, etc.). *Trustori* and *devil stori* are only produced as spoken narratives, while the *bugaregara* (the "law") may also refer to traditional songs, ceremonies and rituals of which there is a great variety."[13] These categories relate to orally transmitted texts, some of which are reproduced in conjunction with forms of inscription such as body painting, and that may be told only at certain places or in conjunction with particular cultural events. Cutting across all three categories are questions concerning who has the authority to tell a story, that may depend on any or all of the following: a person's gender (in the case of secret-sacred men's stories or women's stories); kinship connections; rights to particular tracts of land; and whether or not a person has been recognized as an appropriate custodian of a story by the group that owns it (for stories are the property not of individuals but of kinship groups).

Fictional texts do not appear in Roe's scheme, where all stories are regarded as true because they are produced according to proper protocols and practices. Moreover, the shift from oral to printed modes of textuality disrupts narrative traditions in traditional Aboriginal cultures, where the efficacy of narratives depends on presence—the presence of the person authorized to tell stories, and that of an audience entitled to hear them. Fiction thus departs from Australian Aboriginal traditions in two ways: it derives from absence, as authors tell stories to people far distant and without connections of kinship or authorized relationships; and it diverges from the principle that stories are always true.[14] It is clear from this outline of Paddy Roe's views on narrative that there exists a gulf between Australian Aboriginal and Western epistemologies in regard to crucial concepts such as what constitutes truth; the functions, and purposes of narratives; and who is entitled to tell stories and to hear them. To assume that *everyone* understands what constitutes fiction is to assume that Western paradigms of literary production are universal. Of course, many contemporary Australian Aboriginal authors write fiction; but if these authors have been socialized into Aboriginal modes of understanding and producing stories, their work will inevitably be informed by their cultural experience of Aboriginal narrative practices. I am not arguing here that Australian Aboriginal conceptions of narrative apply across Indigenous cultures; however, comparable dissonances between Indigenous and non-Indigenous traditions are evident in all settler cultures.

On oral retellings of traditional narratives by non-Indigenous storytellers, Joseph Bruchac suggests that instead of relying on published versions, which may be assimilated into Western genres or may include sacred material, storytellers should learn from Indigenous people and should undertake research into the stories they tell, their provenance, and the functions they play within Indigenous cultures.[15] Published retellings of Indigenous narratives constitute a more problematic body of texts, and in chapter 3 I discuss reworkings of Indigenous narratives by two non-Indigenous authors, Paul Goble and Patricia Wrightson. I take a hard-line position, in that I believe that traditional narratives are best retold by those to whom they belong, whether directed at Indigenous or non-Indigenous audiences, and that the processes of retelling should accord with practices of authorization and custodianship of stories as they are observed in the diverse Indigenous cultures of New Zealand, Australia, Canada, and the United States.[16] My reasons for this position are, first, that traditional narratives are woven into cultural values and beliefs and are apt to be reduced or distorted when they are treated in isolation from Indigenous traditions; secondly, that the history of colonization is littered with instances of appropriation of stories and the time for such practices is now over; and thirdly, that Indigenous people are best equipped to determine which of their stories should be retold and by whom, and which versions are authorized by individuals and communities.

Greg Young-Ing, the managing editor at Theytus, lists the following principles as they apply to editing and publishing Aboriginal texts at Theytus:

- utilizing principles of the Oral Tradition within the editorial process;
- respecting, establishing, and defining Aboriginal colloquial forms of English ...;
- incorporating Aboriginal traditional protocol in considering the appropriateness of presenting certain aspects of culture; and
- consulting and soliciting approval of Elders and traditional leaders in the publishing of sacred cultural material.[17]

Young-Ing's formulation of editing principles is echoed in statements of policy and practice by Indigenous publishers across settler societies. The implications of this approach to cultural production are far-reaching, especially as they affect the reception of Indigenous texts, since they require styles of reading different from those appropriate to mainstream texts. For instance, "principles of the Oral Tradition" and the use of "Aboriginal colloquial forms of English" produce texts that depart from the literary traditions associated with quality writing in mainstream cultures.

## Strategies of Interpolation: Language and Narrative

The imposition of English as the national language of British settler colonies resulted in the loss of large numbers of Indigenous languages, and with them rituals, songs, narratives, and cultural practices. In Australia, out of around 250 languages spoken before the arrival of Europeans only about a third are still spoken.[18] In the territories that are now Canada and the United States, some 300 distinct languages were spoken at the end of the fifteenth century, of which some 134 have survived.[19] New Zealand stands out from other former British colonies in that its Indigenous people have a common language, Maori, although the number of Maori speakers declined sharply through the years of colonization and assimilation up to the late 1970s, when a program known as Te Kohanga Reo ("language nests") introduced Maori language to preschool children. Since 1987, when Maori became an official language of New Zealand through the Maori Language Act, the number of Maori children's texts has increased markedly, even though many of these texts are translations from English rather than written in Maori.

Indigenous (and, occasionally, mainstream) publishers producing children's texts address language loss in the most fundamental way through the deployment of Indigenous languages. In New Zealand, there are enough Maori and Pakeha readers of Maori to make the production of Maori texts a viable publishing strand, and Huia has produced a number of children's texts in both Maori and English editions. In Australia, Magabala has published several dual-language texts in English and Indigenous languages. For instance, *Tjarany Roughtail* (1992), by Gracie Greene, Joe Tramacchi, and Lucille Gill, is written in English and Kukatja, a language from the north of Western Australia; and Aidan Laza and Alick Tipoti's *Kuiyku Mabaigal: Waii and Sobai* (1998), a story about two warriors of the Torres Strait Islands, uses a combination of English and dialogue in Kala Lagaw Ya, the language of the western islands of the Torres Strait. In Canada, Theytus has published a Cree-English text, Beth Cuthand and Mary Longman's *The Little Duck* (1999), including a Cree symbol version; and Pemmican has taken the important step of publishing *Li Minoush* (2001), written by Bonnie Murray, illustrated by Sheldon Dawson and translated by Rita Flamand, a dual-language book in English and Michif in which, sentence by sentence, the English text is followed by the Michif version.

The example of *Li Minoush* demonstrates the cultural and political work carried out by Indigenous children's books in regard to the maintenance and promotion of endangered languages. Michif is the language spoken by Plains Métis and comprises French nouns and noun phrases used in conjunction with Plains Cree verbal systems. It is predominantly a spoken language, so that Flamand's translation involved the development of an orthography to represent Michif sound systems. In addition, the narrative thematizes ideas about endangered languages through its story about a young boy, Thomas, who asks his mother for a pet kitten. Because in Métis culture animals tend to be viewed in relation to their functions in hunting, trapping, and such activities, his mother is at first taken aback by his request, which signals a shift in conceptualization toward the idea of "cat" as "pet." When she agrees, she suggests that the cat should be called Minoush, which means "cat" in Michif, and thus Thomas's acquisition of the kitten incorporates his introduction to Michif language. The final illustration shows Thomas standing in front of his classmates showing them his kitten and telling him "how Minoush got its name,"[20] a textual moment in which the idea of endangered languages is foregrounded as a serious cultural question.

Whereas texts produced in Indigenous languages and in dual-language editions foreground linguistic and cultural difference directly, texts written in English use the language of the colonizers to represent Indigenous cultures and identities. To write in English, however, is not necessarily to write as a member of the dominant culture, since as Bill Ashcroft points out, "while ideology, discourse or language constrain subjects, they do not imprison them, nor are subjects immobilized by power."[21] Concerning the use of English by Canadian Aboriginal writers, Emma LaRocque writes, "Colonization works itself out in unpredictable ways. The fact is that English is the new

Native language, literally and politically. English is the common language of Aboriginal peoples. It is English that is serving to raise the political consciousness in our community; it is English that is serving to de-colonize and so unite Aboriginal peoples. Personally, I see much poetic justice in this process."[22] As LaRocque notes, the English of Indigenous people is a new language, shaped, and adjusted to convey meanings particular to colonized groups. To counter the deterministic implications of Althusser's notion of interpellation, Ashcroft proposes the term *interpolation* to signal the variety of ways through which Indigenous subjects exercise agency in textual production: "This strategy involves the capacity to interpose, to intervene, to interject a wide range of counter-discursive tactics into the dominant discourse without asserting a unified anti-imperial intention, or a separate oppositional purity."[23]

If the process of interpolation allows dialogue between languages, concepts, and ideologies in postcolonial texts, the act of reading also involves dialogue between readers and texts. Readers bring their specific and particular knowledge and experience to texts produced within their cultures, and readers locate themselves as subjects within these texts. For readers culturally distant from the world of the text, as is the case for many non-Indigenous readers of Indigenous texts, language constructs distance between cultures even as it affords a means of reaching across this distance.

Indigenous authors interpolate the dominant discourse by inserting into the texts they write words, modes of expression, syntactic arrangements, and narrative forms that do not merely refer to cultural difference but embody it through language. One of the most usual forms of interpolation in children's texts is the use of words in Indigenous languages, some glossed and others unglossed. The picture book *Caribou Song: Atíhko Níkamon* (2001), written by the Canadian Cree author Tomson Highway and illustrated by Brian Deines, affords a vivid example of the uses and effects of strategies of interpolation and demonstrates that interpolation operates at various levels simultaneously, since strategies such as language variance always refer to and mobilize cultural values and ideologies. The text is written in English and Cree, and thus, for non-Cree readers, the fact of linguistic difference is powerfully evident in the appearance of the Cree language, with its diacritical marks over individual letters and its syntactic contrasts with English, obvious in the placement of words such as "pápá" in "'mush!' ká-ta-tépwét mána pápá" ("'Mush!' Papa would yell"). In addition, Cree words enter the English narrative in passages of direct speech. The narrative is set in the snowy landscape of northern Manitoba, where two boys, Joe and Cody, live with their parents, hunters of caribou:

> All year long, they followed the caribou with a sled pulled by eight huskies. "Mush!" Papa would yell, and the dogs would run straight forward. "Cha!" he would shout, and they would turn right. And when he yelled "U!" they turned left.[24]

To determine the meanings of the words "cha" and "u" and to a lesser extent "mush" (that will be familiar to some readers) in this passage, it is necessary to read to the end of the sentences in which they occur to access Highway's explanation of their meanings, so that the words perform a function characterized by Ashcroft as "installation of difference."[25] That is, "cha," "u," and "mush" stand metonymically for the language and culture from which they derive, and thus *install* cultural difference. Readers whose experience of the world does not incorporate these words or information about the cultural practices to which the narrative refers must engage in a style of reading that involves seeking the meanings of unfamiliar words through cues of various kinds—for instance, comparing the English with the Cree text, or checking one form of a word against another in the Cree text—for instance, "atihk" (caribou, singular) with "atihkwak" (caribou, plural).

When words are glossed, as in the sentence "Joe played the accordion, the kitoochigan,"[26] on the one hand readers are provided with information that will assist them to decode the text, while on the other hand the explanation itself installs difference through its momentary disruption of the sentence in which it occurs, and because it points to the foreignness of the term; moreover, since subsequent occurrences of *kigoochigan* in the narrative are unglossed, readers must remember the appearance and meaning of the word the next time they meet it.

Interpolation is achieved not only through the Cree language but also through the text's assumptions about the world. When Joe and Cody wander away from their parents, they engage in a form of play that refers to ritual and ceremonial uses of language, song, and dance:

> One day, at the end of May, the family stopped on an island. After a lunch of whitefish and bannock, Joe and Cody wandered off and found a meadow surrounded by forest. In the middle stood a great big rock.
>
> "Cody," said Joe. "This is the perfect spot. Let's sing and dance for the caribou. You dance with your arms up like antlers. I'll sing 'Ateek, ateek' and play kitoochigan. And before you know it, ten thousand caribou will burst out of the forest."[27]

Accordingly, when Cody dances like a caribou to Joe's music, ten thousand caribou stampede through the meadow, so that the boys are in serious danger of falling beneath the animals' hooves. Joe makes his way through the "snorting, steaming bodies,"[28] and reaches Cody: "When [Joe] took Cody's hand they seemed to float right through the herd. The next thing they knew they were perched on the big rock, Cody on Joe's lap, kitoochigan between them."[29] In this textual moment, Western conventions rub up against Cree traditions: whereas in Western narratives distinctions between realism and fantasy are commonly incorporated into distinctions between genres of writing, Highway's narrative combines the realistic with the magical. The Cree scholar Neal McLeod notes that "there are discursive differences between the colonized and the colonizer as they are embedded within different interpretative vantage points,"[30] and in *Caríbou Song: Atíhko Níkamon*, events are interpreted according to a view of the world where what is real includes spiritual, mystical, and magical experiences. As the caribou stream past Joe and Cody, "out of the drumming came the voice of the herd, whispering, and moaning and wailing.... 'Cody! Joe!' it said. 'Come, come!' And the boys opened their arms to embrace the spirit."[31] Discussing the writing of the Cree author Joy Harjo, Craig S. Womack points out the significance of deer in Cree narratives, particularly those involving the transformation of humans into deer.[32] By claiming these ancient stories and working them into a narrative about boys growing up in the post-Contact world, Highway asserts the vibrancy and tenacity of Cree traditions.

The narrative concludes with the laughter of the two boys as they sit on top of their rock, and with the answering smile of their father, who observes them, in a moment of narrative closure that celebrates a world view held in common across the generations. Such moments are pervasive in Native American and First Nations texts for children, in line with the theory of the Cherokee scholar Jace Weaver, whose study *That the People Might Live: Native American Literatures and Native American Community* (1997) proposes the idea that the principal distinguishing feature of Native American literatures is what Weaver terms "communitism." This is a term whose blend of "community" and "activism" suggests that Native literatures embody "a proactive commitment to Native community,"[33] a concern for cultural endurance. Native American writers produce texts, Weaver says, "to and for Native peoples,"[34] and engage in strategies of remembering and of promoting ways of surviving and persisting as a community.

To read Indigenous texts across New Zealand, Australia, Canada, and the United States is to become conscious of the high valency attributed to relations between young children and elders in these texts. There are literally dozens of Indigenous picture books involving interactions between grandparents and children, often utilizing the device of embedded narratives, such as occurs in Michael Kusugak and Vladyana Krykorka's *Northern Lights*, where Kataujaq's grandmother tells her a story that illuminates events in the framing narrative. Such texts propose ideological practices operating as interactions between old and young members of families and clans, and hence model both social formations and attitudes to the past and to Indigenous traditions. As grandparents and elders represent cultural continuity, so represented interactions between old and young insist that the transmission of narratives from old to young, and the interpersonal relations that accompany these exchanges, enable the formation of Indigenous subjects.

Highway's text, pervaded as it is by Cree values and perspectives, at once constructs difference and enables non-Cree readers to engage with the significances constructed through the narrative. For such readers, its depiction of a Cree world view produces a sense of alterity—that is, it constructs an other located in place, history, language, and religion. The concept of alterity is quite different from the Other of Lacanian theory, applied in colonial discourse theory to the way in which the imperial centre (seen as "mother England" or in relation to imperial discourse) locates the subjectivity of the colonized by defining what the colonized is not. Rather, notions of alterity provide for a sense of difference without the absolutism and hierarchy of the self-Other relationship. In Ashcroft's terms, the language of *Caribou Song* offers meanability,[35] since it renders meaningful modes of behaviour, interpersonal relations, and emotion located in Cree culture and traditions; at the same time, the text maintains a sense of the apartness and specificity of the characters' physical and conceptual world. As I argue in chapter 3, the principal danger in non-Indigenous representations of Indigenous peoples and cultures is that they convert difference into sameness by imputing universal meanings. Highway's evocation of Cree culture in *Caribou Song* demonstrates how strategies of interpolation resist such reductionist interpretations.

Greg Young-Ing's list of the protocols for editing texts at Theytus includes "respecting, establishing and defining Aboriginal colloquial forms of English,"[36] a form of interpolation through which Indigenous authors destabilize the idea that there exists a hierarchy of Englishes with standard English at the apex. Because mainstream publishers have often tended to regard Indigenous dialects of English as inferior and riddled with errors, they have frequently reworked texts by Indigenous people to render them "correct," or ghostwriters have been employed to convert oral narratives into standard written forms. In the words of the Aboriginal novelist Mudrooroo, "Indigenous Englishes... threaten the hegemony of a standard English."[37] In fact, dialects such as Aboriginal English in Australia, Maori English in New Zealand, and Red English in the United States and Canada (sometimes termed Rez English in Canada) have their own grammatical features and vocabulary and are stigmatized because they are associated with speakers on the margins of mainstream culture, not because they are intrinsically inferior forms of English.

The Australian picture book *Tracker Tjugingji* (2003), written by Bob Randall and illustrated by Kunyi June-Anne McInerney, tells the story of a small boy, Tjugingji, as he follows his parents' tracks across the country over the course of a day: "Tracker Tjugingji [say chook in gee] lived out bush with his family. They camped in little windbreak shelters, and Tjugingji used to sleep on the ground next to his parents. One time Tracker Tjugingji's parents decided to go to a big lake, a long way east of where they were camped."[38] The language of *Tracker Tjugingji* combines Aboriginal English with standard English, colloquial Australian usages, and parenthetical explanations, such as the one referring to Tracker's name, of the pronunciation of the Pitjantjatjara terms used in the narrative. This strategy of code-switching across languages and dialects instantiates the complexity of Aboriginal identities as they negotiate the distances between cultures; at the same time, through its insistence on the interface of subjectivity and place in the experience of the characters, it constructs a strong sense of the alterity of the nomadic way of life enjoyed by Tracker Tjugingji and his parents.

The use of "Tracker" as an appositive title with "Tjugingji" constitutes another strategy of interpolation that accords with Terdiman's coinage of the term "re/citation" to refer to a counter-discursive strategy that he compares with the human body's reaction to disease, and that couples the "duplication of the other's discourse with the willful mockery intended in parroting it."[39] Terdiman points out that dominant discourses inform a variety of language features—such as clichés, proverbs, colloquialisms, and institutional names—that tend to pass unnoticed because they involve received and naturalized ideas; re/citation involves imitating such features in ways that denaturalize them, making readers aware of the ideological load they carry. Seen in this light, the name "Tracker" as applied to a small boy both evokes and displaces colonial significances, since Aboriginal trackers were employed by colonial authorities such as police and landowners to search for white people lost in Australian deserts or forests and (more problematically) to locate Aboriginal and non-Aboriginal people accused or convicted of crimes.

The expression "lived out bush" combines the term "bush," which in colloquial Australian usage refers to the opposition between urban and rural locations (the city and the bush), with the more specific meanings of Aboriginal English, where to "live out bush" is to pursue the routines whereby Aboriginal nomadic peoples travelled from one site to another, determining their progress and direction according to the season, the availability of game and other food, and the occasions when kinship groups gathered for recreational and ritual gatherings.[40] The term "camped" refers in Aboriginal English to the nomadic practice whereby people remained in one place as long as they needed to. Its meaning in *Tracker Tjugingji* is far removed from Western concepts of camping, which typically involve equipment, vehicles, and food that is carried to camping sites and cooked there. In contrast, Tjugingji and his parents carry very little with them, sleeping within natural windbreaks of shrubs or small trees that protect them from the wind, or using boughs cut for this purpose, and gathering food—game and vegetation—where they camp. To go camping in Western cultures is to leave one's permanent home for a time; for Tjugingji and his parents, "home" is constituted by the territory around which the family moves, rather than a place from which they depart and to which they return.

The uses of the terms "bush" and "camped" in *Tracker Tjugingji* afford a cogent demonstration of how postcolonial texts construct meaning. As Ashcroft notes, "the inscription of the vernacular modality of local speech is one of the strategies by which a 'marginal' linguistic culture appropriates the imported language to its own conceptions of society and place."[41] Far from carrying universally understood meanings, words such as "bush" and "camp" in postcolonial texts must operate across the considerable distance between writer and reader, for whom such words relate to larger structures of meaning—in this case, around understandings of "home" and discourses of place. More than this, words are situated in relation to cultural ideas that shape narratives. Thus, *Tracker Tjugingji*, whose story is based on the experience of a small boy learning to read his country, uses the term "camp" within a narrative structure where people move from one place to the next, and where events along the journey constitute the main focus of the narrative. Such a structure is quite different from the narrative pattern common in Western stories, where a child leaves home, goes on a journey, and later returns home, now seeing home differently in the light of these experiences of being away.

When Tjugingji is still asleep early in the morning, his parents decide to set out for the lake: "'Oh well, let's leave him,' they said. 'He can catch up later.'" That the narrative bears many of the features of oral transmission is signalled by the narrative intervention, "That's the Aboriginal way—you don't wake your children when they are fast asleep";[42] it is a moment of direct address that draws attention to cultural difference in regard to child-rearing practices. The narrative shape of *Tracker Tjugingji* constructs a set of relationships between Aboriginal people and their country by showing Tjugingji performing the role of one who is apprenticed to country and taught by its inhabitants. As he follows his parents' tracks, he encounters a snake, a perentie (lizard), a kangaroo, a dingo, and finally an emu with its chicks. In each case Tjugingji asks for guidance and is directed toward the lake where his parents have gone, and in each case his mode of address is a relational one: he calls the snake "grandpa" and the other creatures "uncle." The cumulative effect of this pattern is its insistence on the principles that children are at home in their country, that country nourishes and protects the young, and that humans are related to the flora and fauna of their country in ways that connect to the Dreamings of their kinship group.

By the end of the narrative, when Tracker Tjugingji rides on the emu's back to his parents' camp, all the creatures have followed him "to make sure he was okay,"[43] and his father proposes that the group celebrate by dancing and singing: "Let's all have an *inma*. Let's dance."[44] McInerney's final illustration (fig. 3) locates viewers facing the scene, with Tjugingji and his family seated on the red desert earth. At the left of the picture the snake plays a didgeridoo, the perentie plays clapsticks, and the dingo sings, while the kangaroo and emu perform a dance, together with the emu chicks. In this depiction of energetic movement and rapt attention, McInerney conveys a powerful sense of the interdependence of humans and animals. The red and purple tones of the background conjure a landscape whose luminosity is echoed in the skin tones and clothing of Tjugingji and his parents and accords with Aboriginal traditions in which the land is, in Stephen Muecke's words, "totally inscribed, written, densely named, but not necessarily a country which is *seen*."[45] Tjugingji's progress through country is based not on specularity—how the land looks, the extent to which its contours accord with Western notions of the picturesque—but on the signs it affords and the uses that the young Tracker can make of these signs as he engages with the land and its inhabitants. In this way, the verbal and visual narratives of *Tracker Tjugingji* adhere to traditions in which country is a text redolent with stories whose telling ensures the safety of land and people and the maintenance of proper relations between them.

## "Recreating the Enemy's Language": Narratives and Hybridity

Rather than merely inserting the significances and thematics of Indigenous cultures into Western forms and genres, strategies of interpolation achieve transformative effects by "recreating the enemy's language," to use Joy Harjo's phrase.[46] As I have suggested in my discussion of *Tracker Tjugingji*, these effects extend beyond words, syntax, and grammatical features to the way narratives are shaped and the ideologies they propose. A text that illustrates the effects of interpolation upon narrative practice is Joseph Bruchac's *Skeleton Man*, a novel based on a story common in Native American traditions about a person who, having cooked and devoured her or his own flesh, becomes a skeleton preying on humans.[47] *Skeleton Man* commences *in medias res* with Molly, the novel's Mohawk protagonist and narrator, introducing a story in which processes of storytelling are foregrounded: "I'm not sure if I'm a minor character or the heroine. Heck, I'm not even sure I'll be around to tell the end of it."[48] Rather than the predictable move of backtracking to recount events

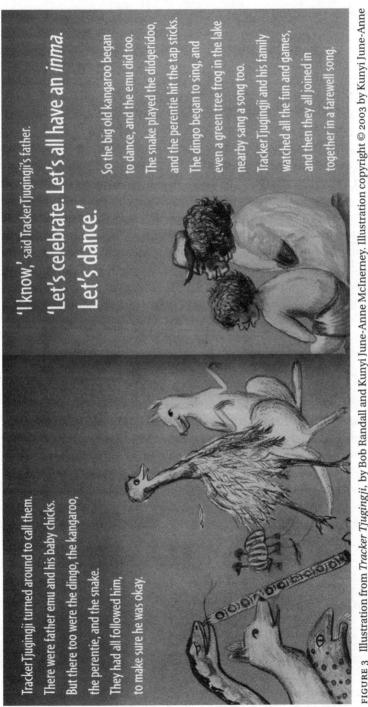

Tracker Tjugingji turned around to call them.
There were father emu and his baby chicks.
But there too were the dingo, the kangaroo,
the perentie, and the snake.
They had all followed him,
to make sure he was okay.

'I know,' said Tracker Tjugingji's father.

'Let's celebrate. Let's all have an *inma*.
Let's dance.'

So the big old kangaroo began
to dance, and the emu did too.
The snake played the didgeridoo,
and the perentie hit the tap sticks.
The dingo began to sing, and
even a green tree frog in the lake
nearby sang a song too.
Tracker Tjugingji and his family
watched all the fun and games,
and then they all joined in
together in a farewell song.

FIGURE 3   Illustration from *Tracker Tjugingji*, by Bob Randall and Kunyi June-Anne McInerney. Illustration copyright © 2003 by Kunyi June-Anne McInerney, reproduced by permission of IAD Press.

as they have occurred to this point, the narrative then turns to Molly's description of her sixth-grade teacher Ms. Shabbas, known by her class as Ms. Showbiz because of her habit of bursting into songs from Broadway musicals; after this, the narrative shifts to Molly's recollection of her father's telling of the story of "the skeleton monster"[49] in a version where a young girl, the sole survivor after her uncle has devoured her family, outwits Skeleton Man with the help of a rabbit who repays an act of kindness, and restores her family to life.

By inserting this summary of the "Skeleton Man" story at the beginning of the novel, Bruchac anticipates the novel's shape and closure, so that the tension of the narrative hinges not so much on whether Molly will vanquish Skeleton Man and rescue her parents, but rather on how she will do so, and on the intersections between the ancient story and Molly's everyday life in the urban setting of the novel. In this way, the narrative refers to and draws on oral traditions that rely on the repetition of stories and their deployment through cultural practices. Echoes of orality in *Skeleton Man* also appear in Bruchac's strategy of embedding one story within another, which suggests the storytelling practice of inserting a secondary story within a framing narrative, and in the novel's construction of Molly as a listener addressing a listener close to her in time and space: "You probably saw me on *Unsolved Mysteries*."[50] Most of the narration is unfolded in present tense, which underscores the presence of a narrator mediating the story and determining what can be seen and known.

A crucial component of the narrative of *Skeleton Man* is a sequence of dreams experienced by Molly, whose parents have disappeared; she is locked in her room each night by the Skeleton Man, who poses as her uncle. In the first dream, Molly saves a rabbit from a trap; in subsequent dreams, the rabbit acts as her helper, telling her that her parents are "buried but not dead;"[51] and, in the final dream, the rabbit guides Molly in her escape. Just as the story of Skeleton Man as recalled by Molly at the beginning of the novel prefigures the shape of the narrative, so Molly's final dream prefigures her escape, her flight, and Skeleton Man's death (or disappearance) when he falls from a bridge to the rocks below. These strategies of double telling depart from more conventional suspense narratives, which generally rely on a chronological and once-only unfolding of events. Shifts of time are also constructed through the settings of Molly's dreams, which occur in a pre-Contact world recognizable to Molly as landscape familiar from the waking world but not yet cleared of giant trees, a landscape in which Molly herself is a Mohawk girl wearing moccasins, a deerskin dress, and a rawhide bracelet. This fluid movement from one time to another interpolates into a modern genre (the suspense story) an insistence on the power and durability of Mohawk traditions, integral to Molly's sense of self. In *Red on Red*, Womack observes that the use of overlapping time frames in the work of Joy Harjo and Louise Erdrich has the effect of emphasizing "what links events rather than the order in which events occur,"[52] and the interplay of contemporary and ancient settings performs a somewhat similar function in *Skeleton Man*, promoting a view of Mohawk female identities that incorporates ancient stories and historical figures such as the eighteenth-century Mohawk Molly Brant into the narrative's evocation of Mohawk female subjectivity.

Molly's dreams also play an interpolative function in what they assert about Mohawk epistemologies; for Bruchac's representation of dreams and their functions is far removed from psychoanalytical traditions in which dreams are depicted as products of the dreaming psyche, associated with wish-fulfillment and repressed memories. Rather, Molly's dreams connect human experience with the world of spirits: "Trust your dreams. Both my parents said that. That's our old way, our Mohawk way. The way of our ancestors."[53] Molly's response to her dream incorporates a set of connected values: respect for her parents, veneration for "our old way," and adherence to Mohawk systems of knowledge. Vine Deloria's observation that "the Indian understands dreams, visions, and intraspecies communications ... as a natural part of human experience"[54] applies equally to Tomson Highway's *Caribou Song* and to *Skeleton Man*; both interpolate dominant discourses by refusing a hierarchy of knowledge that values empirical and "scientific" knowledge more highly than that gained from dreams and visions.

As well as the Mohawk stories and lore that Molly recalls, and the dreams that sustain her during her uneasy coexistence with her "uncle," the narrative of *Skeleton Man* is studded with references to mainstream popular and literary texts. Ms. Showbiz communicates her concern for Molly through the songs she sings, so that "Tomorrow," from *Annie*, serves as a promise that "it is going to be better on the day after this one."[55] On Molly's side, her reading of Avi's *True Confessions of Charlotte Doyle* (1990) affords respite from her anxiety about her parents and a model of an independent and courageous female hero. At the level of genre, Bruchac incorporates references to conventions common in horror stories in a passage where Molly compares formulaic elements such as spiderwebs, bats, clanking chains, and ghostly moans with the appearance of normality that Skeleton Man deploys to disguise his designs on Molly and her parents.[56] Another category of intertextual reference in *Skeleton Man* comprises allusions to the various discourses that inform official and institutional approaches to the surveillance and control of children, evident in the language and behaviour of the social services worker who places Molly in the care of Skeleton Man, and the school counselor and Child Welfare officer who enforce her imprisonment in the house where her "uncle" fattens her up with the intention of devouring her.

One effect of these intertextual references is to foreground the dialogue between texts and cultures that shapes Molly's sense of self, since, far from adhering to the common stereotype of the Native child as a pathetic figure caught between cultures, Bruchac depicts Molly as a Mohawk subject, aligned with the values of her parents and with a world view informed by Mohawk stories and lore. A broader effect of the intertextual references in *Skeleton Man* is that, by grounding Molly's subjectivity within a Mohawk discursive system and showing how this discourse relates to Western textuality and institutional practices, Bruchac alludes to the colonial and postcolonial experience of Mohawk people. In this way, the figure of Molly functions metonymically to propose a mode of being where Mohawk (and, by implication, other Indigenous) subjects affirm identities at once distinct from and in dialogue with the discourses of the dominant culture.

The term "hybridity" is frequently used in postcolonial theory to refer to the myriad practices of exchange that characterize postcolonial textuality—the trading of languages, genres, narratives, and symbols by which colonized and colonizers engage in cultural dialogue. As I have argued elsewhere,[57] discourses of hybridity are unstable and susceptible to collapsing back into the binaries of colonial discourse. On one hand, discussions of hybrid texts and practices are apt to foreclose on the continuing negotiations (often fraught and difficult) between cultures by implying that colonized and colonizers have attained a state of unproblematic accord; on the other hand, hybrid texts and their authors are seen to depart from "pure" or "authentic" forms of cultural expression. Craig Womack satirizes such formulations of hybridity in his introduction to *Red on Red*, where he alludes to non-Indian critics who regard Indian authors and characters as "a bunch of mongrelized mixed-bloods who weren't sure if they were Indians as they muddled about in some kind of hybridized culture, serving as the footpath between whites and Indians."[58]

What is often overlooked in discussions of hybridity is that power relations apply in a highly differential way to cultural production within settler societies. Indigenous peoples have generally had no option but to engage with dominant cultures, whereas members of colonizing groups and their descendants enjoy a privileged position where they need not engage with Indigenous people or textuality except at a superficial level, for instance through the ritual gestures by which settler nations allude to Indigenous cultures in public, ceremonial occasions such as the opening ceremony of the Sydney Olympics in 2000, when "Australia" was defined by way of Aboriginal symbols.

Nevertheless, as *Skeleton Man* demonstrates, Indigenous textuality is capable of decentring and destabilizing the meanings of the dominant culture. At the end of the novel, the school psychiatrist falls back on her stock of psychological theories: "'What was it,' the school psychiatrist said to me, 'that made him want to have total control over a family like that? Was it a chemical imbalance? Perhaps it was because of things that happened to him as a child. Or perhaps not.' Then she tapped her pencil against her chin and looked wise. Right."[59] Molly's ironic "Right" exposes the inadequacy of the psychiatrist's imaginings, her fruitless desire for an explanation congruent with the theories of human behaviour that order her world view. In contrast, her father's words locate Skeleton Man within a typology of creatures known yet mysterious: "There are still creatures that may look like people but are something else. The reason creatures like Skeleton Man do what they do is they like to hunt us. The only way to defeat them is to be brave."[60] Bruchac's strategic subversion of the givens of psychology and the codes of horror narratives refuses any easy accommodation between Indigenous and non-Indigenous cultural formations and practices.

It is a truism to describe picture books as a dialogic form in which meanings are produced through the interplay of verbal and visual texts. The text with which I conclude this chapter, Daisy Utemorrah and Pat Torres's *Do Not Go Around the Edges* (1990), adds to this already complex form another set of dialogic relations, which play out in Utemorrah's memories of a life experienced over a period when colonial practices and policies impacted savagely on Aboriginal cultures in the Kimberley region of Western Australia. The design of the book dramatizes both coherence and complexity: Utemorrah's autobiographical story is placed along the bottom of the book's double-spreads (fig. 4), while a series of poems by Utemorrah is placed in the body of each opening, framed within Pat Torres's illustrations. The border that runs along the lower edge of each opening features the three sacred beings known in Wunambal culture as Wandjinas, orienting the various narrative and thematic strands of the book in relation to the ancient stories of the Dreaming. Readers accustomed to the reading practices usual in picture books will search for thematic and symbolic interactions between verbal and visual texts, but in *Do Not Go Around the Edges* such relationships are elusive, as most of the poems in the book connect only tangentially with Utemorrah's autobiographical story; moreover, Torres's illustrations, which combine representational art with traditional motifs and figures, refer to meanings that relate to the narratives and practices of Utemorrah's Wunambal people and can be understood only to a limited degree by those outside the boundaries of kinship and country.

The strategies of meaning-making deployed in *Do Not Go Around the Edges* demonstrate conceptual and textual complexities far removed from any

FIGURE 4

*Story  About  My  Life*

FIGURE 5

*When I was young in Kunmunya with the other girls, I was a Girl Guide and others were Brownies.  We had Girls' Scouts too and when I came to Derby I was Assistant Cub Mistress.*

FIGURES 4 and 5  Illustrations from *Do Not Go Around the Edges*, by Daisy Utemorrah and Pat Torres. Illustrations copyright © 1990 by Patricia Torres, reproduced by permission of Magabala Books.

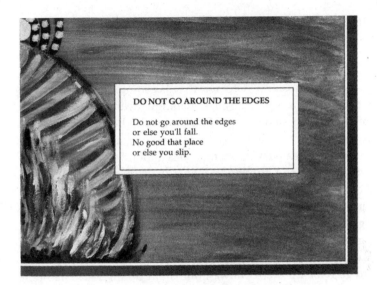

> **DO NOT GO AROUND THE EDGES**
>
> Do not go around the edges
> or else you'll fall.
> No good that place
> or else you slip.

*I was born in Kunmunya Mission in February 1922. From my childhood I lived with my parents, in a humpy.*

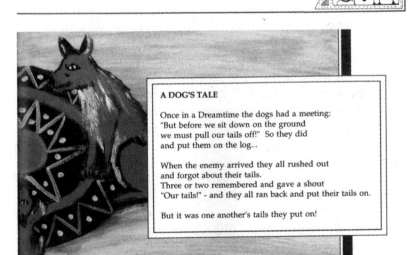

> **A DOG'S TALE**
>
> Once in a Dreamtime the dogs had a meeting:
> "But before we sit down on the ground
> we must pull our tails off!" So they did
> and put them on the log...
>
> When the enemy arrived they all rushed out
> and forgot about their tails.
> Three or two remembered and gave a shout
> "Our tails!" - and they all ran back and put their tails on.
>
> But it was one another's tails they put on!

*I was happy doing that but leaving my tribal land I often think how nice it would be to go back up there. Mowanjum is our home now. The name Mowanjum means settled at last. But I left my traditional country.*

simplistic notion of a mixture or blending of elements from different cultures. Rather, its multiplicity of narratives and systems of meaning destabilizes the domination of British culture and standard English, forcing readers into new modes of reading. In the double-spread featuring the poem "A Dog's Tale" (fig. 5), for instance, Utemorrah tells a humorous version of an event from the Dreaming, when the dogs, holding a meeting, resolve to take their tails off before they sit on the ground. However, when the enemy suddenly arrive, the dogs in their confusion take the wrong tails. Torres's illustration shows three dogs seated (without their tails) around two concentric circles marked with dots and lines and echoing the circles and geometrical patterns of other illustrations throughout the book. This light-hearted, even carnivalesque poem is placed above Utemorrah's account of her experience as a young girl at Kunmunya Mission, where she was a Girl Guide, and later, of her role as assistant Cub mistress in the town of Derby. Utemorrah says, "I was happy doing that but leaving my tribal land I often think how nice it would be to go back up there. Mowanjum is our home now. The name Mowanjum means settled at last. But I left my traditional country."[61]

Utemorrah's involvement in Western institutions is graphically demonstrated by her membership of mainstream bodies such as the Girl Guide movement. At the same time, her references to the places where she has lived—Kunmunya, Derby, Mowanjum—allude to the journeys forced on her and her clan by the various state and church authorities that have been charged with controlling the lives of Aboriginal people; previously, for instance, she has used passive voice to describe the time "when we were shifted from Kunmunya to live in Derby."[62] Utemorrah's story is not one of oppression and suffering, as is clear in her statement "I was happy doing that;"[63] rather, her account of her life insists on a contradictory co-existence of emotions. For instance, she derives pleasure from her involvement in the Girl Guide movement; but she longs for the tribal land from which her clan was forcibly removed before her birth. Again, Mowanjum is now her home; but it is not her country, the place from which she derives her identity, and while the meaning of "Mowanjum" is "settled at last,"[64] the term "settled" evokes the processes of desettlement and displacement that led Utemorrah and her clan to Mowanjum.

The concept of hybridity must always be treated cautiously as a way of understanding and describing texts and subjectivities produced through negotiations between cultures, since, as the Australian Aboriginal author Ian Anderson notes, it has historically been deployed as a way of situating Indigenous people and cultures in a neither/nor state, a chasm between cultures. Writing of his experience as an Aboriginal child growing up in the period of postwar assimilation in Australia, Anderson describes his encounter with the language and conceptualization of hybridity as a teenager, when he read the work of the historian N.J.B. Plomley:

> The "hybrid" Aborigine was constructed as ambiguous (bit of black, bit of white). This ambiguity is well captured by the historian N.J.B. Plomley when he declared in 1977 that "structurally, physiologically and psychologically, hybrids are some mixture of their parents. In social terms, [these people] belong to neither race (and are shunned by both), and lacking a racial background they have no history...." In this infamous description, Plomley was referring to my families. I read this as a teenager, and it is difficult to describe the feelings this statement evoked. It was something like grieving; but a grieving over a tremendous loss which is in itself then denied as being yours.[65]

Just as Indigenous subjectivities are not composed of elements of this and that ("bit of black, bit of white"), so Indigenous texts do not comprise a combination of Indigenous and non-Indigenous tropes and discourses that can readily be torn apart and identified as black or white. Rather, Indigenous textuality engages in processes of self-representation, using the language of the colonizers to construct Indigenous narratives and meanings. Indigenous texts for children, like Indigenous texts more generally, are produced primarily for Indigenous readers, even as they represent to wider audiences the values, practices, and narratives of Indigenous cultures. They thus imply two audiences: the children of the cultures in which they are produced; and non-Indigenous children for whom they are both comprehensible and emblematic of alterity. Addressing these two audiences, Indigenous texts offer a path toward cultural understanding for the youngest citizens of postcolonial societies.

## 3 White Imaginings

> ... our [Indigenous] subjectivites, our aspirations, our ways
> of seeing and our languages have largely been excluded
> from the equation, as the colonising culture plays with
> itself. It is as if we have been ushered on to a stage to play
> in a drama where the parts have already been written.
> —Michael Dodson, "The End in the Beginning"

The fact that most representations of Indigenous peoples
and cultures in settler societies have been and continue to be produced by
non-Indigenous writers and artists is readily explained by the fact that in
these nations it is white, Eurocentric cultures whose practices, perspectives,
and narrative traditions dominate literary production and representational
modes. I do not want to suggest that non-Indigenous people should not or
cannot represent Indigenous people and cultures, although I make a distinction between works of fiction that thematize Indigenous cultures and
characters, and retellings of Indigenous narratives. I have argued in chapter
2 that texts in the latter category are best retold by people from whose traditions they derive, and in forms that respect cultural practices. Works of fiction present a different set of issues, enmeshed within the complex politics
of representational and discursive practices.

As the Canadian scholar Linda Alcoff notes in her essay "The Problem
of Speaking for Others," it is difficult to "distinguish speaking about from
speaking for in all cases,"[1] since representation does not work as a simple op-
eration whereby an author delivers the truth of others, but incorporates advocacy and judgements and acts of valuing as well as information. Alcoff
concludes that those speaking for others should be cognizant of the power
relations embodied in discursive practices and should interrogate the positions from which they speak, that they should take responsibility for what
they say, and that they should "analyze the probable or actual effects of the
words on the discursive and material context."[2] Applied to fiction for children,
these principles suggest that non-Indigenous authors should recognize the

Notes to chapter 3 on pages 237–40.

privileges they enjoy as members of majority cultures, and (crucially) the subject positions they construct for Indigenous and non-Indigenous readers.

Alcoff's recommendations to those who speak for others imply a high level of self-awareness on the part of speakers; but symbolic systems are informed by naturalized assumptions and expectations, which exist in most cases below the level of conscious thought. Discussing representations of Native American historical figures, Hilary Wyss notes that, "Euro-American definitions of Native Americans have long been rooted in specific genres of written discourse—the captivity narrative, the travel narrative, European eyewitness accounts of 'authentic' Native communities—diverse forms that nevertheless complement each other in their attempts to explain Native Americans to a Euro-American audience."[3] Unless representations of Native American people and cultures accord with the narrative and discoursal features of these genres, Wyss argues, they are regarded as inauthentic or erroneous, since they disrupt constructions of racial hierarchies embedded in national mythologies. In a similar vein, Michael Dodson, the Australian Aboriginal academic and activist, observes that Aboriginality is generally defined within Australian culture in terms of its relations with the dominant culture, with the result that, "our [Aboriginal] subjectivities, our aspirations, our ways of seeing and our languages have largely been excluded from the equation, as the colonising culture plays with itself. It is as if we have been ushered on to a stage to play in a drama where the parts have already been written. Choose from the part of the ancient noble spirit, the lost soul estranged from her true nature, or the aggressive drunkard, alternately sucking and living off the system. No other parts are available for 'real Aborigines.'"[4] Wyss's argument that Native American cultures are depicted within specific genres and Dodson's sense that Australian Aborigines are "ushered on to a stage to play in a drama where the parts have already been written" are borne out by an examination of children's texts by non-Indigenous authors. In the main, these texts represent Indigeneity within a narrow range of character types, such as sage figures, political activists, and alienated young people caught between cultures. The predominant narrative patterns cluster around a small number of possibilities: stories in which white children befriend Indigenous characters, thereby enhancing their own growth as individuals; problem novels featuring the identity formation of Indigenous characters; and a substantial body of historical novels, many of which conform to the pattern common in contemporary realistic novels, featuring Indigenous–white friendships that contribute to the maturation of non-Indigenous figures.

A crucial consideration in representations of Indigeneity in children's literature relates to how point of view and focalization encode subjectivities and position readers. As John Stephens argues, point of view is "the aspect of narration in which implicit authorial control of audience reading strategies is probably most powerful."[5] It is especially through focalization that readers are positioned to align themselves with characters, a strategy that can effect what Stephens refers to as "textual subjection."[6] That is, if a reader's sense of self is submerged in the represented selfhood of a focalizing character, such a reader may find it difficult to stand back from the narrative sufficiently to interrogate textual ideologies.

When non-Indigenous authors construct Indigenous focalizers, they must imagine how these characters think, value, and feel, a highly complex task that demands a capacity to represent the other. It is not surprising, then, that non-Indigenous authors are more likely to construct non-Indigenous than Indigenous focalizers, since in this way they are able to represent Indigenous cultures from the outside and from the perspective of majority cultures. Nor is it surprising that non-Indigenous authors who best represent Indigenous cultures—that is, whose depictions of Indigeneity are diverse, nuanced, and informed—tend to be people with long-standing and deep associations with Indigenous cultures.

The Disney animated film *Pocahontas* (1982), directed by Steven Spielberg, affords many instances of how naturalized versions of colonial ideologies resurface in contemporary texts. As S. Elizabeth Bird points out in *Dressing in Feathers*, this film was "greeted with a barrage of contradictory reactions"[7] when it opened in 1995. Much early discussion of *Pocahontas* focused upon questions of historicity, especially the fact that whereas the Pocahontas of the film is clearly a young adult and Captain John Smith around the same age, the historical Pocahontas was aged between ten and twelve years, while John Smith was a mercenary soldier in his thirties. I do not intend to go into the limitations of this mode of criticism here, since I discuss questions relating to historiography and historicism in chapter 4. For now I want only to say that while *Pocahontas* makes use of historical figures and events, its creators were concerned principally with producing a film calculated to attract family audiences and to provide a context for marketing products (such as dolls, fast food, clothes, toys, and books) based on images and characters from the film. My focus here is not on what is and is not "historical fact" in *Pocahontas*, but on the uses made of the story of Pocahontas and the ideological imperatives they serve.

The film's opening sequence commences with a scene suggestive of a high-angle camera panning over the city of London and showing a vast, crowded metropolitan setting, with the Thames hemmed in by buildings and streets. Within this purview, where visual motifs such as steep rooflines and jostling traffic emphasize a habitus in which humans are constrained by the built environment, Captain John Smith's entry into the shipboard scene promotes him as a man of action, leaping astride a cannon as it is lowered onto the ship. The sexual implications of this narrative moment, together with the depiction of Smith as a blond, blue-eyed, square-jawed hero figure, establish him as youthful and virile, anticipating the film's sexualized representation of Pocahontas.*

Following the credits, the action moves to the forests, rivers, and mountains where Pocahontas and her people live, with the use of hazy pinks and blues suggesting an idyllic and dreamlike state. Scenes of happy maidens gathering corn and young men fishing, following on the depiction of London in the opening scenes, enforce a sharp contrast that distinguishes between European and Native American cultures in accordance with colonial binaries: culture against nature; complexity against simplicity; knowingness against ignorance; adult against child. Pocahontas is represented as the only child of the chief, Powhatan, and scenes where she engages in active pursuits, such as diving from a high rock into the river and paddling her canoe over rapids, construct her as an atypical representative of her culture. Her reluctance to marry the worthy but dull warrior Kocoum exemplifies her readiness to depart from customary practices. Thus, while the film represents the contrast between cultures in stereotypical terms, both Pocahontas and Smith are singled out as exceptional within their cultural contexts: Pocahontas as less Native and more like Western women in her desire for individual identity; Smith as less English and more like a Native in his athleticism and energy, and in his regard for Pocahontas and her culture.

Pocahontas's long black hair, full lips, and slanted (Asian) eyes inscribe her as exotic; at the same time, her body shape conforms with the hour-glass figure of the Barbie doll, and her buckskin dress, which displays her cleavage and her shapely legs, gestures toward "Indian" practices while transforming Pocahontas into what Betsy Sharkey, in a review in the *New York Times* at the time of the film's release, described as "an animated Playboy playmate."[8] Thus sexualized and re-placed within a popular-culture site, she is transformed into a commodity. Kent Ono and Derek Buescher observe, "In comparing Barbie with Pocahontas (or Native American Barbie), form, body, race, ethnicity, sex, and gender are all fetishized for consumer culture, further commodifying the Native American woman. This process effectively erases Native American identity from the form itself, while merely appearing to be based on a real Native American identity."[9] The figure of Pocahontas, detached from historical and cultural referents, is resignified by representational modes whereby colonial cultures have established and maintained conceptual hierarchies. Two such modes coalesce in the film's treatment of

---

*Unfortunately it has proved impossible to obtain permission from Disney for stills from *Pocahontas*.

Pocahontas: that of the sexually available Native American woman, and that
of the exceptional Native American individual who becomes the helper and
protector of white people. The first of these evokes colonial anxieties about
racial purity and the degrading effects of miscegenation upon settler cultures.[10] The second serves as a vindication of colonization, since it simultaneously exposes the inferiority of the colonized by contrasting the exceptional Native helper with other, hostile Natives, and implicates the Native
in her own subjection by foregrounding her readiness to be colonized.

The erasure of Native American identity identified by Ono and Buescher
plays out in *Pocahontas* through elements of story and representation that are
mapped onto traditions of cinematic representation. Thus, Pocahontas is
attended throughout the film by appealing animal companions—Meeko the
raccoon and Flit the hummingbird—in line with conventions of Disney an-
imations, notably in *Snow White* and *Cinderella*, where much of the action
centres on the birds and animals who attend the heroines of these films. Notions of the Indigenous person as "natural" ecologist abound in children's
texts as in popular culture, and in *Pocahontas* this stereotype, which aligns
Pocahontas with nature rather than with civilization or culture, is mapped
onto Disney conventions in a sentimental and reductive way.

Again, the figure of the wisecracking female sidekick to the main female
character is common in mainstream film, particularly in romances, where
such characters, conventionally coded as less attractive than lead characters, typically offer advice and emotional support, often undercutting romantic excess with humour. In *Pocahontas*, the character of Pocahontas's
friend Nakoma accords with this figure: she is less glamorous than Pocahontas, less noble, and far less adventurous, and her principal function in the
storyline is to utter warnings that Pocahontas ignores. Moments of slapstick,
such as when Pocahontas tips Nakoma out of her canoe and into the water
toward the beginning of the film, establish Pocahontas as the daring, playful
character and Nakoma as her foil. Like many of the "best friends" of romantic comedy, Nakoma is secretly in love. The object of her desire is Kocoum,
and it is when Nakoma divulges the secret of Pocahontas's love for John
Smith that the film's storyline departs from the Hollywood formula; for
whereas the best friend in comedy generally advances the course of romance,
Nakoma's action causes Kocoum's death. This divergence from Hollywood
convention accentuates the film's insistence on Pocahontas's exceptionalism,
since Nakoma's fear of white strangers is compared with Pocahontas's "natural" desire to engage with John Smith and his culture.

A third manifestation of mapping the story onto cinematic tradition
occurs in the figure of Grandmother Willow, the four-hundred-year-old tree-

spirit from whom Pocahontas seeks advice. As Pauline Turner Strong remarks, Grandmother Willow "appears to be a kindly descendant of the animated trees in *Babes in Toyland*,"[11] but her figure also evokes Arthur Rack-
ham's illustrations, an intertextual reference that locates her within a
European and canonical frame. By deploying the figure of Grandmother Willow instead of a human grandmother as Pocahontas's adviser, the film evades
more difficult dynamics; for although Grandmother Willow speaks in the
gnomic utterances that are coded as "Native" in the film's dialogue ("If you
listen, the spirits will guide you" and "Listen with your heart and you will
understand"), she also encourages Pocahontas in her dreams of romance
with John Smith. In a pivotal scene, Pocahontas introduces Smith to Grandmother Willow, whereupon Grandmother Willow invites him to come closer.
The two stand almost nose to nose in an encounter that emphasizes his
blond good looks and her gnarled and ancient features. Gazing directly at
Smith, Grandmother Willow announces "He has a good heart," whereupon,
turning toward Pocahontas, she adds, "And he's handsome, too." The smile
with which she utters these words can be read as benign or as lascivious; in
any case, by mapping the figure of the wise Native American elder onto that
of the fairy godmother of Western folktale, the film proposes that ideals of
Western good looks are normal and natural, and that romance readily tran-
scends racial and cultural difference.

At the end of the film, John Smith, wounded by the incompetent and
greedy Governor Ratcliffe, is sent back to England to recover. Given a choice
between accompanying him and staying with her people, Pocahontas
chooses the latter path. This moment of decision is prefigured near the beginning of the film, when her father places the necklace on her with the
words "Your mother wore this at our wedding. It was her dream to see you
wear it. It suits you." Pocahontas loses the necklace when Kocoum is killed,
and in the film's last scenes it is restored to her by her animal helpers. Her act
of saving John Smith and staving off war between the English and the
Powhatan is construed as proof that, in her father's words, she possesses
"wisdom beyond her years." In this way she is inscribed as the mother of her
people, the restored necklace suggesting both continuity and duty. In the
final scenes, Pocahontas is viewed silhouetted on a high rock as she observes
the boat carrying John Smith to England. At first, the colours of this image are
the pinks, purples, and blues associated with natural settings throughout,
but in the last moments they shade into sepia tones. This choice of colour invests the scene with a claim to historicity, suggesting the effect of an engrav-
ing where Pocahontas appears as a static figure performing her final act of ab-
negation; having saved John Smith's life, she now resigns herself to living
without him.

Strong observes that the words of the film's theme song, "Colors of the Wind," suggest a degree of tension between "listening with your heart" and "walking in the footsteps of a stranger." While the song's refrain makes the promise "You'll learn things you never knew you never knew," Strong notes that, "This is not the Pocahontas we never knew we never knew, but the Pocahontas we knew all along, the Pocahontas whose story is 'universal'—that is, familiar, rather than strange and shocking and particular. This is a Pocahontas whose tale … fits into the mold of the Western coming-of-age story."[12] Certainly Pocahontas's progress from self-centredness toward acceptance of responsibility for her people accords with the dominant schema of children's literature—the shift from solipsism to empathy with and openness to others. However, the figure of Pocahontas standing alone on the headland refers not only to the coming-of-age of the individual, but to myths of American nationhood that represent as normal and natural the idea that its Indigenous inhabitants should subordinate their interests to those of white settlers.

A further strand of signification is evident in the film's closure, in the contrast between stillness and motion. The immobile figure of Pocahontas, set against the energetic movement surrounding the departure of John Smith, produces an opposition common in colonial discourses where Indigenous peoples and cultures are represented as static and incapable of adapting to modernity. By avoiding an outcome in which Pocahontas and John Smith become sexual partners (or one that alludes to the historical Pocahontas, who married John Rolfe, an Englishman, travelled to England, and died there), the film avoids evoking a most troublesome figure, that of the Indigenous person whose multiple affiliations disrupt boundaries between races and ethnicities. While seeming to promote Pocahontas as an independent and agential figure, then, the film affirms myths of nationhood through its reproduction of colonial stories about the inevitability of Native American dispossession, the primacy of European culture, and the ideal of the self-sacrificing Indigenous figure whose principal function is to facilitate colonization.

## Authoritative (White) Experts and Indigeneity

The history of colonization in British settler societies is studded with stories, reports, anthropological and ethnographic studies, and official documents produced by non-Indigenous "experts" on Indigenous peoples and cultures. Edward Said's landmark work *Orientalism* first analyzed the discursive and rhetorical similarities that characterized a wide range of European texts on the Orient and its peoples, and studies of colonial discourses by scholars such as Mary Louise Pratt, Peter Hulme, Gayatri Spivak, and Homi Bhabha have built on Said's work. Said argues that "Everyone who writes about the Orient must locate himself vis-à-vis the Orient; translated into his text, this location includes the kind of narrative voice he adopts, the type of structure he builds, the kinds of images, themes, motifs that circulate in his text—all of which add up to deliberate ways of addressing the reader, containing the Orient, and finally, representing it or speaking in its behalf."[13] Said's thesis is that Orientalist writing always places the Orient in a position of inferiority by constructing Orientals as other to Europeans. It is by representing themselves as *knowing* about the Orient, "speaking in its behalf," that Orientalists capture and maintain power, since to represent the other is to determine the "kind of images, themes, motifs" that "contain" the Orient.

It is generally agreed, almost three decades on from *Orientalism*, that in this work Said represents Orientalists as a more unified group than they are and Orientalist texts as more univocal than they are.[14] When Said's theory is applied to the textual production of settler societies, it is clear that colonial discourses are subject to fissures and ambivalence, even if they accept as a given the principle that colonizers occupy a position of superiority; and post-colonial textuality is even more multifarious in its scope and variety of forms. As Homi Bhabha points out, the stereotyping by which the West represents non-Western cultures incorporates a contradictory mixture of fascination and distaste: "Stereotyping is not the setting up of a false image which becomes the scapegoat of discriminatory practices. It is a much more ambivalent text of projection and introjection, metaphoric and metonymic strategies, displacement, over-determination, guilt, aggressivity; the masking and splitting of 'official' and phantasmic knowledges to construct the positionalities and oppositionalities of racist discourse."[15] Settler society children's literature by non-Indigenous authors manifests much of the ambivalence that Bhabha describes, notably in the way white authors continue to claim specialist knowledge of and access to Indigenous cultures. My focus here is on two authors, both highly regarded for the uses they make of Indigenous narratives and mythological figures: Paul Goble, most of whose books comprise retellings or reinterpretations of Native American stories; and the Australian author Patricia Wrightson, who during her long career has produced many novels featuring Aboriginal spirit figures.[16]

Both Goble and Wrightson have explained and justified their use of Indigenous material. In her essay "Ever Since My Accident: Aboriginal Folklore and Australian Fantasy," in *Horn Book* in 1980, Wrightson describes her search for an "Australian" folklore that would enable her to introduce fantasy figures into her novels. She tells how, during the writing of her 1972 novel *An Older Kind of Magic*, she searched through "the works of anthropologists and early field workers and of laymen who had lived in sympathetic friendship with Aboriginal Australians"[17] for accounts of spirit figures and the narratives in which they appeared, selecting only "spirits that anyone might meet at any time and that could therefore enter new stories; spirits not held to be secret or sacred, not involved in creation or preservation but only in the chanciness of daily life."[18]

Wrightson's description of her research is striking for its Orientalist assumption that non-Aboriginal experts, "anthropologists and early field workers," are the proper sources of information about Aboriginal traditions, rather than Aboriginal people, who, she says, "told [their stories] haltingly in a foreign tongue or with skilled techniques that could not be conveyed in print; and so [the stories] lay buried in scientific books or brief retellings,"[19] to be recognized and explained by (non-Aboriginal) folklorists. The unquestioning faith in experts reflected in Wrightson's essay occludes the fact that the early anthropologists and field workers on whose work she relies were themselves deeply Orientalist and ethnocentric, interpreting and retelling Aboriginal narratives to make them fit Western categories of traditional stories such as myths, legends, fairy tales, and so on. Such classifications have little relevance to Aboriginal conceptions of narrative, which order stories according to the places and clans from which they derive, their functions within cultural practices, and the audiences to whom they are available.

Although Wrightson has always maintained that she avoids drawing on secret and sacred narratives, it cannot be assumed that early anthropologists and folklorists were cognizant of the complex, subtle rules that regulated who was eligible to tell and hear narratives within the Aboriginal cultures they studied; rather, as the artist Pat Torres says, from the beginnings of colonization in Australia "people in powerful positions such as police, protectors, missionaries, academics, government personnel and their spouses or family members often have used their position of power and authority to gain access to privileged information."[20] This is not to say that Wrightson deliberately draws upon sensitive or sacred traditions, but rather that she views Aboriginal narratives in a way that is doubly Orientalist, in that she both relies on Orientalist "authorities" and is herself deeply imbued with Orientalist perspectives, as she reveals in the following statement: "to recognize story and drama in a halting phrase, to hear in a few broken words the poetry and terror of strangeness experienced, and to convey these things in the techniques of print—that is the writer's job."[21] The phrase "the poetry and terror of strangeness experienced" eloquently supports Bhabha's view that stereotyping of the kind that Wrightson employs demonstrates a contradictory admixture of elements: fascination and fear; respect and disdain; desire and suspicion.

Goble bases his claims to knowledge of Native American traditions on his first-hand knowledge of Plains traditions and on his research into written sources and museum holdings. In his autobiography, *Hau Kola—Hello Friend* (1994), Goble describes his friendship three decades earlier with a Lakota elder, Chief Edgar Red Cloud, and says that "An Indian lady once wrote to me: 'I've always thought the *wanagi* (spirits) are close to you. Some of your illustrations reveal that the ancestors come to visit you in your dreams.'"[22] In *Adopted by the Eagles* (1994), Goble includes the following dedication: "*Ehanni iyayapi ki, wichunkiksuya pi*. I have made this book remembering Chief Edgar Red Cloud, 1896–1977. He gave me a Lakota name, and called me 'Son.' *Woplia ate.*"[23] In his author's note in the same book, Goble again refers to his friendship with Chief Edgar Red Cloud: "There are two main ideas inside this Lakota story which appear often in North American Indian literature: treachery between two warriors or hunters when they are far from home, and animals or birds who help people in need. Both were surely familiar ideas to our Stone Age ancestors all over the world.... I like to think that Edgar somehow sensed, right from the start (1959), that I would one day make books of some of the stories he told me."[24] This passage contains a telling slippage between past and present tense. Goble refers to two ideas in *Adopted by the Eagles* (treachery between warriors, and creatures that assist humans) that, he says, "appear often in North American Indian literature." He then shifts to the past tense in his judgement that these stories were "surely familiar ideas to our Stone Age ancestors all over the world." By implication, Lakota culture is close to "our Stone Age ancestors" in its mobilization of these narrative motifs. Opposite the author's note in *Adopted by the Eagles* is a photograph of Chief Edgar Red Eagle, and at the end of the book there appears another photograph of the chief, taken with Paul Goble in 1959. Goble's claims to authority, supported by the words of the "Indian lady" who wrote to him and by the photographs included in the book, imply that he has been endowed with a particular and even a spiritual connection with Native American traditions, suggested by the words of the letter, "Some of your illustrations reveal that the ancestors come to visit you in your dreams," and by Goble's impression that Edgar "sensed" that he would "make books" from "some of the stories he told me." The distinction between "books" and "stories" implies that Goble is charged with the responsibility of adding value to stories by transforming them into books.

Goble's credentials to retell Native American narratives, as he describes them in his autobiography and his picture books, seem to rest on his friendship with Chief Edgar Red Eagle, as though this relationship constitutes a once-and-for-all endorsement of his treatment of Lakota narratives; yet the three decades during which Goble has produced his picture books have seen

significant developments in Native American politics, expressed in the recla-
mation of identities, narratives, and traditions. Moreover, Goble's allusions
to his friendship with an individual Native American do not bear on broader
questions of power concerning his position of enunciation, as a privileged and
successful white author-illustrator who maintains and enhances his status
by retelling the stories of less privileged Native Americans. As I noted in
chapter 1, Goble's Iktomi stories undermine the contemporary struggles of
Native Americans by imputing ulterior motives to Iktomi, whose thoughts he
conveys by way of marginal commentaries. In *Iktomi and the Coyote*, Iktomi
announces that "That white guy, Paul Goble, is telling my stories again. Only
Native Americans can tell Native American stories. So, let's not have anything to do with them."[25] By deriding the notion that "only Native Americans can tell Native American stories," Goble here constructs himself as a
trustworthy and reliable intermediary, a figure parallel to Said's characterization of the Orientalist who assumes the role of "addressing the reader,
containing the Orient and finally representing it or speaking in its behalf."[26]
Like Wrightson, Goble expresses reverence for the spiritual and mystical
qualities of Indigenous narratives even as he downplays the capacity of Indigenous people to tell their own stories.

Just as Wrightson's authorities are deeply implicated in Orientalist perspectives, so Goble relies on anthropological and ethnographic sources rather
than on the living traditions of Native American people. His retelling of *The
Legend of the White Buffalo Woman* (1998), for instance, lists as primary
sources Joseph Epes Brown's *The Sacred Pipe* (1953) and John G. Neihardt's
*Black Elk Speaks* (1932), while among his secondary authorities are nineteenth-century and early-twentieth-century folklorists, anthropologists, and
ethnographers, including George A. Dorsey, James Mooney, and Clark Wiss-
ler; the artist George Catlin; and the photographer Edward S. Curtis. The
retellings on which Goble relies are inevitably informed by the cultural discourses that prevailed at the times they were produced, as well as by the preoccupations and agendas of white "experts." For instance, Julian Rice's *Black
Elk's Story* (1991), which explores the religious philosophies of Black Elk, argues that John Neihardt, whose interviews with the Lakota holy man provided the basis of *Black Elk Speaks*, possessed "a strong, consistent view of
history as providential progress. His relatively conventional vision foregrounds Platonic dualism and Christian universalism in his epic poetry, and
from that standpoint he edited the Black Elk interviews for *Black Elk
Speaks*."[27]

Given Goble's reliance on the work of white authorities, and the large
body of contemporary writing by Indigenous and non-Indigenous scholars
on the appropriation of traditional narratives,[28] it is surprising that his picture

books have been received so uncritically by reviewers and critics. In *Native Americans in Children's Literature* (1995), Jon Stott describes Goble's picture books as follows:

> [Goble's] adaptations of traditional myths and legends display a general pattern. After an author's introduction and bibliographical note the legend is narrated. The conclusion relates the event to the audience, referred to as "we" or "you," and traditional poems about the legend's topic finish the book.... The introductory materials clearly identify the sources of the stories and give them a firm cultural and historical context; these are the stories the people actually told, and these are some of the reasons they told them. The narratives, free of authorial comment, are then placed immediately before readers to be experienced directly.[29]

Stott's use of passive voice in "the legend is narrated" removes agency from Goble, suggesting that "the legend" exists in a pure or authentic form to be reproduced, while the past tense of "these are the stories the people actually told" is problematic for two reasons: its assumption that the retold stories on which Goble relies are unchanged from the narratives on which they are based; and the implication that contemporary Native American people no longer tell their stories. The claims that the narratives are "free of authorial comment" and "placed immediately before readers to be experienced directly" promote the idea of a pure, authentic, intact tradition passed on and received without reference to the historical and cultural contexts of production and reception.

A dissident voice in the canonization of Goble's work is that of Doris Seale, who criticizes his treatment of Iktomi as "offensive, insulting, and mean-spirited."[30] Seale's strongest argument relates to the questions of power and positioning that I discussed at the beginning of this chapter. She takes issue with Goble's statement, in the author's note of *Brave Eagle's Account of the Fetterman Fight*, that his primary intention in producing retellings of traditional stories is to pass on these narratives to Native American children. Seale responds, "Along with many anthropologists, [Goble] assumes, apparently, that we have so lost our traditions, cultures, and histories that we must be taught them by a white person."[31]

Given that the story of the white buffalo woman is, in Goble's words, the "most important of all Lakota sacred legends,"[32] his retelling of the story both mobilizes and repeats the old acts of appropriation signalled in his list of primary and secondary sources. Contrary to Stott's claim that Goble merely passes on narratives "free of authorial comment," he frames his version of the story by surrounding it "with other related myths."[33] In effect, he sandwiches the narrative between an opening sequence comprising stories of flood, regeneration, and war, and, after his account of white buffalo woman and her gift of the sacred pipe, a closing phase consisting of a story about the red stone from which pipes are made, and finally (connecting the end with the beginning) the explanation that the red stone is "the flesh and blood of the people who drowned at the end of the Old World."[34] Since the ordering of phases of narrative is one of the most powerful means of signifying relations between events, characters, and symbols, and hence of constructing meanings, Goble's textual intervention here directs readers to understand the story of white buffalo woman within the larger narrative frame he has devised. That is, he has constructed meanings by arranging the stories in this sequence.

Patricia Wrightson's deployment of Australian Aboriginal traditions differs from Goble's retellings in that Wrightson draws on narratives, motifs, and spirit figures from a wide range of clans and places in order to construct a pan-Aboriginal mythology. Her trilogy *The Song of Wirrun*, which comprises *The Ice Is Coming* (1977), *The Dark Bright Water* (1979), and *Behind the Wind* (1981), is Wrightson's most sustained attempt at creating such a mythology; the series follows the progress of a hero, Wirrun, who is charged with the task of restoring order to the land when it is threatened by hostile spirits. Throughout the trilogy, characters are divided among four groups: the Happy Folk, white people who live hedonistic and superficial lives on the coastal fringes of the country; the Inlanders, who live in the interior and farm the land; Wirrun's kinsfolk, the People, described as "dark-skinned, with heavy brows and watching eyes," who "belong to the land; it flows into them through their feet";[35] and the spirits of the land, progeny of "red rocks and secret waters, dust-devils and far places, green jungle and copper-blue saltbush."[36] Wrightson's sharp distinction between the city and the bush, and between city-dwellers and bush-dwellers, reinvokes literary and popular traditions that represent the "real" Australia as rural and inhabited by white settlers. However, in *The Song of Wirrun* Wrightson imagines a hierarchy where the People alone are capable of interacting with the spirits of the country, while the Inlanders observe their signs but have no access to them, and the Happy Folk are unaware of their existence.

On the face of it, this representation might seem to constitute a homage to Aboriginal knowledge; but the fantasy genre within which Wrightson works is so shaped and informed by European traditions that the Aboriginal characters, motifs, and spirit figures that it deploys are drawn inexorably into Western frames of reference. Central to the trilogy's narrative development is the story of Wirrun as a hero, beginning as an tentative boy faced with tasks apparently beyond his capacities, developing into a figure respected by the People, and attaining powers that enable him to restore order to the land when it is threatened by conflict between spirits. After his death, he enters the spirit world but continues to travel through the earth and to show himself to the People at their campfires.

As this summary suggests, Wirrun's progress as a hero is strongly reminiscent of Joseph Campbell's formulation of the hero's progress through the stages of separation, initiation, and return, that constitute what Campbell, in his influential work *The Hero with a Thousand Faces*, refers to as the monomyth, the universal heroic quest. Thus, Wirrun's encounter with "the dark" at the beginning of his journey corresponds to Campbell's conception of the "threshold guardian,"[37] the mythological presence that marks a distinction between the everyday and the monstrous, while at the end of the trilogy, Wirrun's struggle with Wulgaru, the spirit of death, corresponds to Campbell's description of the final act in the hero's story, "that of the death or departure"[38] that epitomizes the essence of the heroic identity.

I do not here suggest that Wrightson has been directly influenced by Campbell's work, but rather that her conception of the heroic journey is founded in her immersion in Western narrative traditions, and particularly of the story of Christ, one of the "universal heroes" who, according to Campbell, "bring a message for the entire world."[39] Literary historian Maurice Saxby observes that Wirrun's encounter with Wulgaru, the spirit of death, evokes "Gilgamesh crossing the waters of death to the faraway; Odysseus exploring Hades; Maui entering the Underworld; Beowulf in Grendel's Cave, Christian walking through the Valley of the Shadow of Death."[40] While Saxby is correct in reading Wirrun's progress in relation to stories of heroes from Gilgamesh to Christian, he misses the point that Wrightson's treatment of the Aboriginal hero merely reinvokes power relations that privilege white, Western traditions by treating them as normal. Thus, whereas Aboriginal traditions are highly localized and centred on particular tracts of land, Wrightson's Wirrun is a pan-Aboriginal hero, ranging across the continent and exercising his power over diverse spirits and places. Again, while knowledge in Aboriginal cultures is produced and reproduced according to protocols of seniority and kinship, Wirrun's understanding of the spirit world derives from an immanent and transcendent order. The colonizing effects of Wrightson's approach depend precisely on their invisibility to non-Aboriginal readers, who are positioned to read the story of Wirrun in the light of Western traditions of the heroic quest.

### The Spectre of Authenticity

While myths of national origin vary across settler colonies and across time, white imaginings of Indigenous peoples have had much in common with one another: the primitive other; the noble savage, the dying race metonymized by figures memorialized as "the last of" a tribe or people (the last of the Mohicans, the last of the Tasmanians, the last of the Beothuk). All of these tropes incorporate notions about "authenticity," an overworked and problematic term in discussions of Indigenous peoples and texts. A widespread prejudice across settler nations has been the association of "authenticity" with "pure" or "full-blood" Indigenous people, and, in regard to cultural production, with "traditional" forms and practices. The Australian Aboriginal art curator Hetti Perkins criticizes "determinist perceptions of authenticity," which, she says, promote the notion of a "pure or iconic expression of Aboriginality"[41] and that allow little room for invention, cultural change, or dialogue between Aboriginal and Western traditions. Similar issues bedevil discussions of authenticity across settler cultures, where the schizoid effects of colonization are evident in contradictory impulses wherein the "disappearance" of pure, authentic forms of Indigeneity is deplored at the same time that Indigenous people are blamed for not being Indigenous enough.

Welwyn Wilton Katz's *False Face* (1987) affords an instructive example of how discourses of authenticity inform representations of Indigeneity. The critical reception of this text since its publication is also instructive for the diverse views held of it by scholars and for how those views have changed over time.[42] In *False Face*, a white girl, Laney McIntyre, and her Mohawk friend Tom Walsh discover two masks, one of which has covered the face of a man who has been buried in a bog for many centuries, and the other a miniature version of the first. These masks are found to possess magical powers that control those who possess them (or, rather, whom they possess). Thus, when Laney's materialistic mother appropriates the larger mask in order to sell it, the evil influence of the mask means that when she is negatively disposed toward a person or animal, the result is sickness or even the threat of death.

This melodramatic use of the mask as a signifier of occult forces relegates Native American traditions to a realm of savagery that implicitly evokes its opposite, the civilized world where rationality and scientific knowledge are privileged. When Laney's mother is controlled by the power of the mask, her "natural" civilized identity is destabilized, whereas the Indian who fashioned the mask had been "naturally" aligned with a world of savagery, his "crooked body"[43] figuring his deformity of spirit. While Katz's author's note lays claim to her reliance on Mohawk traditions relating to false-face rituals, the language of her summary is striking for its use of terms that enforce the savage/civilized dichotomy: for instance, members of the Society of Faces are said to make "a terrible racket with horns and rattles, as well as by dancing and chanting."[44]

If the masks in *False Face* gesture toward notions of "authentic" Iroquois traditions as savage and barbaric, the characterization of Tom Walsh is equally problematic. Tom is a stereotypical "in-between" figure, caught between his father's Mohawk heritage and his mother's whiteness, and feeling himself to be "neither one thing nor the other."[45] Having grown up on a reserve, he has moved to London, Ontario, following his father's death, and he experiences the hostility of white students at the school that he attends with Laney. When Tom finds the face mask in the bog, his access to Indigenous traditions is represented as an instinctive response to its power: "Danger. Danger. Impossible to bury it again. Impossible not to. Tom ran, breath sobbing, feet thudding. He was all Indian now, an Iroquois fleeing for his life."[46] To be "all Indian" is clearly an undesirable state in the world of the novel, since it is associated with Tom's powerlessness against the mask.

When Tom seeks advice from the "real" Indians on the reserve where he has grown up, he encounters only hostility. A boy who was previously his friend barely acknowledges him, and the old man whom he meets at the longhouse speaks in the gnomic utterances so often attributed to Indigenous people in children's novels, rejecting Tom's claim to Indian ancestry. When Tom visits his father's grave, he realizes that his father had "not belonged on this Reserve. He had not belonged on any Reserve. He had seen people as people, regardless of the colour of their skin."[47] "Real" Indians, then, are shown to be locked into relations of hatred and resentment of white people, and of those other, less "authentic" Indians, who engage positively with white culture. To return to Alcoff's discussion about speaking for others, it is clear that the narrative of *False Face* is enunciated from a Eurocentric position that conceals the false universals and the position of superiority on which it relies. Thus, the idea that Tom accepts at the end of the novel, that "Everybody had to choose what to let himself be,"[48] is built on Western norms of individual progress that claim universality. The novel positions its readers to accept that the authentic Indian is the one who is most like "us."

While *False Face* presents a strikingly negative account of "authentic" Indigenous culture, many children's texts are informed by romantic discourses whose ideological effects are not dissimilar. Eve Bunting and John Sandford's *Moonstick: The Seasons of the Sioux* (1997) juxtaposes an account of the lives of Sioux early in the history of colonization[49] against a depiction of their descendants, whose lives play out against a backdrop of industrialization. The first-person narrator through most of the book is a Sioux boy who describes "the seasons of the Sioux" with reference to natural phenomena such as the end of snow, the budding of the box elders, and the eating of strawberries and juneberries: "When the snows of winter disappear my father cuts a moon-counting stick that he keeps in our tipi. At the rising of the first moon he makes a notch in it. 'A new beginning for the young buffalo,' he says. 'And for us.' Everything is new."[50] Sandford's painterly illustrations construct an idyllic and ordered world in which the young narrator, guided by his father, is inducted into Sioux practices and sociality. The narrative follows the sequence of thirteen moons commencing with spring and concluding with the "moon when the grass comes up."[51] In the last few pages of the book, there is an abrupt shift to a time when modernity has taken hold of Sioux culture: "Many moons have died. Many winters have passed. My father is with the Great Spirit. The buffalo have gone and the eagles are few in the sky. Our lives are different now. My eldest brother works in a barbershop. His hair is white as winter snows. My wife does beadwork and I make headdresses of feathers that sell well. We do not hunt."[52] What is striking about Bunting's narrative is that her reliance on stereotypical versions of Native American speech—the use of short, portentous sentences; metonyms such as "many moons"; references to the spirit world; similes drawn from natural phenomena ("white as winter snows")—is standard across the two narrators, suggesting that Sioux culture stands still, immune to change. This impression is reinforced by the parallels between two illustrations, the first (fig. 6) depicting father and child in the early colonial period, and the second (fig. 7) showing the narrator and his grandson in the modern period. In the text accompanying the second illustration, the narrator rehearses what he will say to his grandson: "To him I will say, 'Do not despair. One time follows another on life's counting stick. Changes come and will come again.' I was told once that it is so arranged."[53] The effect of the two matching illustrations and of the narrator's tone of melancholy acceptance is that the destruction of Sioux culture is inescapably positioned as part of a historical cycle in which "one time follows another," an unfortunate but inevitable consequence of modernity. In this way, readers are positioned to acquiesce to the disappearance of "genuine" Sioux just as surely as is the case in *False Face*, with its ostensibly more negative representation of contemporary Indigeneity.

Discourses of authenticity as they work through this book locate "authentic" Sioux culture in an idealized, romanticized past. Hence, the modern narrator's proposal that he will cut a counting stick as his father did, and show it to his grandson, appears as no more than a pathetic gesture with little point in a world where there are no buffalo to hunt and where Sioux culture has in effect been assimilated into modernity. While this book does not present Native American culture in as negative a light as does *False Face*, it nevertheless produces similar ideological outcomes: "authenticity" is associated with a past utterly discontinuous with modernity, modern Native American cultures are represented as "inauthentic," and the implication is that the only hope for Indigenous survival is to discard the cultural practices and beliefs of the past and assume those of the majority culture.

FIGURES 6 (*above*) and 7 (*opposite*) from Eve Bunting and John Sandford, *Moonstick: Seasons of the Sioux.* Copyright © 1997 by John Sandford. Used by permission of Harper-Collins Publishers.

## The Cherokee Princess Effect

In Joseph Bruchac's *The Heart of a Chief* (1998), Chris, the Penacook protagonist, has an encounter with a classmate, Katie, who confides in him that she too is an Indian. Musing on this avowal as he travels home to the reservation on the bus, Chris consults his friend Belly Button:

> "She said she was Indian?"
> "Unh-hunh."

"Anybody can say they're Indian. What kind of Indian?"

Gartersnake, who is listening to it all, turns around in his seat, lifts up his shades, and joins in.

"Yeah," Gartersnake says, "what kind? Hollywood? Calcutta?"

Pizza leans over from the seat next to us. Of course he's been listening too.

"Cherokee Princess?" he asks.[54]

The boys' skepticism derives from their awareness that they are second-class citizens, "the kind of Indian who gets ignored at best and treated like dirt at worst,"[55] and from their intense suspicion of white people who claim Native American ancestry while maintaining a careful distance from Native Americans.

In her essay "'White Indians': Appropriation and the Politics of Display," Deborah Root argues that the myriad appropriations of Native traditions that occur in contemporary popular culture in Canada and the United States are founded in a reflex acceptance of colonial notions of Native people as "heroic victims, or, perhaps more accurately, as people who are heroic precisely because they have been victimized."[56] In line with the binary oppositions characteristic of Western thought, Native nations must be "inherently abject and doomed to defeat"[57] if white people are to be absolved of responsibility for the depredations of colonialism and the continuing disadvantage of contemporary Native people. Root argues that acts of appropriation where white people adopt Native modes of apparel, adornment, and ritual constitute performative strategies that enable non-Native people to "seize discursive space from Native people,"[58] locating themselves at the centre of attention as compassionate and sensitive. Perhaps, Root suggests, such strategies of appropriation derive from the sense that "Native people may be oppressed, but the traditions have power; white people may be 'in charge' within a colonial context, but our culture has lost its heart, soul, and life—its power."[59]

Katie, the "Cherokee Princess" of Bruchac's *The Heart of a Chief*, turns out to be Indian, though Mohawk and not Cherokee, a development that enables Bruchac to construct a Native American subject who identifies as Indigenous even if her Mohawk ancestry is not obvious in her appearance. At first glance, Sharon Creech's *Walk Two Moons* (1994) might seem to involve a similar mode of identification, as the narrator-protagonist, Salamanca Tree Hiddle, defines herself in relation to her Seneca great-great-grandmother. However, the novel's treatment of Salamanca's Indianness is folded into representational patterns that characterize the Cherokee Princess effect: the deployment of scraps and fragments of Native American traditions that stand for Indigeneity while displacing any reference to the materiality of Native American peoples and cultures. The novel's title, which alludes to the proverb used as the novel's epigraph, "Don't judge a man until you've walked two moons in his moccasins," establishes this strategy at the outset.

*Walk Two Moons* has been widely praised for its "authentic" representation of Native American culture; indeed, Michelle Pagni Stewart goes so far as to assert that "novels such as Michael Dorris's *Sees Behind Trees* and Beatrice Culleton's *In Search of April Raintree* deserve attention in the classroom, yet neither of these novels introduces students to the complexity of Native American literary traditions to the extent that…*Walk Two Moons* does."[60] This claim is contestable on many fronts. Stewart's imagined classroom is populated by the non-Indigenous students who are the implied readers of *Walk Two Moons*, and who will readily comprehend the figure of Salamanca Tree's mother precisely because her character is based on familiar, stock, white versions of Native Americans—as children of nature, tragic figures torn between cultures, and wild, free spirits. In comparison, *Sees Behind Trees* and *In Search of April Raintree* are less comfortably familiar and hence more challenging to read, since in these texts Indigenous subjectivities are normative and the world of the dominant culture different and other. The implication of Stewart's comparison between *Walk Two Moons* and two texts by Indigenous authors, *Sees Behind Trees* and *In Search of April Raintree* is, perversely, that the two latter texts are not Native enough. Stewart proposes that *Walk Two Moons* adheres to Native American traditions of narrative, such as interpolated narratives, references to dreams, and multiple narratives, and that in this sense the text "introduces students to the complexity of Native American literary traditions." I would respond that interpolated and multiple narratives are common in late twentieth-century texts for children in general, and that "authenticity" cannot be defined through reference to a checklist of "Native American literary traditions." It is necessary to go beyond the surface features of texts to the discourses that inform linguistic and narrative strategies, in order to discern how ideologies are promoted to readers.

When Salamanca describes how her parents named her in the erroneous belief that her maternal great-great-grandmother belonged to the Salamanca tribe, this error is treated as a charmingly eccentric episode, as though the circumstances of her ancestor's life and tribal origins are inconsequential; and Salamanca tells a related story concerning her mother's name: "My mother said that Grandmother Pickford's one act of defiance in her whole life as a Pickford was in naming her. Grandmother Pickford … named my mother Chanhassen. It's an Indian name, meaning 'tree sweet juice,' or—in other words—maple sugar."[61] Salamanca's glossing of "tree sweet juice" can be contrasted with the glossing of terms by which Indigenous authors install difference; here, it denotes as quaint and primitive the expression "tree sweet juice," implying that "maple sugar," is the "correct" meaning toward which "tree sweet juice" can merely point.

The narrative of *Walk Two Moons* is built on two interrelated strands, each involving a mystery that is solved by the end of the novel. The first strand relates to the death of Salamanca's mother, while the second involves a story about Salamanca's friend Phoebe, a story related by Salamanca as she travels with her paternal grandparents, Gramps and Gran, from Ohio to Lewiston, Idaho, where her mother has been buried. The mystery at the centre of the story of Salamanca's mother relates to why she left her family and how she died, and references to her Native American ancestry permeate the novel's unraveling of this mystery. When Salamanca and her grandmother watch "a group of Native Americans dance and beat drums"[62] at the Wisconsin Dells, where they have broken their journey, Salamanca recalls her mother's insistence on using the term "Indian" rather than "Native American," because, she said, "*Indian* sounds much more brave and elegant."[63] This memory leads to another: "My mother and I liked this Indian-ness in our background. She said it made us appreciate the gifts of nature; it made us closer to the land."[64] Salamanca's sense of self here relies on her internalization of romantic notions concerning "Indian-ness," which is represented as a bundle of inherent characteristics and values, transmitted through the generations without reference to cultural associations or engagement with Native Americans.

The actual Native Americans whom Salamanca observes, the men in "feather headdresses and short leather aprons" and the women wearing "long dresses and ropes of beads,"[65] are homogenized figures in whom Salamanca takes no more than a spectatorial interest. When her grandmother joins with the dancers, ending up in the centre of the circle of women and wearing "an enormous headdress, which had slipped down over her forehead,"[66] it seems that Salamanca's claim to an Indigenous identity is enhanced by her grandmother's capacity to take on Indigeneity. Later in the journey, at the Pipestone National Monument in Minnesota, her grandparents and Salamanca smoke a peace pipe that similarly stands for Indianness even as the narrative maintains a resolute distance from the Native American man who hands the pipe to Salamanca's grandfather.

The narrative gradually reveals that Salamanca's mother, deeply depressed following the death of her infant daughter, left her family to "clear her head, and to clear her heart of all the bad things,"[67] and that she died when the bus on which she was travelling plunged down a steep cliff. Her repudiation of her life with her husband and Salamanca is explained, at least in part, by a disjunction between a selfhood identified with her Native American ancestry, and her sense that her husband is "too good" for her. When he seeks to reassure her that she does not need to go away to discover who she is, she responds, "'I need to do it on my own … I can't think. All I see here is what I am not. I am not brave. I am not good. And I wish someone would call me by my real name. My name isn't Sugar. It's Chanhassen.'"[68] Her insistence that her real name is Chanhassen enforces the idea that Salamanca's mother must be true to an Indian identity in order to regain her sense of self. Further, the contrasts between Salamanca's father (sweet-natured, calm, kind, reliable) and her mother (volatile, unpredictable, close to nature) signal both an unbridgeable gap between the two and the seeming inevitability of a tragic end to their relationship, thus gesturing towards colonial stories concerning interracial sexual relationships that are doomed to end in disaster. As I have signalled, the attractiveness of *Walk Two Moons* to white audiences can be explained in part by the fact that its treatment of Indigeneity is so reassuringly familiar and unthreatening: the novel's representation of Salamanca's mother—doomed, beautiful, tormented—accords precisely with white imaginings of the Native American feminine. Moreover, Salamanca herself represents an adapted and "improved" version of Indianness, one that claims emotional and psychic depth while evading any reference to memories of colonization or of the lived experience of Native American people either in relation to Salamanca's great-great-grandmother or in the contemporary world of the novel's setting. The fact that *Walk Two Moons* is a skillfully written book with appealing characters and an engaging narrative means that it is difficult to interrogate its hackneyed treatment of Indigeneity; similarly, Patricia Wrightson's novels so eloquently evoke the Australian landscape that it is all too easy for readers to acquiesce to her homogenized and Westernized versions of Aboriginality.

## Ancient Cultures: Good Medicine

Just as the Cherokee Princess effect relies on strategies of appropriation, a related constellation of meanings is evident in the very many texts by non-Indigenous authors where white characters derive psychological or spiritual benefits from engagement with Indigenous cultures. The trope of the Indigenous environmentalist appears in many children's texts, including Brian Doyle's *Spud Sweetgrass*, which I discussed in chapter 1. Some of these texts involve issue-based narratives whose thematics refer to ecological and environmental concerns specific to their place and time of production. For instance, Lesley Choyce's *Clearcut Danger* (1992) calls on the long history of political activism by the Mi'kmaq nations of Eastern Canada, around hunting and fishing rights and claims to ancestral lands.[69] When Alliance Forestry Products, a powerful milling company, seeks to establish a new timber mill on land sacred to her ancestors, the Mi'kmaq girl Alana, together with her white friend Ryan, conduct a campaign against the development, with the support of members of the Spruce Harbour Indian Reserve and Greenpeace. Ryan is the novel's first-person narrator, and its action hinges on his growth in environmental awareness and respect for Mi'kmaq culture. Thus, while the narrative proposes a model of activism where non-Indigenous people learn from the traditions and practices of Indigenous cultures, subjective agency is never granted to Indigenous characters, whose actions and thoughts are always filtered through Ryan's perspective.

Other texts thematizing environmental issues draw on more generalized notions of Indigenous characters as *naturally* attuned to the land. In *Walk Two Moons*, Salamanca and her mother are instinctively drawn to appreciate nature because of their Seneca heritage; and in *Owl*, the New Zealand novel considered in chapter 1, Indigenous characters know and value the natural environment in ways unavailable to non-Indigenous figures. At the other end of the spectrum are texts that mobilize New Age discourses where Indigeneity is valued for its capacity to heal the ills of industrialized societies whose inhabitants are oppressed by their powerlessness in the face of ecological destruction and neoliberal politics.[70] The Australian text *A Long Way to Tipperary* (1992), for instance, incorporates an Aboriginal elder-figure, Kajabbi, who is treated as the last hope for the land's recovery from deforestation, pollution, and degradation.

It is, of course, not in question that within the complex and diverse Indigenous cultures of New Zealand, Australia, Canada, and the United States, spiritual beliefs and cultural practices centre on relationships between humans and the natural world. Nor would I argue with the principle that the non-Indigenous inhabitants of settler societies have much to learn from the original custodians of lands and waters. In general, however, non-Indigenous representations of Indigenous environmentalists fall back on nostalgic and reductive conceptions of a Golden Age when humans lived in harmony with the land. Moreover, as Patricia Seed argues in *American Pentimento*, her study of the continuing effects of colonization in the Americas, the figure of the Indigenous environmentalist reinscribes colonial distinctions between settlers who actively and intentionally used the land for profit, and Indigenous peoples who occupied the lowly place of hunter-gatherer in the Social Darwinist hierarchy of races. Seed argues that, in contemporary settler cultures, "demanding that present-day conduct conform to preconquest (or what are considered to be preconquest) characteristics denies native peoples the opportunity to progress or to participate in history,"[71] relegating them to a primordial state.

A common trope through which Indigenous cultures are depicted as a boon to non-Indigenous characters is the character type described by Michael

Dodson as "the ancient noble spirit."[72] An example of such figures occurs in Ben Mikaelsen's *Touching Spirit Bear* (2001), in which fifteen-year-old Cole Matthews, charged with physically attacking a younger boy, pleads guilty in order to participate in Circle Justice, a system by which young offenders, rather than going to jail, undertake activities intended to develop empathy for the victims of their crimes and to take responsibility for their actions. Cole is required to live alone on an Alaskan island under the supervision of two Tlingit men, Garvey and Edwin, respectively a parole officer and an elder charged with guiding Cole toward self-knowledge and remorse. Mikaelsen's depiction of the relationship between Cole and his two mentors focuses squarely on the benefits to Cole of his introduction to Tlingit beliefs and practices, and suffers from a malaise common in this trope—that is, the sole narrative function of Indigenous elders is to heal the wounded spirits of damaged white characters, while the elders themselves seem to inhabit a mythic past without reference to their personal and communal histories.[73]

The many problem novels that trace the progress of troubled young Indigenous figures generally depict these characters as feeling, like Tom Walsh in *False Face*, that they are "neither one thing nor the other,"[74] as though mixed ancestry is in itself a cause of psychic trauma. Symptomatic texts include Mary-Ellen Lang Collura's *Winners* (1984), James Moloney's *Gracey* (1994), William Taylor's *Beth and Bruno* (1992), and Monica Hughes's *Log Jam* (1989). Deborah Savage's *Flight of the Albatross* (1989), the text with which I close this chapter, combines several of the tropes that I have discussed. It incorporates Mako, a troubled Maori youth; Hattie, an ancient Maori woman; and Sarah, a fifteen-year-old white girl newly arrived from New York to stay with her mother, an ornithologist, on the remote Great Kauri Island, in the Hauraki Gulf near Auckland. Sarah, a gifted flutist, resents her mother's abandonment of her and her father ten years previously; Mako, whose father is a well-known Auckland activist, has been in trouble with the law and has been sent to Great Kauri Island to work for his stepfather, a fisher.

Sarah finds an injured bird, a rare wandering albatross, and takes it to what she thinks is an empty cottage. The rundown building turns out to be the home of the Maori elder Hattie, whose speech is strikingly similar to that of Grandmother Willow in *Pocahontas*: "'You will leave the bird with me. She is not for your mother. You found her; she is yours. You did not find her by chance—you do not believe you did. You will care for her here. She is yours, and you will help her fly free again. That is what you want.'"[75] Given Hattie's intimations about the connections between Sarah and the bird (and the psychic powers thus signalled), it is not surprising that Sarah's romance with Mako is preordained, or that she finds herself speaking Maori words that she does not understand, or that she is irresistibly drawn to Goat Hill, a place that is *tapu* because of its associations with Maori rituals of death.

The dénouement of the novel sketches the progress of Sarah and Mako from alienation to an enhanced capacity for empathy and engagement with others. Mako discovers that his ancestor Tawahi sided with the European conquerors and betrayed the Ngati Moana, the people of Great Kauri Island, and that his father's radicalism is merely a disguise for the ancestral guilt that oppresses him. Sarah forgives her mother for abandoning her in order to pursue her career in ornithology. The wise woman Hattie dies at the very moment that the albatross, healed of its wounds, takes to the skies. The ideologies of the novel, evident in its closure, privilege Sarah and her access to classical music and high culture over the impoverished and illiterate Mako, just as Maori radicalism is undermined through the link between Mako's father and his treacherous ancestor Tawahi. If Hattie is represented as the embodiment of ancestral wisdom, it is also the case that she dies alone, the "last of her tribe," ushering in a new world in which "it is time for the voices of all people to grow, for nations to grow."[76]

At the end of the novel, Sarah has returned to the United States to study music at an Ivy League college. Sitting on the shores of a lake near the college, she plays her flute, the wind "carrying the notes out over the lake." As she reads a letter from Mako and a poem he has written in Maori and English, she glimpses a seabird wheeling high overhead, and a "perfect white feather" falls into her lap: "She picked it up and held it in her hand, a perfect white feather, bigger than any gull's. She drew it lightly across her cheek, and in that faintest whisper of sound, she heard the words as surely as if they had been spoken: 'I love you, I love you.' She recognized the voice."[77] What Sarah has gained from her engagement with Maori culture is an enlarged sense of the possibilities that lie before her, symbolized in her enhanced abilities as a musician. Like Pocahontas, Mako remains "at home," a self-sacrificing figure offering unconditional affirmation to a beloved white person. *Pocahontas* and *Flight of the Albatross* rework colonial narratives in which Indigenous people are seen to benefit from Western knowledge— Pocahontas by learning to speak English; Mako by learning to read—in ways that will equip them to prosper in a white world (in contrast, neither John Smith nor Sarah learns an Indigenous language). However, the non-Indigenous characters, John Smith and Sarah, gain far more: a sense of their own worth, a consciousness of their magnanimity in valuing non-Indigenous cultures, and a reaffirmation of racial hierarchies. In both film and novel, Indigeneity is subsumed into the invisible and unmarked norms of white cultures.

## 4 Telling the Past

We know the past affects the future, but can the present change the past? And is it always clear what is real and what is not?
— Felice Holman, *Real*

The prevalence of historical novels in settler culture children's literature underlines the ideological work that these texts carry out as they seek to explain and interpret national histories—histories that involve invasion, conquest, violence, and assimilation. More than any other category of settler culture texts, historical fiction is caught between opposing and sometimes incompatible imperatives, since it seeks to position child readers as citizens of nations even as narratives located in colonial settings necessarily advert to the violent dispossession and struggle that characterize the origins of settler societies. It is not only in historical fiction that texts deal with the past. In chapter 8, I discuss texts that deploy allegorical and metaphorical modes to interrogate not only imperial history but also the ideology that informs it, an ideology characterized by Bill Ashcroft as "sequentiality, inevitability, purpose, authority; a teleology that is divinely ordained."[1]

Historical fiction is not history, despite the fact that the peritextual materials included in many novels (such as maps, timelines, authors' notes) claim varying degrees of historicity for the events and characters they represent, and despite their deployment of realist narrative modes. Rather, historical novels select, order, and shape events to serve the purposes of their narratives; and historical fiction no less than other genres is informed by deep-seated cultural habits and practices. It is not the case that there exists a body of empirically derived "historical facts" of colonization that can be unproblematically portrayed in fiction, or that historical novels for children can be evaluated in terms of their adherence to historical actuality. Said's comment about truth and representation is apt here: "… the real issue is whether there can be a true representation of anything, or whether any and

Notes to chapter 4 on pages 240–42.

all representations, because they *are* representations, are embedded first in the language and then in the culture, institutions and political ambience of the representer. If the latter alternative is the correct one (as I believe it is), then we must be prepared to accept the fact that a representation is *eo ipso* implicated, intertwined, embedded, interwoven with a great many other things besides the 'truth,' which is itself a representation."[2] Moreover, when historical events and characters are introduced into fictive narratives, they are construed in ways that accord with the directions and ideologies of these narratives, rather than with any "objective" body of historical knowledge, since they are framed by the conventions and practices of fiction, and not those of history.

While historical fiction is not history, the production and reception of historical fiction always responds to and engages with shifts and developments in how "history" is understood. Since the 1970s, the emancipatory drive of postcolonial studies has had a marked effect on the discipline of history. Leela Gandhi notes that, whereas Europe was formerly the subject and centre of national and international histories, "postcolonial historiography declares its intention to fragment or interpellate this account with the voices of all those unaccounted for 'others' who have been silenced and domesticated under the sign of Europe."[3] Many historians, Indigenous and non-Indigenous, have undertaken revisionist projects that seek not merely to view colonial events through Indigenous perspectives (often by calling on the oral histories and narrative traditions of colonized peoples),[4] but—more radically—to engage with Indigenous epistemologies and theories of history, which often depart in fundamental ways from Western traditions.

To describe what I refer to as Indigenous historiography, I turn now to the work of Japanese scholar Minoru Hokari, who in a series of essays describes his encounters with Gurindji historians in the Northern Territory of Australia. Gurindji epistemologies are attuned to particular places and traditions, and I discuss them not to produce generalizations about Indigenous views of history, but to focus on an exemplary instance of cultural difference. Hokari visited the Northern Territory to gather oral histories, learning Gurindji history from an elder, Jimmy Manngayarri (Old Jimmy), who used sand drawings to teach him how colonial events were explained within Gurindji traditions. Many of these narratives relate to Jurntakal, a snake that during the Dreaming emerged from the earth and travelled through country, creating humans and establishing law (the proper relations between humans and country, as well as between one clan and another). Jurntakal's progress through country was "the right way,"[5] proceeding from west to east: "Jurntakal is 'right' because he rose from the earth and gave people the law. In the beginning, the earth was alive and conscious. Then 'movement' occurred. According to Old Jimmy's philosophy, this single line [drawn in the sand] representing the 'movement from west to east' opens up the ontological and moral dimensions of the world."[6] Old Jimmy's understanding of the law derives from the Gurindji stories he has heard and from dreams in which Jurntakal has spoken to him. His view of colonization is that the English flouted the law by travelling in the wrong direction, from north to south, thus cutting across the "right way" established by Jurntakal. The "wrongness" of the colonizers' actions is understood in both a moral and a spatial sense, for to invade and claim country not one's own is profoundly immoral, especially when invaders do not seek permission to enter Aboriginal land but violently assume ownership and control over it.

I have touched here on just a few aspects of Minoru's discussion in order to demonstrate some of the many ways in which Old Jimmy's view of history departs from Western historiography. The sources of Gurindji history are generations of elders, Dreaming spirits, and the land itself, whose features, topography, and sacred places are infused with knowledge of the past. History as Old Jimmy understands it is localized, *placed* in Gurindji country, and it incorporates a moral framework. Story and history do not belong to different discoursal modes, but history is realized through story. Nor is the past merely a passive body of facts and events to be interpreted, but Gurindji people interact with the past, which is alive and active in the present. For instance, Hokari tells how Gurindji people taught him histories "when and where the past spoke to them,"[7] so that as he travelled in their company, elders recounted events that had occurred in particular places (for instance, colonial massacres), and described how the spirits communicated with them in these locations. It is, then, impossible to overestimate the importance of locality in Gurindji historiography. As Hokari notes in his "Localised History: 'Dangerous' Histories from the Gurindji Country," localized history is different from local history, in that the latter "tends to be a part of 'universal' history (or national history, in many cases),"[8] whereas localized history resists being incorporated into Eurocentric models that claim universality, and it testifies that Western historiography is only one way of explaining historical practices.

In chapter 2, I discussed some of the strategies by which Indigenous texts interpolate dominant discourses without "asserting a unified anti-imperial intention, or a separate oppositional purity,"[9] to return to Bill Ashcroft's treatment of interpolation. One mode of interpolation comprises fiction that contests Eurocentric versions of settler society pasts. Just as non-Indigenous historians such as Minoru Hokari address Indigenous views of history by acknowledging and honouring their difference, so it is open to non-Indigenous as well as Indigenous authors to interpolate the givens of mainstream historical fiction. However, as I will argue in this chapter, historical fiction that is produced by non-Indigenous authors and concerns itself with precolonial and colonial events continues with few exceptions to represent the past from Western perspectives and in line with Western conceptions of history.

### Alternative Histories

I noted earlier that postcolonial historiography seeks to dismantle the disciplinary givens of Western traditions of history by introducing the perspectives and views of colonized others. It might be imagined that the many historical novels for children that are focalized through the perspectives of Indigenous characters or first-person narrators, such as Brian Burks's *Walks Alone* (1998), Diane Johnston Hamm's *Daughter of Suqua* (1997), Sally M. Keen's *Moon of Two Dark Horses* (1995), and the *Dear America* novels, including Ann Turner's *The Girl Who Chased Away Sorrow* (1999), accord with this agenda; but in fact they routinely subsume Indigenous identities within Western paradigms.[10] An example is Jan Hudson's novel *Sweetgrass* (1984), whose eponymous narrator is a Blackfoot girl living early in the nineteenth century. In this novel, the shape of the narrative accords with the many Western stories about young women, of which *Little Women* is the paradigmatic example, in that Sweetgrass's progress from youth to maturity involves a sequence of events in which a "rebellious" girl is transformed into a woman compliant with the domestic and heterosexist expectations of her society. The alterity of Blackfoot society is signalled at a superficial level by details of everyday life (food, domestic arrangements, clothing), but the deeper values and ideologies of the culture are unaddressed. The informing assumption of the text is that Sweetgrass desires the same outcomes (such as individuation, physical attractiveness, and heterosexual romance) that are prevalent in conservative versions of the feminine in Western narratives.

Two Indigenous texts that exemplify alternative approaches to narrativizing the past are the *Papunya School Book of Country and History* and Michael Avaarluk Kusugak and Vladyana Krykorka's *Arctic Stories* (1998), which both locate historical events within Indigenous systems of narrative and history, contesting dominant versions not only of historical events but also of how the past is conceived and represented. The opening pages of the *Papunya School Book of Country and History* assert the text's reliance on a specifically Anangu historiography in which *ngurra* (country) is at the centre of knowledge: "We learn about our history and our country from our elders and our community. We learn by going to our country, by living there and being there. We learn through the *Tjukurrpa Yara*—the Dreaming stories. We learn through the different songs and dances and paintings, that belong to different *ngurra*."[11] By claiming the Dreaming stories, along with presence

in country, as a mode of learning about history, the *Papunya Book* departs
from European formulations of the past, which separate mythological traditions from the real and the historical. It departs, too, from Western notions
of time as a linear progression capable of being divided into eras, centuries,
and other units. Rather, the Dreaming is, in the words of the archaeologist
Claire Smith, "both 'then' and 'now.' It encompasses events of the ancestral
past but also exists in the present."[12] At the end of the *Papunya Book*, a fold-
out page extends the final double-spread to show a diagrammatic version of
Anangu history, presented as a sand painting on the red earth of the desert.
Progress through time is depicted as a spiral pattern that loops around, continually returning to the Dreaming. Whereas Western historical practice privileges action, played out within places functioning as mere backdrops of history, the visual and verbal texts of the *Papunya Book* treat country as a space
imbued with life and with significations.

In the picture book *Arctic Stories* (1998), written by Michael Arvaarluk
Kusugak and illustrated by Vladyana Langer Krykorka, Kusugak alludes to
histories of abuse and exploitation in residential schools through the strategic use of oral history and mixed-genre writing. He constructs an account of
Inuit life during the 1950s through the perspective of a focalizing character,
Agatha, who lives with her family in Repulse Bay on the Arctic Circle. The
first two stories establish a habitus where Agatha's life revolves around the
practices of her close-knit family and community, shadowed by the incursions
of the world outside. In the third story, "Agatha Goes to School," she is obliged
to leave Repulse Bay to attend boarding school in Chesterfield Inlet, to "a
world [Agatha] had only heard about, a place where people spoke English and
the language-of-the-priests."[13] Finally, Kusugak's afterword comprises an
autobiographical note in which the author describes his experience as one of
the many Inuit children enrolled in residential schools during the 1950s.[14]
In both "Agatha Goes to School" and in his afterword, Kusugak negotiates the
topic of child abuse, drawing on oral history to produce an account of the experience of Inuit children, trapped in a strange world where they struggled to
determine meanings.

A key sign of institutional corruption in the mission school at Chesterfield
Inlet in Kusugak's stories is the disruption of connections between signifiers
and signified. In "Agatha and the Ugly Black Thing," the first of the stories,
Agatha's relationship with her father is characterized by warmth and mutuality. In "Agatha Goes to School," however, the term "father" is at odds with
these significations, calling attention to the gap between words and practices: "The nuns did not make very good mothers and the priests, who were
called fathers, did not make very good fathers."[15] Again, while the nuns sing
"so beautifully that Agatha thought they must sound like angels,"[16] in reality

"they were not angels. If you did not kneel just so and hold your hands just so in church, they would get mad and hit you on the knuckles."[17] These guarded references to the emotional, physical, and sexual abuse experienced by Inuit children are set alongside the benign story of Father Fafard, who skates on thin ice and falls into the freezing water, to be rescued by Agatha. The afterword offers a more explicit counter-narrative: "Many people who went to that school have now charged the Catholic Church, the Government of Canada and all those involved with harassing boys and girls. Some of the priests, brothers and nuns who took care of us are now gone. And I am sure some of them have not gone to heaven. But there were some good things that happened; we got a good education. And then there were the skis, the skates and Father Fafard. If he is not with us any longer, I am sure he has gone to heaven."[18] If Father Fafard is a character in "Agatha Goes to School," he is also an historical figure retrieved through the author's memories of his time at residential school. Just as Kusugak disrupts generic boundaries, so he refuses to engage in neat generalizations: while the priests, brothers, and nuns who abused the children in their charge "have not gone to heaven," the same children have received "a good education." The difficult and contradictory meanings of *Arctic Stories* unsettle distinctions between fiction, autobiography, and history, foregrounding the interplay of memory and narrative.

I conclude this section by considering Orson Scott Card's *Red Prophet* (1988), which is often described as an alternative history of the United States and which spans young adult and adult readerships. *Red Prophet* is the second volume of the series *The Tales of Alvin Maker*. The narrative situates historical figures such as Napoleon Bonaparte, William Henry Harrison, Tecumseh, and his brother Tenskwatawa within a rite-of-passage plot involving ten-year-old Alvin Miller, the seventh son of a seventh son, whose paranormal powers enable him to heal broken bones and bodies. Alvin is transparently a version of Joseph Smith, and the ideologies of the text gravitate toward an affirmation of white, patriarchal power, which shapes the novel's representations of Native American characters and cultures.[19]

Card's strategy of focalizing events through a variety of perspectives (including those of Hooch Palmer, Mike Finch, Ta-Kumsaw, Tenskwa-Tawa, and Gilbert de La Fayette) seems to construct a kaleidoscopic world characterized by radical differences of vision and understanding. At the same time, the narrative is structured by binaries: the pure, idealistic Alvin against the principle of negativity known as the Unmaker; the determinedly pacifist Prophet compared with Ta-Kumsaw, whose aim is to "drive the White man back into the sea";[20] the idyllic community of Alvin's hometown, Vigor Church, set against the venality and violence of Harrison's Carthage City.

Within this conceptual scheme, Native American culture is marshaled to endorse Alvin's standing as the "true" Native. Thus, the Prophet's role resides in his duty to "teach [Alvin] how to be Red instead of White,"[21] while Alvin's power extends to restoring to the Prophet his sense of oneness with the land, lost to him because of the shock of his father's murder and the alcoholism in which he has taken refuge.

Toward the end of the novel, Harrison's forces attack Tenskwa-Tawa's settlement of Prophetstown, abetted by the villagers of Vigor Church (including Alvin's father), whom Harrison has incited to violence. The men, women, and children of Prophetstown stand in Speaking Meadow, "just looking out at the White men who were killing them"[22] until they are mowed down by musket fire. This description of mass slaughter, like that of the novel's final scene of battle when Ta-Kumsaw and his French allies are defeated by Andrew Jackson and his forces, enforces their representation as doomed and passive victims. In both episodes, the narrative lingers on the maimed and dying bodies of Native Americans, producing an aesthetic that associates death, suffering, and blood with Redness. That this aesthetic is founded in notions of a lost and romanticized Indigeneity is clear: "So Ta-Kumsaw was remembered in song as Red villages and families moved west across the Mizzipy to join the Prophet; he was remembered in stories told beside brick hearths, by families who wore clothing and worked at jobs like white men, but still remembered that once there was another way to live, and the greatest of all the forest Reds had been a man called Ta-Kumsaw, who died trying to save the woodland and the ancient, doomed Red way of life."[23] Card's comparison between an "ancient, doomed Red way of life" and the lives of those who "wore clothing and worked at jobs like white men" effects a radical discontinuity between ancient, "authentic" Red traditions, and Native American people pursuing occupations and living in settings similar to those of the mainstream culture, a strategy that detaches those ancient traditions from Reds and associates them instead with the figure of Alvin.

Red Prophet offers a clear demonstration that the mere inclusion of Indigenous figures and themes does not construct alternative versions of history; for meanings are produced not only through story but also through language—through discursive and narrative strategies that position readers and propose ideologies. By taking on Redness, Alvin is shown to become all the more "American": at the end of the novel he "walked like a Red man, all at one with the living world,"[24] so claiming ownership of the land and its future. In Red Prophet, then, representations of Indigeneity exemplified in the figures of Ta-Kumsaw and Tenskwa-Tawa are subordinated to narrative directions in which the true, proper American is masculine, white, and godly.

## Pre-contact Settings, Contemporary Meanings

Realist historical fiction is in the main a non-Indigenous genre, with the exception of a small number of texts by Indigenous authors, such as Louise Erdrich's *The Birchbark House* (1999), Joseph Bruchac's *The Arrow over the Door* (1998), and Michael Dorris's *Morning Girl* (1992), all of which focus on the experience of Indigenous subjects encountering Europeans in early colonial settings where, to return to Mary Louise Pratt's description of the contact zone, "disparate cultures meet, clash, and grapple with each other."[25] As I noted in chapter 2, Indigenous children's authors generally focus on the production of texts modeling the identity formation of contemporary Indigenous subjects. It is perhaps the case, too, that the field of realistic historical fiction dealing with colonial events has been so dominated by Eurocentric versions of the past that it is unrecuperable to Indigenous authors. Thomas King suggests as much in *The Truth about Stories*:

> It would be reasonable to expect Native writers to want to revisit and reconstruct the literary and historical past, but … with few exceptions contemporary Native writers have shown little interest in using the past as setting, preferring instead to place their fictions in the present….
>
> What Native writers discovered, I believe, was that the North American past, the one that had been created in novels and histories, the one that had been heard on radio and seen on theatre screens and on television, the one that had been part of every school curriculum for the last two hundred years, that past was unusable, for it had not only trapped Native people in a time warp, it also insisted that our past was all we had.[26]

King goes on to conclude that, faced with the impossibility of writing a past already so thoroughly inscribed with the meanings of the dominant culture, Native writers "began to use the Native present as a way to resurrect a Native past and to imagine a Native future. To create, in words, as it were, a Native universe."[27]

Constructions of Indigenous life prior to European colonization would seem to demand of authors that they imagine social formations and identities that depend upon frames of reference very different from those that apply in more modern settings. In this section, I consider a group of novels, all except one by non-Indigenous authors, located in settings that precede colonization: Joanna Orwin's *Ihaka and the Prophecy* (1984), in a Maori settlement in the eleventh century; Joan Clark's *The Dream Carvers* (1995), in what is now Newfoundland in the eleventh century; Allan Baillie's *Songman* (1994), in northern Australia half a century before the arrival of James Cook;

and Joseph Bruchac's *Children of the Longhouse* (1996), in a Mohawk village late in the fifteenth century. All four novels tell coming-of-age narratives involving young boys, and while *Ihaka and the Prophecy* and *Children of the Longhouse* are set in Indigenous settlements that have no connections with non-Indigenous populations, *Songman* and *The Dream Carvers* trace cross-cultural relations: in *Songman* between Aboriginal people and Macassan fishermen from what is now Indonesia, and in *The Dream Carvers* between a Norse boy and the Beothuk clan who capture him.

Writing on historical novels from the North East of England, Pamela Knights notes how these texts invoke deep histories instantiated in features such as "Norse place-names, artefacts, documents, scars on the land itself"; these histories "deploy the region's past as the sphere of healing for the dysfunctions of the present."[28] Whereas these novels promote a reconciliation of past and present through continuities of identity and place (even when they rehearse ancient conflicts, as the reference to Norse place names signals), settler culture texts located in pre-contact settings always contend with the ruptures of colonization, since the cultures and events that they describe cannot be imagined without at least implicit reference to subsequent narratives of invasion and destruction. Whereas the texts described by Knights imply readers who share with focalizing characters some sense of regional or national affiliation, the texts I discuss, with the exception of *Children of the Longhouse*, imply (in the main) non-Indigenous readers positioned in quite complex ways—as outsiders to Indigenous cultures but also as citizens of nations where tropes of Indigeneity contribute to cultural identities.

Such pre-Contact narratives are inevitably shadowed by readers' awareness of the impending events of colonization, which are imminent in two of the novels: *Children of the Longhouse* and *Songman*. In *The Dream Carvers*, as in the novel I discuss later in the chapter, Kevin Major's *Blood Red Ochre* (1989), the narrative's setting in a Beothuk community gestures toward the colonial trope of the vanishing Indigene, since Shawnadithit, the so-called "last of the Beothuk," died in 1829. By subordinating large-scale historical events to narratives of individual development, the four novels position readers to align themselves with protagonists whose progress from childhood to adulthood is figured through narrative sequences consistent with those that dominate children's literature, in that experiences of danger and testing tend toward closures where characters achieve an enhanced sense of selfhood.

As John Stephens observes, historical fiction often "incorporates strategies for defamiliarization which are peculiar to this discourse."[29] In all four novels, the principal strategy of defamiliarization is their use of what Stephens terms the "register of antiquity,"[30] the use of grammatical features, syntax, and vocabulary that construct a world contrasted with modernity. As Stephens also notes, such a register is "unequivocally an artefact of high culture and is inevitably fraught with the ideological concerns of particular social groups with an idea of history as a moral structure."[31] Specifically, the novels I discuss here implicitly interrogate the values of contemporary settler cultures through their constructions of Indigenous pasts.

The prophecy referred to in *Ihaka and the Prophesy* relates to a chant uttered by the dying *tohunga* (priest) Takaroa, who predicts that the people of Takurangi will migrate from their present dwelling place in the north of the South Island, across the stretch of water now known as Cook Strait, to resettle in the warmer climate of the North Island. In order to fulfill this prophecy, the men of Takurangi must construct a seaworthy, double-hulled canoe capable of carrying the entire settlement, and the events of the narrative are organized around the progress of the boy Ihaka toward the realization of his identity as a carver of stone and wood, a highly privileged role associated with sacred places, tools, and rites. Ihaka is apprenticed to the old carver Paoa, who dies after the new canoe has been launched and Ihaka has been inducted as a *tohunga.*

By plotting Paoa's death against the ascendancy of Ihaka, Orwin foregrounds cultural continuity, but a particular kind of continuity that depends on the maintenance of hierarchies of class and lineage. Not only is Ihaka the son of an elder, but his gift for carving manifests as an innate quality recognized by Paoa, so that social order is seen to inhere in a combination of hereditary rights and meritocracy. The boy Toihau, whose niggling resentment Ihaka experiences intermittently through the narrative, finally accedes to Ihaka's superiority after the latter receives the facial tattoo that marks him as a *tohunga*:

> [Ihaka] could see Toihau watching him steadily, not a smile on his face. Ihaka met his eye quietly.
>
> Toihau stared a bit longer. Then he said slowly, "None of us begrudge you this honour, Ihaka."[32]

This interaction serves to consolidate Ihaka's position within the group of young men as a future leader with an inborn right to command, enforcing the novel's construction of a conservative, hierarchical class structure.

In *Ihaka and the Prophecy*, Orwin uses language coded as archaic principally in direct speech, heightening the impression of solemnity and occasion by introducing such language into the narration as well at key moments. The following passage, for instance, describes the death of Paoa:

> For a moment, Paoa's grip was firm. His eyes seemed to clear and he smiled at Ihaka. Then he said in a voice that they all heard,

"E, Ihaka. E, tama, spread your wings and fly."

In the hush that followed, Paoa closed his eyes. Ihaka felt the pressure of the old man's grip relax…

"Paoa's spirit has flown," said Mawera softly. "His last words have been spoken."

…From across the water, the lament for the dead rose and fell as the people gathered on the shore to farewell Paoa's spirit as it left his body for the last long journey over the western horizon.[33]

The metaphorical usages of "spread your wings," "Paoa's spirit has flown," and "the last long journey," the impression of solemnity conveyed through the passive construction of "His last words have been spoken," the snatch of Maori "E, Ihaka. E, tama" ("Tama, my son"), and the alliteration of "last long journey" and "lament" underscore the weightiness of this episode, when the old *tohunga*'s dying words address the new *tohunga* in an affirmation of tradition and heritage.

Directed toward young New Zealanders (Pakeha and Maori), this novel constructs Maori culture as an inheritance, the land as peopled by proud and noble ancestors. The episode I have discussed, that of Paoa's death and Ihaka's inheritance of his *mana* (prestige), can be read as promoting values such as stability and respect for authority. At the end of the novel Ihaka looks to his future: "He knew… that no matter where the great canoe would take him, one day he would find his way back. Like the kuaka [godwit], Ihaka would return to this place where he had grown to adulthood."[34] This promise of a return to origins resonates with cultural anxieties over the fact that many young New Zealanders leave the country to travel and work, making lives for themselves as expatriates. The closure of the narrative thus positions readers to extrapolate from the precolonial setting a set of values presented as transcendent and timeless: love of one's place of origin, loyalty, and the resolve to return. The novel's appeal to notions of cultural continuity effectively displaces the cultural and historical differences between its setting and that of its readers, producing Ihaka as a model young New Zealander.

Whereas the ideological intentions of *Ihaka and the Prophecy* are implicit, *Children of the Longhouse* promotes ideologies far more overtly, both in its narrative and also in Joseph Bruchac's afterword. Here Bruchac claims cultural continuity from pre-Contact to contemporary Mohawk cultures, suggesting that the establishment of the Great League of Peace was "one of the greatest and most hopeful epics of humanity, a tale of peace and true forgiveness"[35] capable of speaking to nations engaged in ethnic and cultural conflict at the time of the novel's production: "a bit like the contemporary struggle in the Balkan States of Europe."[36] This is an uncommonly explicit expression by a novelist of the cultural work carried out by historical fiction. *Children of the Longhouse* is also the only novel of the four I discuss in this section to have been produced by an Indigenous author. Its treatment of the past departs from that of the three other novels in that its narrative is structured as much by a story of negotiation and conciliation between putative enemies as by a coming-of-age narrative. In its emphasis on the processes whereby a Mohawk village maintains order within its own sociality and peaceful relations with other communities, *Children of the Longhouse* adheres to what Jace Weaver terms "communitism,"[37] since it promotes communal rather than individual interests. At the same time, the coming-of-age story that it incorporates seeks to engage non-Mohawk children in a narrative consonant with the usual directions of mainstream literature for children.

The protagonists of the novel are the twin brother and sister Ohkwa'ri and Otsi:stia, and a key meaning promoted by the narrative, embedded in its alternation of focalization between the two children, is an insistence that female power and a balance between male and female authority are fundamental to Mohawk culture. The pivotal event of the narrative is a game of Tekwaarathon (the ball game from which lacrosse derives), involving a contest between the Old Men's and the Young Men's teams.[38] In this game, two narrative strands intersect: Ohkwa'ri is established as a future leader of the community, playing as a surrogate for the old man, Thunder's Voice, in whose honour the game is played; and Grabber, a young man who is resentful and jealous of Ohkwa'ri, suffers a nearly fatal injury in his attempt to harm Ohkwa'ri. When Ohkwa'ri staunches the blood flowing from Grabber's broken leg and stays with him as he waits for help, singing "the song to be sung when you were in need of a friend,"[39] he is shown to demonstrate the wisdom and forbearance expected of a leader, while his physical prowess is evident in his success in the game of Tekwaarathon.

Like *Ihaka and the Prophecy*, *Children of the Longhouse* centres on a hierarchical social order and protagonists who (at least potentially) occupy the higher echelons of that order: Ohkwa'ri and Otsi:stia's grandmother, She Opens the Sky, is a Clan Mother, and their mother's brother Big Tree is one of the Roia:ne or clan leaders. As in *Ihaka and the Prophecy*, status and power depend upon a combination of ancestry and innate ability. While the third-person narration of *Children of the Longhouse* adheres in the main to Present Standard English, more elevated and archaic forms of language are evident in narrative moments involving public oration and in sequences where characters navigate interpersonal and familial relations.

A sequence that demonstrates the latter use of language appears when Otsi:stia encounters her brother, her father, and her two uncles following a scene where Ohkwa'ri has been given a new stick for the approaching game, one intended for Thunder's Voice but never used by him. Otsi:stia is the more reflective and careful of the two children, and the narrative places high significance on her capacity to watch out for her brother, to anticipate dangers, and to counsel him, functions that stand in a metonymic relationship to the surveillance exercised by senior women in the community over the activities of men and children. At the point where this excerpt begins, Otsi:stia has observed the satisfied expressions on the faces of Ohkwa'ri and the men, and has seen the new stick, but she does not know how to read what she observes:

> But even though she knew she would be teased for her impatience, she could stand it no longer.
>
> "Tell me," she said.
>
> Big Tree laughed. "My sister's daughter," he said, "we are going to have to give you a new name. Otsi:stia, 'The Flower,' is not a good enough name. Maybe you should be called 'Watches Everything.' What do you think, my sister's husband?
>
> Two Ideas laughed. His laughter, like Big Tree's, was not at all unkind. In fact, it had an approving sound to it. "I think my daughter is much like your honored mother," he said. Then he paused, for it was not proper for a man to tease his mother-in-law or for her to tease him. "By this," Two Ideas said, no longer laughing, "I mean that my daughter is one of those who always seems to know what is going on in our village, just like her grandmother."[40]

The vocatives "my sister's daughter" and "my sister's husband," used by Big Tree, as well as Two Ideas's use of "my daughter," "your honored mother," and "her grandmother" instead of the names commonly used in the community, underline the importance of kinship relations—specifically, between a man and his mother-in-law, and between children and their maternal uncles, who take particular responsibility for training and guiding them. While Big Tree adopts a gently teasing tone in his suggestion that Otsi:stia should be given the new name of "Watches Everything," he shifts into a different register in the careful formality of "your honored mother" and in his cessation of laughter. As if to emphasize the significance of such relationships, Bruchac interpolates an explanation as to the protocols of respect and distance proper between Two Ideas and She Opens the Sky: "for it was not proper for a man to tease his mother-in-law or for her to tease him." The modulations of register here are quite subtle, and they achieve a defamiliarization that draws attention to the alterity of Mohawk culture.

Similar language features and explanations of practices and protocols occur throughout *Children of the Longhouse*, so that this novel may very likely appear "slow" to mainstream audiences accustomed to realist narratives more dependent on events and actions. In other ways, too, such as the double narration of some episodes seen first through Ohkwa'ri's and then through Otsi:stia's perspective, and the interpolated narratives through which adults instruct the children, the narrative slows down considerably. It is useful here to return to Patricia Linton's discussion of resistant texts, which I referred to in the introduction,[41] where Linton distinguishes between readers enculturated in the world of the narrative and those she refers to as "cultural outsiders."[42] While Bruchac is at pains to offer explanations concerning Mohawk practices and customs, the very visibility of these explanations draws attention to the educational and formative purposes of the text as they are directed to the non-Indigenous children who comprise the majority of readers. *Children of the Longhouse* thus directs itself toward two audiences: non-Mohawk children, and the Mohawk readers referred to in the novel's dedication, "For the children of the longhouse—past, present, and future,"[43] who are positioned to recognize and affirm the values and ideologies of contemporary Mohawk life.

Whereas *Ihaka and the Prophecy* and *Children of the Longhouse* locate their narratives exclusively within Indigenous communities, Joan Clark's *The Dream Carvers* and Allan Baillie's *Songman* thematize cross-cultural exchanges that precede colonization. In *The Dream Carvers*, Thrand, a fourteen-year-old boy from Greenland, is kidnapped by a group of Beothuk when he accompanies his father on a voyage to Leifsbudir (Newfoundland) to obtain wood; and in *Songman*, Yukuwa, a young Yolngu man from what is now the Northern Territory of Australia, travels with his mentor, Dawu, to the island of Sulawesi in Java, present-day Indonesia, where he encounters Dutch colonizers who use Macassar as a centre of trade and exploration.[44]

The encounters between Indigenous and non-Indigenous figures in these books disrupt colonial histories that construct the arrival of European colonists in the New World as epoch-making, foundational events, foregrounding instead Indigenous histories of cross-cultural relations stretching back through many centuries. Nevertheless, both novels implicitly refer to and prefigure colonial events, and both map these events onto ancient encounters. In *The Dream Carvers*, Thrand is captured to replace Awadusut, a young Beothuk man of the Osweet clan who has been killed by the Norsemen; Thrand is renamed Wobee. The first-person narrative is focalized partially through the perspective of Thrand/Wobee, and to a lesser extent by Abidith, Awadusut's sister, with whose family Wobee lives. The novel is structured by the story of Wobee's enculturation into Osweet culture, and its closure is effected through his resolution to establish a permanent relationship with Ahune, a girl from a neighbouring clan.

Wobee's narration is conducted in Present Standard English. The register attributed to Abidith, including the passages of direct speech interpolated in her narration, is distinguished by simple sentence structure, frequent use of rhetorical devices such as repetition and balance, a limited and mainly concrete vocabulary, and occasional archaisms. This contrast, together with the fact that Wobee's narration takes up the bulk of the novel and both introduces and closes the narrative, produces the sense that Wobee's is the normative mode of thinking and speaking, and that his world view accords with Western perspectives and ideologies. Moreover, Abidith's narration incorporates sequences where she accesses Wobee's dreams and thoughts and "speaks" to him through his mind, while Wobee cannot enter Abidith's thoughts. Like the (Indigenous) alien beings I discuss in chapter 8, whose planetary homes are colonized by humans, the Beothuk of *The Dream Carvers* engage in telepathic communication that locates them in a world of dreams, interiority, and imagination, in contrast with Enlightenment concepts of rationality and externally driven action.

As Wobee engages more empathetically with his Osweet captors, the narrative constructs him as questioning the values of his own culture. First, whereas the Beothuk do not ascribe higher status to chiefs than to clan members, Norse culture is represented as riven with distinctions between lords and peasants, and between free and enslaved individuals. Second, Wobee reflects on Greenlanders' concepts of individual and familial ownership of property, compared with the communal rights to material goods and land that prevail within Osweet sociality. Wobee recognizes that "If no one owns anything, it's impossible to steal,"[45] whereas in his culture, where people are "greedy for goods,"[46] acts of theft are serious crimes. Third, Wobee's memories of fierce conflict between individuals and groups are set against the Osweets' preference for negotiation and communal decision-making, such as when the council of clans decides to welcome Wobee and another captured Norseman, Cheething, as permanent members. By aligning readers with Wobee as he learns to value Beothuk ways, the novel interrogates ideologies—hierarchies of worth, materialism, and the resolution of conflict through violence—that characterize contemporary Western cultures.

Nevertheless, there exists an acute tension between, on one hand, the teleological directions of the novel, which involve Wobee's movement from a state of alienation to one of incorporation within Beothuk culture (instantiated in his romantic relationship with Athune), and, on the other hand, the larger teleologies of Canadian nationhood in which the Beothuk represent cultural annihilation and the dominance of colonizers. To put it bluntly, by

the end of the novel Wobee has aligned himself with the "wrong side," cast-
ing his lot with an Indigenous group described by Ingeborg Marshall in her
*History and Ethnography of the Beothuk* (1996) as "the only tribe whose extinction is popularly [in Canada] linked to persecution by Europeans," and
which has thus "received more posthumous attention than any other native
groups, and ... led to more recrimination."[47] While the novel positions Canadian readers to admire and even venerate Beothuk culture, it also provides an
explanation for its destruction that, by implication, enforces colonial distinctions.

In a somewhat similar way, the narrative of Baillie's *Songman* teeters between its construction of a conventional trajectory of identity formation and
its treatment of cross-cultural relations between Aborigines and Macassans
prior to colonization. In his afterword, Baillie makes a claim to historicity
by referring to events and facts: the establishment of the convict colony of
Sydney half a century after the events of the novel, nineteenth-century evidence of cross-cultural relations between Macassans and Aboriginal groups
in the north of Australia, and the cessation of Macassan fishing fleets in the
1880s as the waters around Australia came under colonial rule. By implication,
the transactions of friendship and commerce between Aborigines and Macassans to which the novel alludes are set against colonial histories that involve
more antagonistic and destructive dynamics, signalled in references to Dutch
colonial rule in Macassar; yet the novel's representation of the violence of
Dutch rule and the poisonous relations between Macassans and colonizers
produces a too-simple analogy with the impending depredations of British
rule in the north of Australia. This is not to say that British colonization was
"better" than Dutch, but rather that each colonial setting is unique in its interface between the geographical, political, and cultural factors that shape
its peculiar dimensions.

Yukuwa, the novel's protagonist, is an inept hunter, which brings him
shame; but he has a gift for inventing songs, just as Ihaka in *Ihaka and the
Prophecy* has a gift for carving, and like Ihaka he achieves a sense of selfhood when his gift is recognized by his community. As in *Ihaka and the
Prophecy*, the coming-of-age narrative adheres to Western paradigms of individual growth that jostle against representations of ancient societies where
the interests of the community are valued over those of individuals.

In *The Dream Carvers*, *Ihaka and the Prophecy*, and *Songman*, Indigenous
cultures are idealized and romanticized. *Children of the Longhouse* stands out
from this group of texts because of its emphasis on how the ideologies and
values of Mohawk culture are realized through rituals, practices, and behaviours. In the other three texts, readers are positioned to admire Indigenous
cultures destined (according to the historical teleologies that these narra-

tives evoke) for extinction or colonization. As well, the narratives of individual achievement that structure *The Dream Carvers, Ihaka and the Prophecy,* and *Songman* position readers to align themselves with characters "like them"—that is, characters whose progress from youth to maturity accords with schemata familiar from countless mainstream Western texts, literary and popular, in which protagonists encounter obstacles or dangers and attain enhanced levels of awareness or self-regard. Thus, despite the claims to historicity that are articulated in the afterword of *Songman,* the author's note of *The Dream Carvers,* and the glossary of *Ihaka and the Prophecy,* these three texts afford representations of Indigenous cultures that are all too readily caught up in universalizing formulations of the human subject.

## Colonial Histories, Binary Narratives

The narrative structure referred to by Robyn McCallum as "interlaced binary narrative,"[48] which involves dialogue between the perspectives of two narrators or focalizers, would seem to offer the possibility of mediating between historical and contemporary perspectives. *The Dream Carvers* involves a narrative of this kind, although the bulk of narration is mediated through Wobee's perspective. I conclude this chapter with a discussion of three binary narratives, which all shift between contemporary and colonial times and are set in a colonial past when violent events occurred. In the New Zealand text *Cross Tides* (2004), by Lorraine Orman, sixteen-year-old Bel has been sent to stay with her aunt, uncle, and cousins on Taupahi Island in the north of the South Island. Her first-person narration alternates with that of a sixteen-year-old British girl, Lizzie, sold by her drunken stepfather to settle his gambling debts and forcibly married to Jack Dawson, the captain of a whaling station on Taupahi Island in the 1820s. Kevin Major's *Blood Red Ochre* (1989) is set in Newfoundland and alternates between chapters incorporating narrator-focalized and first-person narration, tracking the lives of two fifteen-year-old boys: David in the contemporary setting, and a young Beothuk man, Dauoodaset, in the early nineteenth century. In Felice Holman's *Real* (1997), the framing narrative is itself historical, set in 1932 in southern California and featuring a young boy, Colly, whose father is a stuntman working in movies. Colly's story is set alongside that of a Cahuilla boy, Sparrow, who is stranded in a "Forever Day" in 1774, condemned day after day to replay his death and that of his grandmother at the hands of scouts accompanying a wagon train, because their bones have not been accorded a ceremonial burial (*nukil*) and their spirits must therefore wander without rest.

Each of the novels incorporates uncanny moments or sequences when contemporary and historical figures meet—in *Cross Tides,* a ghostly Lizzie visits Bel at Dawson's Beach, the site of the whaling station; at the end of *Blood Red Ochre*, David encounters Dauoodaset and his lover Shanawdithit on Red Ochre Island in the 1820s, where Dauoodaset is killed by a woodsman; and in *Real*, Colly and Sparrow meet, sometimes in the 1770s world and sometimes in the 1930s setting. The white protagonists of these novels are alienated or depressed young people. In *Blood Red Ochre*, David has discovered that the man he has always believed to be his father is in fact his stepfather; the boy Colly, in *Real*, is mourning the death of his mother in a traffic accident; and in *Cross Tides*, Bel has been sent to Taupahi Island while her parents finalize their divorce. In line with the well-worn narrative pattern that dominates in texts by non-Indigenous authors, Indigeneity figures as a site of healing and insight, enabling white characters to develop an enhanced capacity for other-regarding and self-reliant modes of being.

The potential advantage of binary narratives is that they are capable of producing a dialogue that interrogates the givens of both cultures by showing them to be constructed, relative, and contingent. However, such dialogue depends on the extent to which cultural and historical discourses are accorded alterity. Of the three texts, *Cross Tides* is the least complex, and its treatment of historical contexts is most clearly subsumed into the norms of contemporary Western culture. This is largely because the structuring schema in both the contemporary and the colonial narratives is that of interracial romance. In the colonial story, Lizzie falls in love with Matthew, a Maori preacher who visits the island. Their romance is a shameful secret because Lizzie is married to Jack Dawson, but more tellingly because it flouts colonial attitudes that regard as unthinkable the possibility that white women should form romantic and sexual liaisons with Indigenous men, although Indigenous women are always prone to seduce white men.[49]

The contemporary story tracks Bel's romance with Daniel Kelly, the Maori grandson of Mere Ihaka, an elderly activist who with other clan members conducts a symbolic protest about land rights on Dawson's Beach. While colonial interdictions against interracial romance are not articulated in the contemporary setting, the fact that Daniel is Maori invests the romance with a sense of riskiness: according to Bel's young cousin, Daniel is "a bit crazy. He likes to be off by himself all the time, he won't join in with sport and things."[50] In a melodramatic scene during which Bel and Daniel are stranded in a remote cave where they discover Matthew's skeleton, Bel resists the temptation to have sex with Daniel because she experiences a ghostly visitation from Lizzie who convinces her that "this is *wrong*. Wrong for me, maybe even wrong for Daniel too."[51]

In both the narrative strands of *Cross Tides*, Maori cultures and characters afford an exotic background to the main action, which centres on the female characters, Lizzie and Bel. In Lizzie's narrative, Maori men feature as tough, tattooed whalers and Maori women as the common-law wives of white whalers, while another Maori "type" is present in the person of Te Rauparaha, the warrior and leader, represented here as a dangerous and posturing figure. The contemporary narrative, too, incorporates tough, tattooed men who are, however, absorbed into the category of activists, since they form part of Mere Ihaka's group of protestors. Just as Lizzie's Maori friend, Marama, possesses second sight, so Mere Ihaka communicates with Daniel by telepathic means; thus the category "Maori" across the two time frames is occupied by a limited repertoire of character types: sexually available women, manual labourers, revolutionaries, and seers.

Both Matthew and Daniel stand out from other Maori as atypical figures whose difference is explained in relation to their connections with non-Maori practices and behaviours. Matthew, who tells Lizzie that he was "left to die by [his] own people,"[52] was taken in by missionaries, educated, and converted to Christianity, while Bel sees Daniel as "different to the others, totally different. Really spunky.... He reminds me of the Native American Indians on TV. Sort of graceful, not all clumpy and awkward like the boys at school."[53] The novel's representations of Matthew and Daniel as exceptional Maori characters renders them acceptable as objects of romance, even as their Maori ancestry invests them with glamour.

In *Cross Tides*, the historical narrative is subsumed into the contemporary Western schema that informs the novel's account of Bel's progress toward selfhood. In a final strategy of incorporation, Bel discovers at the end of the novel that she is descended from Lizzie's son, who was adopted by Marama and her husband, and that Lizzie is thus her ancestor and not Marama, as the family has always believed. The Cherokee princess effect, which claims spiritual connection and power through an imagined or remote biological connection with Indigeneity, is realized in this narrative twist, which draws otherness into a normative Western selfhood.

I noted in discussing *The Dream Carvers* that the dominant narrative perspective is occupied by the Greenlander, Wobee, whose language is represented as Present Standard English and hence as figuring Westernness. In *Blood Red Ochre*, a similar pattern is evident. The chapters tracking David's identity formation shift between character-focalized and narrator-focalized perspectives, while Dauoodaset's first-person narration is laden with defamiliarizing strategies that alert readers to the alterity of Beothuk culture. The opening lines of the first "Dauoodaset" chapter are as follows: "It is winter still. Seven of our people came many days over land from the great lake. We wait in this place by the river until the ice melts into pieces to run down to the saltwater. We will go with the running water to find salmon and the beaches heavy with mussels at the drawing down of the tide. There will be seals thick with fat and many seabirds for our arrows. We will not hunger. Spring will be a new life for our people."[54] That the actions described here are ancient, habitual, and ritualized is suggested by references to places—"the great lake," "in this place by the river," "with the running water"—whose exact locations are givens within the culture of the band ("our people"). The predominance of present and future tense, too, throws emphasis on actions repeated time and again according to seasonal routines; and the terms "running water" and "drawing down of the tide" make strange familiar natural phenomena. Affirmations of future prosperity crowd the last four sentences, evoking expectations, instead, of lack and poverty. The exchange between Dauoodaset and his mother Waumaduit that follows this paragraph gathers up these gloomier predictions as Waumaduit anticipates that the group will not have sufficient caribou meat for the winter. Later in the chapter, Dauoodaset refers to other signs of decline: a lack of success at hunting, the encroaching presence of colonists, and the tubercular cough of Baethasuit, Dauoodaset's aunt.

The sense of diminishment and poverty so potently evoked in the chapter that introduces the Beothuk is modified to some extent during a later sequence when Dauoosadet has a modest success at hunting and is rewarded by a "hunter-thanking song."[55] However, immediately following this the men of the group engage in a game of dice using arrows as currency; Dauoosadet challenges the leader, Edeshon, and wins all his arrows. Such individualistic and competitive behaviour is unacceptable in a group organized around principles of cooperation, so ill-feeling attends the moment when Edeshon hands over his arrows: "The arrows [Edeshon] gives me are marked as if they must make kills. He expects me to prove again that I can bring food to our people."[56] The implication of this exchange, and of the later sequence in which Dauoosadet builds a birchbark canoe and leaves the *mamateek*[57] in search of food, is that there are only two modes of "being Beothuk"—through the traditional, cooperative practices promoted by Edeshon, or through behaviour, like Dauoosadet's, that in its stress on individual action and agency, accords with Western ideals of personal striving and achievement. The novel's construction of this opposition—between tradition and innovation, old and young—is echoed in many representations of Indigeneity across settler cultures and testifies to the hegemonic control that Western culture exerts over formulations of non-Western cultures.

As the narrative strand focusing on Dauoosadet draws to its deterministic closure, that concerned with David tracks his progress from alienation to a more positive view of his subjectivity and his future. Tensions around masculinities contribute to David's sense of being adrift in the world. He has a testy relationship with his stepfather, whom he despises for his devotion to stereotypically masculine behaviours such as hunting and drinking alcohol, and when he meets his biological father, he can find no point of contact with him. These generational struggles are echoed in Dauoosadet's conflict with his leader, Edeshon. Thematically, the two narrative strands intersect in a project David carries out on the Beothuk and in the old Beothuk pendant he has been given by his grandfather. The most significant connection, however, is played out in David's infatuation with Nancy, a girl in his class whose outsider status is signalled through her odd clothing and isolation from her classmates. As the novel progresses it becomes clear that Nancy is in fact Shanawdithit, the "last of the Beothuk," and Dauoosadet her promised partner.[58]

The last chapters of *Blood Red Ochre* bring together the novel's two narrative strands when Nancy/Shanawdithit, David, and Dauoosadet meet on Red Ochre Island. Here the narrative's treatment of Indigeneity crystallizes into a preoccupation with how David's sense of self is to be enhanced through his access to an ancient (and soon-to-be-extinct) culture. The two boys, initially suspicious of each other, collaborate in building a birchbark shelter, a process that requires Dauoosadet to climb on David's shoulders to tie together poles to form a frame. Their joint activity, and David's capacity to sustain Dauoosadet's weight, reassure David as to his physical strength and hence, in the ideological scheme of the novel, that his anxieties about masculinity are unfounded. Dauoosadet is killed by the woodsman, Nancy disappears, and David returns to his own time, the novel concluding with these words: "And now that the wind had died away, he was gone from the island, back to his home and his family."[59] Figuring Canadian nationhood, this ending can be said to expunge the uncanny presence of the Beothuk and to reaffirm the comforting myth that the settlement of Canada comprised, in the words of the historian Ken Coates, "the 'gentle' occupation."[60]

The final text I discuss in this chapter, Felice Holman's *Real*, is more multistranded than binary in its structure, although the narrative is built on two principal perspectives, those of Colly in 1932 and of the Cahuilla boy, Sparrow, in 1774. The novel commences with Colly observing war-painted Indians attacking a stockade. What Colly is actually watching, however, is the making of a film in which his stuntman father, Matt, plays an Indian, so that from the beginning of the novel it is clear that an important aspect of signification relates to representation itself, and to the uses to which Indians are put in the burgeoning western genre during the 1930s. Later in the novel, when the director Cy Cyrus shoots a western on location and employs "real Indians" from a local reservation, he is obliged to teach the Indians how to perform war cries and to look angry.

When Colly and his father seek out the small adobe dwelling in the Californian desert once occupied by Colly's grandfather, they encounter two "real" Indians, an elderly botanist, Benjamin Gray Fox, and his grandnephew, Ozro. The friendship developed by the two boys incorporates Colly's education in Cahuilla culture and in the desert environment that is Ozro's home. The novel is far too complex to discuss in any detail, since in addition to the elements I have identified it incorporates a romance between Matt and the starlet Dolores Rivera, a subplot relating to the appropriation of Cahuilla artifacts by a fanatical museum curator and his dishonest assistant, and a sequence of dreams in which Colly is visited by his dead mother. My focus here is on one aspect of the novel's concerns—the interplay between Indigenous and non-Indigenous subjects as it develops in relations between the three boys, Sparrow, Colly, and Ozro.

In the 1770s setting, Sparrow and his family have been making their yearly visit to sacred paintings in the caves of the mountains. Sparrow's grandmother has been injured by a puma, and his father, a Cahuilla chief named Net, has asked his son to remain behind to care for her. A wagon train of explorers has been seen crossing the mountains, and Net and his people are intent on avoiding these strangers and returning home. However, Sparrow and the old woman are seen and pursued by scouts accompanying the wagon train. The two are trapped on a cliff and shot, their bodies tumbling to a ledge below.

When Colly walks through the desert in 1932, he encounters Sparrow, whom he at first takes to be a film extra. Transported to Sparrow's time, he observes the moment when Sparrow and his grandmother are killed and learns that a member of Sparrow's tribe is condemned to "pace out the day of his death over and over if there is no *nukil* ceremony to move his spirit from the earth to the land of Mukat."[61] Following his meeting with Sparrow, it is some time before Colly recovers from sunstroke, and then he is only dimly aware that he has been charged with an important task. Meanwhile, Sparrow, in the 1770s world, has attained the shamanistic capacity of transforming himself into animals—a silvery hare, a small bird—and of entering Colly's dreams. It is because of Sparrow's promptings that Colly and Ozro discover a cave full of treasures—Cahuilla pictographs and artifacts—which are restored to the people of the reservation in which Ozro lives. When Colly locates the bones of Sparrow and his grandmother, the elders conduct the *nukil* ceremony that conveys human remains to the land of Mukat.

*Real* departs from most of the texts I have considered in this chapter in that it promotes an ethic of mutuality rather than merely of tolerance or acceptance. The fact that two of the three child protagonists (Ozro and Sparrow) are Cahuilla boys, though from different centuries, destabilizes oppositions between one cultural context and another. Importantly, the *nukil* ritual in which the remains of Sparrow and his grandmother are honoured and their spirits "released forever to join their families"[62] takes place in Ozro's reservation and hence in an Indigenous space apart from that of mainstream society, rather than restoring its white characters to the "normal" settings that generally constitute closure. Nor is Colly represented as appropriating Indigeneity in order to achieve selfhood; as Sparrow reflects toward the end of his Forever Day, "There is room for all of them."[63]

Bill Ashcroft says that "the process of insertion, interruption, interjection, which is suggested by the act of interpolation, is the initial (and essential) movement in the process of post-colonial transformation."[64] The Indigenous texts I discussed earlier in this chapter engage in precisely such transformative processes, inserting Indigenous historical perspectives, interrupting narratives of White heroism through humour and irony, and interjecting Indigenous formulations of history, myth, and truth into accounts of the past. Holman's *Real*, too, undermines the assumption that Western perspectives are normative, by attending to questions of representation and by insisting on the alterity of Cahuilla beliefs and attitudes. This text is, however, unusual in historical fiction, since my sampling of mainstream texts depicting precolonial and colonial settings and characters suggests that representational and narrative habits and patterns privileging Western over Indigenous perspectives are more entrenched in this genre of children's literature than any other. Most of the mainstream texts I have discussed in this chapter subsume Indigenous cultures and characters within universal (that is, Western) narrative schemata, notably those that trace the progress of individuals from youth to maturity and their achievement of goals such as self-actualization and a sense of purpose. Similarly, in the binary narratives of *Cross Tides*, *The Dream Carvers*, and *Blood Red Ochre*, Indigenous characters are set against non-Indigenous protagonists whose perspectives are represented as normative. It seems, then, that what Thomas King says about White constructions of the North American past can be applied to settler societies more generally: that the dominant culture's treatment of the histories of these societies, created through fictional and historical texts as well as through media including radio, film, and television, is so generally accepted as true, natural, and ordinary that it is virtually "unusable" for transformative purposes.

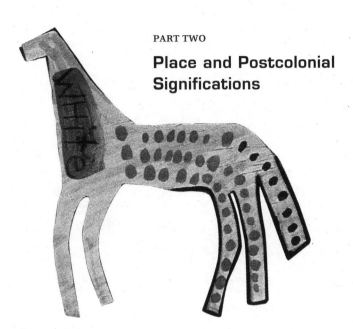

PART TWO

# Place and Postcolonial Significations

# 5 Space, Time, Nation

The burns that rush so swiftly down our hillsides are not the creeks that wander through these deep woods. The high hills are not these low lands and the spirits of our rocks and hills and burns, the old ones who dwell in the unseen world, are not here.

But we are not to grieve. The old ones came to our hills in the ancient times. It began somewhere. It began there long ago as it begins here now. We are the old ones here.

—Janet Lunn, *Shadow in Hawthorn Bay*

During the nineteenth century and well into the twentieth, a historicist world view dominated critical social theory. Michel Foucault describes as follows the nineteenth-century preoccupation with time and history: "Space was treated as the dead, the fixed, the undialectical, the immobile. Time, on the contrary was richness, fecundity, life, dialectic."[1] This historicist orientation was deeply teleological, construing social life and practice in terms of events and movements that were seen to relate to one another chronologically and causally, and that afforded the possibility of projecting how the future might evolve out of the past. Space was regarded merely as the background against which history played out, an inert locus.

As the geographer Edward Soja shows in his seminal work *Postmodern Geographies* (1989), the 1960s saw the beginnings of a reconceptualization of space exemplified by the work of Foucault and the French Marxist philosopher Henri Lefebvre, who sought to show, Soja argues, how "relations of power and discipline are inscribed into the apparently innocent spatiality of social life, how human geographies become filled with politics and ideology."[2] Postcolonial studies focus precisely on the politics and ideologies of human geographies by investigating how colonizing powers incorporated the spaces of colonized lands into their own modes of thought and belief, and by examining the extent to which postcolonial textuality interrogates or supports those colonial conceptions.

The notions of space that dominated British imperialism were predominantly visual. Bill Ashcroft notes that Western "ocularcentrism" involved

Notes to chapter 5 on pages 242–44.

the following components: "its habit of objectivism, the revolutionary de-velopment of modern mapping, the discovery of longitude, the establish-ment of Greenwich Mean Time, the emergence of the discipline of geography, in short, the whole gamut of European ways of constructing space and place."[3] Such strategies of surveillance and categorization effected a distinction be-tween space (as an abstract idea of measurable land or territory), place (as an inhabited and known location), and temporality that was foreign to many pre-Contact cultures. As Anthony Giddens points out, "in premodern societies, space and place largely coincided, since the spatial dimensions of social life are, for most of the population … dominated by 'presence'—by localised ac-tivity."[4] Moreover, practices such as hunting, social gatherings, and cere-monies were generally carried out according to daily and seasonal routines, so that time and place were locked together. As colonizers appropriated land, caused populations of Indigenous peoples to shift from one place to an-other, and effected environmental change, they also disrupted the time–place relations that informed Indigenous cultural practices.

It is clear that the impact of mass communication and global capitalism has radically and irrevocably separated space from place, since even the most remote of Indigenous communities, such as those in the Northern Ter-ritory of Australia and the territory of Nunavut in Canada, engage in transac-tions with people and institutions far removed from them in space. For in-stance, Aboriginal artists in the deserts of Australia and Inuit carvers in Nunavut produce artworks that are displayed in European galleries; deci-sions made by governments located in Canberra and Ottawa affect the lives of people living in these distant places; members of remote communities in Alaska and the Torres Strait watch television sitcoms made in metropolitan centres. To acknowledge that the separation of space from place is integral to modernity, however, does not imply that place–time relations are defini-tively sundered, or that place is not resonant with significances for both In-digenous and non-Indigenous inhabitants of settler societies. In children's lit-erature produced in these societies, a key concern is precisely how selfhood and place relate to each other.

Non-Indigenous inhabitants of settler societies belong to what Stephen Slemon describes as a "neither/nor territory."[5] White settlers were both col-onized and colonizers, simultaneously subject to imperial rule and engaged in processes of colonization in relation to Indigenous peoples; and their de-scendants, as well as other immigrants, are beneficiaries of processes that have ensured that relations of power favour non-Indigenous institutions and practices. The legacy of this "neither/nor" culture is manifested in many contemporary texts by textual moments of ambivalence and unease when characters enter spaces (forests, icy expanses, mountainous regions) that seem hostile, alien, or threatening. Aspects of such settings often serve as metaphors for the otherness of Indigenous people whose systems of valuing and belief depart from those of white child characters.

## Places and Identities

Like most children's novels dealing with the colonial past, Elizabeth George Speare's *Sign of the Beaver* (1983) is focalized through the perspective of a non-Indigenous character with whom readers are positioned to align themselves. Matt Hallowell, left to guard his family's log cabin in Maine while his father travels to Massachusetts to fetch his mother and sister, is the focalizing character, and the narrative can be seen as an instance of how time is preferred over space in a contrast between non-Indigenous and Indigenous cultures. The measurement and codification of time are integral to the narrative's development. When Matt's father leaves him alone, he directs Matt to make notches on a stick to mark the passage of the weeks, and he gives Matt his most prized possession, a silver watch. Matt's progress from fearful boy to self-reliant young man is constructed through a series of setbacks and achievements that occur between his father's departure for Massachusetts some time in June, and his return to the cabin with Matt's mother and sister just before Christmas, which is construed as the time above all when families should be together.

If events unfolding in time are associated with settler culture, the Indians of *The Sign of the Beaver* are represented in relation to space—that is, the wild space of the forest, a domain as yet unclaimed by colonization. When Matt is severely stung while looking for honeycomb, he is saved by an Indian man, Saknis, and his grandson, Attean, who have observed Matt's activities and routines from the shadows. Doreen Massey observes that, within traditions of Western thought, time is typically coded as masculine and space as feminine: "It is time which is aligned with history, progress, civilization, politics, and coded masculine. And it is the opposites of these things which have, in the traditions of western thought, been coded feminine."[6] Although Saknis wants Matt to teach Attean how to read so that he will be able to negotiate treaties between his people and the colonizers, Attean has no use for literacy: "What for I read? My grandfather mighty hunter. My father mighty hunter. They not read."[7] Attean's resistance aligns him with the "stasis, passivity and depoliticization"[8] which, in Massey's view, are associated with conceptions of space and the feminine, so that when, at the end of the narrative, Attean explains to Matt that his people must move away to a place where there is "no more white man,"[9] readers are positioned to acquiesce to Matt's regretful acceptance of a colonial order in which the Indigenous fade away into space and hence into a state of powerlessness.

Even as Matt gives Attean his father's prized silver watch as a parting gift, the narrative shows him ruefully aware that Attean is incapable of recognizing the significance of the gift: "Probably, Matt thought, Attean would never learn to use it. The sun and the shadows of the trees told him all he needed to know about the time of day. But Attean knew that Matt's gift was important."[10] The pathos of this moment lies in the implication that Attean, as a figure metonymic of his people, senses that time is important, but not how or why, and that this clouded perception renders him incapable of accessing Western modes of thought.

A telling moment occurs at the end of the novel, when Matt is reunited with his family. His mother, observing the physical changes in him, remarks, "You look different, Matt. You're 'most as tall as your pa. And awful thin. You're so brown I'd have taken you for an Indian."[11] Matt's joking response, "I almost was one," is tempered by his reflection: "He hoped she'd never know how true it was."[12] From Attean, Matt has learned the skills of hunting, strategies for surviving in the forest, and a smattering of Attean's language; but more importantly, he has in a sense *become* Indian as the land and cabin have become his territory, and this indigenization also enacts the displacement of Attean and his people.

That the question of land ownership is a site of textual tension in the novel is evident in the episode involving Matt's last meeting with Attean. Matt, uncomfortable at the thought that he and his family have occupied land previously owned by Attean's family, asks, "This land … this place where my father built his cabin. Did it belong to your grandfather? Did he own it once?"[13] Attean replies that it is impossible for one man to own the ground, which, he says, is "same as air. Land for all people to live on. For beaver and deer."[14] Matt is disconcerted by this response: "How could you explain, Matt wondered, to someone who did not want to understand? Somewhere in the back of his mind there was a sudden suspicion that Attean was making sense and he was not. It was better not to talk about it."[15] The narration here renders unspeakable the idea that the value system of the colonizers is not absolute and universal. Matt's conclusion that "It was better not to talk about it" effectively dampens down the text's unease concerning the dislocation of Attean and his people, forced to move from their ancestral land. At the same time, Attean's insistence that the land is "for all people to live on" suggests that communal occupation of land does not *really* constitute ownership as envisaged by Matt and his family.

Although the novel concludes with Matt anticipating the family's first meal together and the ritual of his father's prayer for blessing, this comfortable imagining is undercut by Matt's wish that he "could be sure that the Indians had found a new hunting ground."[16] Time here prevails over space as ideas of progress and action dominate, and the book's final sentence, "Then he would tell them about Attean,"[17] incorporates Attean and his people into Matt's narrative about his own self-actualization. *The Sign of the Beaver* is an unsettling text because of its evasiveness concerning place, its uncertainty as to whether land can or should be owned, and its ambivalence about whether it is possible for white people and Indians to coexist when they hold such different views of the value of place.

Across settler society texts for children, there are many narratives in which white child characters are indigenized and, as a consequence, rendered "at home" in places formerly associated with Indigenous peoples. In some novels, such as James Houston's *River Runners* (1979), white characters are welcomed into Indigenous kinship groups and are endowed with names and family relationships; in others, such as the Australian novel *The Children of Mirrabooka* (1997), by Judith Arthy, and the Canadian novel *Ring of Tall Trees* (1992), by John Dowd, non-Indigenous children see visions or have dreams that induct them into Indigenous traditions and provide them with access to places marked by Indigenous histories and practices. The function of the trope of indigenization is to reassure readers of the legitimacy of white settlement by depicting white children as having rights to place and valid attachments to it, but the figure of the indigenized white child is also a problematic one. First, it bears echoes of colonial anxiety about miscegenation, which hinge on the belief that the ideal for a civilized person is whiteness, a principle threatened by narratives in which white people "go native."[18] Second, texts in which white children experience dreams and visions are prone to draw on universalized and romanticized representations of Indigenous traditions.

In the New Zealand novel *Take the Long Path* (1978), by Joan de Hamel, the protagonist, eleven-year-old David Regan, is not indigenized but undergoes a more literal kind of transformation, in what I have described elsewhere as a narrative of inadvertent passing.[19] Such narratives, which generally involve non-Indigenous characters who discover their Indigenous ancestry, trace the uncovering of past interracial relationships that have previously been concealed; in David's case, he discovers that Bob Regan, the man he has believed to be his father, is in fact his stepfather, and that he was born of a marriage between his white mother and his Maori father, who is now dead. The narrative of *Take the Long Path*, published at the end of a decade when Maori land rights for the first time assumed national significance in New Zealand,[20] centres on the connections between place and identity, and around divergent views of place and its meanings.

The Regans live on a struggling sheep farm on the Otago peninsula near Dunedin in the South Island. Their property is close to a Maori settlement, and Bob Regan argues with his Maori neighbours, over a tract of land that they refuse to allow him to use as grazing country for his sheep. The plot turns on David's encounters with a Maori man, Old Tama, who is in reality a spirit returned from the dead to ensure that a ritual promise, the *Oha*, is carried out by his descendant. It is only when David discovers his real parentage that he understands that he is the one required to perform the necessary act of recovering a *patu*, a whalebone club that once belonged to his ancestor, a young boy killed in a tribal war.

To Bob Regan, who represents a settler identity reliant on Britishness, the Maori land he wants to use for pasture is merely empty space, useful land going to waste. However, to the Maori people who cling to the ownership of this piece of land, it is a place marked by ancestral associations and stories, which they invoke to claim their rights according to the Treaty of Waitangi, the founding agreement between Maori and Pakeha. Joy Regan's reluctance to admit to her first marriage to a Maori man is metonymic of lingering cultural prohibitions against "mixed marriages" as the nation struggled to define itself as bicultural. The narrative's closure, which occurs when David realizes that Old Tama is his grandfather, involves not so much the discovery of new knowledge but rather David's sense that he is affirming a truth previously inaccessible but now rescued from his memory: "David leapt towards the truth which he suddenly realized he must have known for a long time. Old Tama's son had gone to Auckland and died. But not before he had had a child ... whose pakeha mother had thought it best to marry again."[21] David's recognition of his Maori self validates his intimacy with the land and with the colony of penguins[22] that he has observed and cared for, as his father did when he was a boy. Through these associations, place is personalized and incorporated into David's new identity as Maori; but the narrative also engages in several evasions at the point of closure. The representation of Old Tama as a spirit figure who disappears once David has fulfilled his obligations to the Oha means that David's Maori identity is strictly personal, unconnected with any broader system of Maori kinship and sociality. Moreover, questions around land ownership and land rights in New Zealand are subsumed into a story about individual identity, thus producing a depoliticized sense of how place and identities intersect. David's recognition of his identity carries the implication that racial identity is innate and inherited, present within the individual as an essence, and that the significances of place are likewise recognized instinctively in accordance with an inherited knowledge. More than this, David's sense of his Maori self as a personal secret without wider social implications can be seen as a metaphor for a supposedly bicultural state in which the dominant Pakeha culture incorporates Maori identity without having to *be* Maori; David wears the *patu* next to his skin, but beneath his clothes.

Whereas *The Sign of the Beaver* and *Take the Long Path* construct ideas about place, identity, and Indigeneity from within settler paradigms, the picture books I will now discuss, Michael Arvaarluk Kusugak and Vladyana Krykorka's *Northern Lights: The Soccer Trails* (1993), and Elaine Russell's *A Is for Aunty* (2000), contest the Eurocentric assumptions about space and time that impacted on the lives of colonized people—in the territory of Nunavut, in *Northern Lights*, and in an Aboriginal mission in Australia, in *A Is for Aunty*. Both texts draw on oral traditions and Indigenous versions of history to produce deeply resistant views of place and its meanings.

*Northern Lights: The Soccer Trails* traces the story of a young Inuit girl, Kataujaq, following the death of her mother. Elaine Russell's alphabet book *A Is for Aunty* is set on Murrin Bridge Mission, on the banks of the Lachlan River in northern New South Wales, in the 1950s, and the book works as a series of vignettes of mission life, focusing on games, food, animals, and family. In both *Northern Lights* and *A Is for Aunty*, the intersections of history and geography are signalled by way of narratives where the experience of adults and children is intermeshed. In *Northern Lights*, when ice forms on the lakes and sea in early winter, the inhabitants of Kataujaq's village gather during the long nights, adults, children, and dogs playing soccer for hours. These communal occasions remind Kataujaq of the absence of her mother, who when Kataujaq was a little girl became ill like many others: she "coughed and coughed and they sent her away, way down south in an aeroplane. And she never came home again. Nobody told Kataujaq what had happened. She was too little. Her mother just never came home again."[23] The older Kataujaq, who is "a big girl; well, almost a big girl,"[24] recalls the confusion and pain of her younger self, which has led to a lingering depression.

Kusugak's description of the events surrounding the death of Kataujaq's mother introduces history to geography by alluding to the effects of colonization, and specifically the epidemic of tuberculosis that so afflicted Inuit inhabitants of Canada's far north that, according to the historian Olive Dickason, "by the mid-fifties and early sixties the Inuit had the highest rate of tuberculosis in the world."[25] Dickason notes that "Those sent 'outside' for treatment often vanished without a trace as far as their families and relatives were concerned."[26] What might seem to constitute an idyllic depiction of the community at play on the ice is shown to be subject to destabilization or destruction by forces outside it, as Kataujaq's life has been torn apart by her mother's death. Nonetheless, Kusugak constructs the arctic landscape as a domain infused with narratives that possess healing and consolatory properties.

As Kataujaq watches a game of soccer, too sad and lonely to play, her grandmother tells her a story. The spirits of people who die, she says, go up into the skies. Because they continue to enjoy soccer they play on the "giant field"[27] of the night sky, using a "huge, frozen walrus head with big tusks for a soccer ball."[28] What humans know as the aurora borealis is really the spirits of the dead playing soccer. The narrative ends as follows: "Sometime, when the moon is out and the stars are twinkling brightly in the frosty air, you should go outside and take a look. Maybe you will see the northern lights way up in the sky. They really are the souls of people who have died and, like us, they like to go out and have a good time. They love to play soccer. And if you look closely, maybe you will see someone special whom you thought had gone away forever. That special person has not really gone away at all. It is the most wonderful thing."[29] Here Kusugak alludes to the possibility of dialogue across temporal and spatial divides, or, indeed, a collapsing of such divides as humans observe the spirits at play. This moment, which is both in and out of time, is set against the linear narrative of Kataujak's loss and her progress toward induction into the story of the northern lights, which offers her a sense of being at home in her world. This is not to say that the text ameliorates the ruptures and dislocations of colonization. Rather, it advocates a world view where humans and spirits do not inhabit separate domains, and in its direct narratorial address at the end of the book it invites readers to imagine such a world: "Sometime, when the moon is out and the stars are twinkling brightly in the frosty air, you should go outside and take a look."

Krykorka's final illustration (fig. 8) shows the northern lights shadowed by the smiling faces of the dead. Here, the vast spaces of the sky are transformed into familiar and known places because they are inhabited by stories and spirits as they conduct a game analogous to that of the villagers. Viewers' eyes are drawn to the *inuksugaq*,[30] which stands squarely in the middle of the page, against the horizon that separates ground from sky. The figure of the *inuksugaq*, at once human-like and archaic, refers in this illustration to a specifically Inuit subjectivity forged out of practices and stories that integrate humans and spirits and that depend on ancestral connections with place.

*A Is for Aunty*, more explicitly than *Northern Lights*, focuses on the material interventions of colonization. The page representing *M Is for Mission* (fig. 9) instantiates the strategies of forced removal, surveillance, and cartography by which spaces deemed empty were transformed into colonized places. The narrative reads, "The government built the houses—all in rows— for the Aboriginal families to live in. There was a school, a church, and a dance hall. The manager and his family lived in their own house on the mission."[31] In this world, where hierarchies of race are spatialized and the man-

FIGURE 8 Illustration from *Northern Lights: The Soccer Trails*, by Michael Avaarluk Kusugak and Vladyana Krykorka. Illustration copyright © 1993 by Vladyana Krykorka, reproduced by permission of Annick Press Ltd.

ager's wife visits each house on Inspection Day to ensure that homes are kept "clean and tidy,"[32] Russell's narrative focuses on episodes involving movement—billycart races, canoeing, running away from emus, and swimming in the Lachlan River. As in *Northern Lights*, the community is radically intergenerational: Aunty Goldy cheers on the billycarts and one-legged Uncle Jim gives the children rides on his bike, three at a time, until "his one leg got tired from pedalling."[33] The formality of Russell's art contains this energetic movement, constructing a world whose inhabitants must live within constraints of time and place.

There are, however, moments in *A Is for Aunty* when the grids and linear patterns that embody the constraints of the mission are disrupted. The first

FIGURE 9   Illustration from *A Is for Aunty*, by Elaine Russell. Copyright © 2000, reproduced by permission of Elaine Russell.

of these occurs in "H Is for Humpy" (fig. 10), where the narrative describes the "oldies" at the mission: "When I first went to live at the mission, a few of our oldies still lived in humpies.... Our oldies believed that the new houses had evil spirits, so they had to smoke the spirits out of the houses before they could live in them."[34] The humpy, a temporary dwelling made of tin, bark, or branches, evokes the regular routes travelled by Aboriginal people as they

FIGURE 10  Illustration from *A Is for Aunty*, by Elaine Russell. Copyright © 2000, reproduced by permission of Elaine Russell.

hunted, conducted ceremonies, and took care of their country, following the tracks determined by their Dreaming stories. The semicircular shape of the humpy in this illustration, echoed by the curve of the lagoon near which an old woman cooks over the fire, attests to the survival of those practices despite the coercion of the mission. The humpy shape and the resistance it suggests are echoed in the illustration for "N Is for Nessy" (fig. 11), where the narrator

FIGURE 11   Illustration from *A Is for Aunty*, by Elaine Russell. Copyright © 2000, reproduced by permission of Elaine Russell.

recalls times when she and her friend Nessy would hide in their cubby house "hidden in the bushes. It was 'Our Place,' our secret, and no one knew about it, not even our brothers and sisters."[35] The humpy shape constitutes a chronotope incorporating time and space and producing a dialogue with the grids and linearity of the mission: the elders in their humpies and the two girls in their cubby house elude the linearity of the mission and gesture toward concepts of temporality outside and beyond the strict routines of mission life. They thus resist internalizing the hierarchies and boundaries that construct them as colonized subjects.

There are striking contrasts between constructions of place and identity in *Northern Lights* and *A Is for Aunty*, on one hand, and *The Sign of the Beaver* and *Take the Long Path*, on the other. In *The Sign of the Beaver* and *Take the Long Path*, the settings of forest and seacoast are places where events occur, backgrounds against which child characters solve problems and attain selfhood. In *The Sign of the Beaver*, the space where the log cabin is located is marked by the presence of the Indians, but it is also space taken over by Matt and his family, and Matt's identity formation is associated with his determination to contend with his environment. In *Take the Long Path*, David discovers the whalebone *patu* at the place where his ancestor died, and his act of bravery in climbing a sheer cliff face to unearth the *patu* proves his right to Maori ancestry. The formulation of identity constructed in *Northern Lights* and *A Is for Aunty* depends on the intersections of self, community, and land. That is, the "I" of the self is incorporated into the "we" of the group through the person's experience of the land and through the socializing processes by which learners are inducted into their cultures, pre-eminent among them the narratives that order experience and situate human subjects in relation to place.

By the significance they attribute to events, *The Sign of the Beaver* and *Take the Long Path* maintain hierarchies that privilege time over place. Both Matt and David must struggle with the land in order to achieve self-actualization, Matt through the trapping and hunting by which he gains self-sufficiency, and David in his dangerous climb up the cliff face. Their domination over place folds into colonial assumptions that the land must be conquered so that it can be transformed into a settled and domesticated space. In contrast, *A Is for Aunty* and *Northern Lights* proceed from the belief that place constitutes a vast text redolent with meanings accessible to its Indigenous inhabitants.

While *The Sign of the Beaver* and *Take the Long Path* have a good deal in common in regard to representations of place and subjectivities, they are informed by rather different conceptions of power as it plays out in systems of land ownership. The ethos of *The Sign of the Beaver* is that of individual rights over place, metonymically represented by the land purchased by Matt's father. The presence of the Indians points to other ways of regarding place, but Attean's question "How can man own land?"[36] discloses a set of ideas so foreign, so other to what is normative, that it merely reinforces notions of place as a resource to be bought and sold. Even when Saknis broaches the subject of treaties, asking Matt to teach Attean to read so that "Attean not give away hunting grounds,"[37] the narrative forecloses on the possibility that treaties may deliver rights to ancestral land, because the Indians of *The Sign of the Beaver* are clearly powerless to resist the appropriation of their hunting grounds. More than this, Attean as an implied future leader is represented as having no faith in even the possibility of treaties to redress colonial appropriation, when in his final conversation with Matt he says, "We go far away. No more white man. Not need to sign paper."[38] For a text published in 1983 following decades of political action by Native Americans in which treaties became symbols of Native identities and rights,[39] *The Sign of the Beaver* promotes a pessimistic and deterministic view of negotiations over place between colonizers and colonized peoples.

In contrast, *Take the Long Path* constructs a New Zealand in which it is possible for Maori to reclaim land from farmers who have purchased it, as the Maori of the Otago peninsula have reclaimed land from Bob Regan. It is clear that, in class terms, the Maori of the novel occupy a status lower than that of the Regans, who employ them as shearers, and that Maori land constitutes a small portion of the terrain; even so, the juridical processes associated with the Treaty of Waitangi are seen to prevail over individuals such as Bob Regan, who resents the court's judgement. Nevertheless, despite what appears as an affirmation of Maori rights, *Take the Long Path* implies a degree of ambivalence concerning Maori claims to land. At the end of the novel, prohibitions against David and his friend Tama visiting a derelict cottage on Maori land are explained in relation to illegal trapping activities carried out by Tama's father, so that claims to cultural connections between local Maori and their land are undercut by these more sceptical inferences about Maori motivations.

References to treaties and negotiations over land in these two texts touch on the complex mesh of beliefs and values around place in settler societies, but they also demonstrate the extent to which realistic genres embody naturalized ideologies. The principles of land ownership naturalized in *The Sign of the Beaver* and *Take the Long Path* rest on concepts of place informed by the ocularcentrism of imperialism: for instance, the belief that place comprises measurable spaces mapped and divided by boundaries, that "empty space" is available to be filled by settler activity, and that what is invisible to colonial eyes (such as the social relations and cultural practices associated with place by Indigenous peoples) is irrelevant to questions of ownership and use of land. In contrast, *A Is for Aunty* accords with Stephen Slemon's view of a resistant literary practice that "fractures inherited representational conventions"[40] through a composite textuality comprising oral history, artwork that draws on traditional symbols, and a narrative enunciated from within Aboriginal culture.

## Habitation, Home, and Nation

There is no more resonant trope in postcolonial textuality than that of home. What was generally regarded in colonial times as inevitable and benign, the appropriation of colonized lands, was experienced by Indigenous peoples as invasion and dispossession. At the same time, settlers experienced forms of dislocation that revolved around the loss of habitual ways of being at home and the necessity of creating ways to inhabit the New World. In chapter 6, I consider how borders, boundaries, and frontiers mark the distinction between settled and unsettled spaces, between home and not-home, and how narratives of travel and journeying construct ideas about belonging and about the desire to belong. In the discussion that follows I focus on representations of homes, and on the metaphorical and symbolic implications of such representations.

The Hallowells' log cabin in *The Sign of the Beaver* typifies countless similar colonial homes in settler society texts and represents a particular kind of dwelling: simple, sturdy, and snug, a haven from what is dangerous and unfamiliar. Many homes in contemporary texts are less comfortable and comforting spaces; indeed, many are marked by what Homi Bhabha calls "the deep stirring of the unhomely,"[41] the moment when a dwelling that might have seemed safe and secure is experienced as uncannily expressive of the psychic and political upheavals of colonialism. Homes function as metaphors for human subjects and for nations, and are thus apt to signify the instabilities of postcolonial experience.

Pierre Bourdieu's conceptualization of *habitus*, "the durably installed generative principle of regulated improvisations,"[42] offers a framework for viewing habitation in the context of habits of behaviour that shape human practices. The concept of habitus is, however, far more than what is implied by the term "habit," because it incorporates a person's knowledge and understanding of the world, as well as interpersonal relations and modes of social behaviour. It does not constitute a deterministic set of expectations, but rather the conjuncture of social structures and personal history; nor is it invariant, because it changes as the material conditions of people's lives change. I propose to take up Ashcroft's suggestion that the notion of habitus can be usefully applied to postcolonial experience as a way of thinking about "the transformation of colonial space into post-colonial 'life-space.'"[43] My focus through the remainder of this discussion is on four postcolonial texts that incorporate representations of home: a New Zealand picture book, Gavin Bishop's *The House That Jack Built* (1999); Louise Erdrich's *The Birchbark House* (1999); the Australian novel *Two Hands Together* (2000), by Diana Kidd; and Janet Lunn's *Shadow in Hawthorn Bay* (1986).

Of these texts, only *Two Hands Together* depicts home in a contemporary setting, that of suburban life in a modern Australian city. *The Birchback House* locates its protagonist Omakayas within Anishinabe society in 1847;[44] *The House That Jack Built* tells the story of the settler Jack and the house that he builds on his migration to New Zealand in 1798; and in *Shadow at Hawthorn Bay*, the protagonist Mary Urquhart migrates from the Scottish Highlands to Upper Canada in 1815. As I argued in chapter 4, representations of the past are always informed by the ideologies of the place and time of their production, and all three texts inscribe contemporary readings of the colonial past and promote ideas about postcolonial subjectivities.

In *The House That Jack Built*, Bishop distances readers from the figure of Jack by depicting him as a type, a representative British settler who travels from London to New Zealand bearing trade goods and a red door intended for the house he builds on land cleared of vegetation. The successive renderings of the house in Bishop's illustrations show its transmutation from a small cabin made of *ponga* (a native tree fern), to a trading post, then to an extended dwelling for Jack and his family, and in its penultimate manifestation as Jackson's hotel, situated next to Jackson's General Store and Mrs. Jackson's Academy in the burgeoning settlement of Jackstown. These depictions of Jack's house signify the encroachment of British culture and institutions, and they are supported by representations of interactions between Maori and settlers that show, on one hand, a fracturing of habitus in Maori culture and, on the other hand, the relentless process by which the country is rendered European through the introduced habitus of commercial transactions and social life. Scenes of the growing settlement of Jackstown show settlers at the centre of activities involving trading, shopping, and social exchange, while Maori occupy the edges of illustrations, passively observing the signs of colonization.

There is, however, another force at play, namely the gods who observe the degradation of the land and the demoralization of Maori, and who eventually intervene by calling Maori to go to war against the settlers.[45] Bishop represents the gods through images of eyes looking out from the sea and sky toward the land, and through the rhetoric of the god of war, Tumatauenga: "Again and again Tumatauenga, the war god called to the people of the land. 'E tu!' he cried. 'Stand up! Protect the earth mother! Rise up! Fight for the spirit of Papatuanuku.' The people took up their weapons and the terrible dance of war was heard over the land."[46] The last scene in which Jack's house appears (fig. 12) shows the red door, singed and battered, in the ruins of his house while around it swirl the stylized shapes that symbolize the gods, and the words of the nursery rhyme reach their conclusion: "And this **was** the house that Jack built."[47] This powerful image of the smouldering building seems to argue that Jack's house has never been firmly established as a home, that it has never properly integrated into the land, and that the habitus of European life has never taken root in the colony. Its destruction represents the unhomely moment to which Bhabha refers, when "the private and the public become part of each other, forcing upon us a vision that is as divided as it is disorienting."[48]

If Jack's house is shown to be tenuously situated in a land inhabited by Maori gods, the home established by Mary Urquhart in *Shadow in Hawthorn Bay* is seen to derive its stability and endurance from spiritual forces that originate in the Old World and find a congenial space in the Canadian wilderness.[49] Mary grows up as a child with "the gift of the two sights. There were times she could see into the past, into the future, into the distance, and even into the hearts of others."[50] When she travels to Canada in search of her childhood companion and cousin Duncan Cameron, she discovers that the Cameron family have already returned to Scotland following Duncan's death by suicide. Lacking the resources to follow them, she has no choice but to attempt to make a life for herself, and this she does by claiming the Camerons' cabin as her home and by establishing a school in it for settlers' children.

Mary's initial sense of not being at home in the colony is signified by her pathological fear of the forest, by the way she hankers after the fairies and spirits of Scotland, and by her repeated experience of hearing the voice of her dead cousin as he calls to her from the lake in which he drowned. Simultaneously, her act of inhabiting the Camerons' cabin—which signifies her project of reproducing in the New World the habitus of her Scots homeland—is represented as her attempt to exorcise the homesickness that drove Duncan to his death. Whereas Bourdieu insists that habitus is "powerfully generative,"[51] comprising a set of dispositions adjusted to "new and unforeseen situations,"[52] Mary's home in the forest merely replicates an Old World habitus.

Within the novel's somewhat melodramatic sequence of events, Lunn depicts Mary's cabin as an island of safety surrounded by a forest that is both empty and threatening. Her friend Luke Anderson tells her that "no people had lived in these forests ever. Even the Indians had never settled here, they had merely traded and travelled the lakes and along the shores of the island. There had always been only the trees."[53] This insistence on the emptiness of the land accords with Erin Manning's discussion of Canadian landscapes as they are represented in the artworks of the Group of Seven,[54] where they appear as unpopulated wilderness evoking a "land with unmediated landscapes peopled by those of strong, pure character."[55] Manning's argument is that while the artworks of the Group of Seven have frequently been marshalled to support a nationalist sentiment, in effect they rely on the imperial desire for empty lands that can be filled with British settlers. A similar pattern is evident

FIGURE 12  [*left and right*]  Illustration from *The House That Jack Built*, by Gavin Bishop (www.gavinbishop.com), reproduced by permission of Scholastic New Zealand Limited.

in Lunn's treatment of the forests in *Shadow in Hawthorn Bay*, which are uncanny precisely because of their emptiness, but which exist as *terra nullius*, nobody's land, waiting for Mary to occupy them and transmute them into homely spaces.

The novel ends with Mary preparing to marry Luke and live with him in the Camerons' cabin, a space once marked by the tragedy of Duncan's death but now redolent with possibilities for the future. Nevertheless, the novel's closure insists on the significance of spiritual and mythical associations, since Mary's access to a world of spirits means that she is endowed with an originary status, a capacity to invent myths of nationhood. On her wedding day, she visits Duncan's grave to place a bouquet of rowan berries there, and she kneels to talk to him: "'It is well, Duncan,' she said. 'And it will be well, for it is meant to be. It is not the same here for me as it was at home—as it was not the same for you.... The high hills are not these low lands and the spirits of our rocks and hills and burns, the old ones who dwell in the unseen world, are not here. But we are not to grieve. The old ones came to our hills in the ancient times. It began somewhere. It began there long ago as it begins here now. We are the old ones here.'"[56]

The novel's strategy of forgetting the Indigenous inhabitants of the land installs Mary as the indigene, the "old one" capable of inventing a Canada that reproduces the Old World in the New. Through this means, the violence of the colonial encounter is elided and the cabin in which Mary and Luke begin their life together serves as a metaphor for a nation built in an empty land. A key aspect of the novel's representation of Mary as the honorary indigene is the language she speaks, which in its repetitiveness and formality and its use of formulaic expressions such as "the old ones," "the unseen world," and "the ancient times" accords with what John Stephens and Robyn McCallum identify as hieratic register, typically associated with mythological and religious narratives and modern fantasy.[57] Mary's deployment of this register invests her with a quasi-religious significance as both mother figure and seer, so that her home in the Canadian forest replicates a site common in European folk traditions, the dwelling of the wise woman who ministers to the physical and psychic needs of a community. It is true that Mary has learned the names and properties of native plants from the Indian woman Owena, but this gift of knowledge, like Owena's wedding present of a deerskin dress, serves only to accentuate the sense that Mary has taken over the role of the wise Native woman.

The metaphor of the home situated in an empty land and signifying a culture transplanted from the Old World is not exclusive to *Shadow in Hawthorn Bay*: by the end of *The Sign of the Beaver*, the Indians have faded into nameless spaces, leaving the Hallowell family to establish a dynasty of settlers. The metaphor is critiqued in *The House That Jack Built*, where the reason for the destruction of Jack's house is that he treats the land as virtually empty, its Maori inhabitants devoid of any rights to its amenities and resources and its gods misrecognized as superstitious fantasies.[58] Louise Erdrich's *Birchbark House* also resists and writes back to European imaginings of unpopulated lands, in its representation of an Anishinabe habitus characterized by patterns of travel in which home is not the point from which one departs but a staged series of dwellings constructed in certain places at different seasons. The birchbark house of the novel's title is a summer house where Omakayas's family come for the fishing, and comprises a permanent frame that is covered with birchbark each year. In winter, the family live in a cedar cabin in the village of La-Pointe; in autumn, Omakayas and her family travel by canoe to the sloughs where wild rice grows, joining with their extended family to live for a time in the rice camps while harvesting food for the winter; in spring, they travel to a sugar camp where they gather maple sap.

Erdrich's representation of home relies less on the physical dwelling than on the play of relationships within a communal life where each member depends on the others for physical and emotional support; this communal life hinges upon ordered and regulated behaviours. Habitus in *The Birchbark House* is both deeply relational and also embodied, as Erdrich shows how Omakayas's obligations to her family are expressed through actions such as scraping a moose hide, rocking her baby brother Neewo in his cradle board, and weaving mats out of reeds. From the beginning of the narrative, the complex of practices and beliefs that constitutes Anishinabe culture is seen to be precariously poised as settlers, missionaries, and traders rapidly establish themselves on Anishinabe land. The book's prologue tells of a baby girl, the only survivor discovered in a village on Spirit Island after her family and their neighbours die from smallpox; by the end of the novel, when Omakayas discovers that she herself was the baby girl so spared from death, her own village and family have been ravaged by the disease, which has killed Neewo, and Omakayas, immune from the disease, has cared for them.

The novel ends with Omakayas and her family rebuilding the birchbark house where they will live during the summer. While the cyclic patterns of seasonal change continue to shape Anishinabe practices of habitation and travel, Omakayas finds strength in her new knowledge of the past: "She was the girl from Spirit Island. She lived in a birchbark house. This was the first day of the journey on which she would find out the truth of her future, who she was."[59] Living between Anishinabe and European cultures, cognizant of tradition and of the interventions of colonialism, Omakayas learns that to be a human subject in her world requires what Bourdieu refers to as "a power of adaptation"[60] that endows her with a sense of being at home even as she recalls Neewo's death. The white-throated sparrows whose song she dimly recalls hearing as she lay surrounded by the dead on Spirit Island also remind her of the presence of Neewo: "She heard Neewo. She heard her little brother as though he still existed in the world. She heard him tell her to cheer up and live. *I'm all right,* his voice was saying, *I'm in a peaceful place. You can depend on me. I'm always here to help you, my sister.*"[61] Erdrich's deft evocation of the moment when Omakayas feels herself to be free of the depression that has haunted her draws on the symbol of the sparrows to show how regeneration can be forged out of loss, and, by implication, how Anishinabe culture can sustain human subjects, maintaining a sense of home and belonging even as familiar patterns of life are disrupted.

In the novels I have considered so far, homes represent practices and ideologies identified with a particular culture: Pakeha, Scots-Canadian, and Anishinabe. In *Two Hands Together,* two suburban houses next door to each other afford a setting where children learn to reach beyond cultural boundaries. An Aboriginal family, the Rileys, move to a house in a predominantly white suburb, and the Riley children, Ella and Danny, form friendships with Lily and Jake, the children next door. The reflex racism of Lily and Jake's father constitutes an obstacle to these friendships until the two families are brought together by a crisis when the Rileys save Jake from drowning. This relatively simple storyline allows the interpolation of a number of embedded stories: for instance, stories by Ella's Aunty Maisie about her escape from an orphanage as a child, the ghost stories that Lily invents, and an urban myth about hitchhikers told by Ella. The trading of these stories symbolizes and enacts cultural exchange at the same time that Lily's father seeks to prevent his children from mixing with the Riley family.

As the four children move between one home and the other, the habitus of each family is shown to be both different and similar. The similarities lie in the affection of family members for one another, their engagement in shared projects, and their interactions with relational networks beyond their homes. The contrasts between the two families play out cultural and historical differences: for instance, Aunty Maisie's stories about her son Frankie refer to a history of racial discrimination that has propelled Frankie toward a life of crime and incarceration; and the stereotypes that characterize the views of Aboriginality held by Lily's father manifest views of white superiority still prevalent in Australian culture alongside more progressive ideologies. Thus, his view of Aboriginal child-rearing practices is built on preconceptions about Aboriginal laxity and white control, as is clear from his injunction to Lily and Jack:

"...I don't want you two getting yourselves into trouble. They're different, those kids. They've been brought up differently from the way Mum and I brought you two up.

"Did you see that girl's hair? That's no way to let your daughter run around—looking like one of those wild street kids."[62]

The terms "trouble," "different," and "wild" oppose Aboriginal to white culture according to notions of safety, conformity, and adherence to middle-class norms, arguing for the maintenance of colonial distinctions between civilized white people and wild Aborigines. Lily recognizes the falsity of such distinctions: "I don't like Dad talking about the Rileys like that. As if they're aliens from another planet. As if they're not like him and Mum and Jake and me."[63]

The two homes next door to each other represent the nation, in which discourses of race mingle and contest. Just as Lily's father mobilizes racist stereotypes about Aborigines, so the Rileys' Aunty Thel expresses misgivings about Aboriginal people who interact with white people, suggesting that as they move away from their traditional lands they become "all high and mighty," forgetting their origins[64] and assimilating into white society. These fears concerning loss of Aboriginal identity imply that urban Aborigines are "less Aboriginal" than those living traditional lives. A response to Aunty Thel's anxieties is suggested by the action that follows, when the Rileys, Lily, and Jake, together with Aunty Thel's grandchildren, play a game that incorporates "Ring-a-rosies" with the frisson of fear occasioned by the Aboriginal figure of the hairyman who preys on children when they stray from their homes, and whom they imagine lurking in the shadows. This hybrid game, which contests the exclusionary discourses of white and Aboriginal cultures, is played as the children dance "round and round the washing line,"[65] and, through this use of an Australian domestic icon, Kidd suggests the possibilities of an Australia at once conscious of cultural difference and engaged in modes of interpersonal relation that efface notions of racial superiority.

The word "home" is both dense—infused with emotionally charged meanings and values—and culturally specific, since what constitutes a sense of home is as particular as the sounds, smells, and sights that evoke it. In postcolonial societies, home often refers to or seeks to replicate an absent or distant place, like Mary Urquhart's home in *Shadow in Hawthorn Bay* and Jack's in *The House That Jack Built*. The Rileys in *Two Hands Together* carry their home with them as they settle in the suburbs but maintain their links with people and places "up the coast."[66] Erdrich's *Birchbark House* constructs a habitus both present and absent, since its episodes of smallpox encode colonialism's destructiveness to Anishinabe life, but the narrative itself reclaims traditional practices and shows how they sustain individuals and groups.

In *Post-Colonial Transformation*, Bill Ashcroft quotes bell hooks's view that "home is no longer just one place. It is part of the constructions of a new world order that reveals more fully where we are, who we can become,"[67] and goes on to argue that "one of the consequences of the disruptions and displacements of colonization has been that 'home,' like 'place,' becomes freed from a simple spatial concept of location."[68] This argument readily feeds into a quietism that accepts that Indigenous peoples whose homelands are appropriated might well make do with any tract of land to call home; or, indeed, that a spiritual attachment to place might render superfluous the recovery or ownership of ancestral lands. For many Indigenous peoples, places regarded as "home" through thousands of years of habitation, ritual, and narrative retain their potency even through decades or centuries of colonial appropriation; for the struggles of Indigenous peoples for recognition and restitution of homelands are still in progress.

I conclude this chapter with a quotation from Deborah Bird Rose's essay, "The Year Zero and the North Australian Frontier," which argues that what is required in the Australian context is a transformation of society and culture: "The challenge is to find ways to imagine a future that will include this place as a productive home, and us as people whose labour will sustain for us a future in this place. The first principle of this endeavour must be reconciliation and reciprocity with indigenous peoples, for their cultures and practices are founded in long term reciprocal interactions with home countries which are neither liminal nor mapped by absence."[69] The particularity and intensity with which Louise Erdrich, Gavin Bishop, Michael Kusugak, and Elaine Russell claim land as home in the texts I have discussed in this chapter demonstrate that Indigenous texts for children constitute a site of political action. If *The Sign of the Beaver* and *Shadow in Hawthorn Bay* accept as normal the historical processes that transformed Indigenous homelands into colonized places, *Take the Long Path* and *Two Hands Together* model the more complex negotiations by which Indigenous and non-Indigenous inhabitants of settler cultures might attain reconciliation—negotiations that centre on questions of space, place, and their significances.

# 6 Borders, Journeys, and Liminality

[Benny Len and Stanley] didn't mind the long journey so
much after that. They were sure they would be back for
the bear dance every year, because now they knew the way
home.                          —Chiori Santiago and Judith Lowry,
                                *Home to Medicine Mountain*

References to borders, boundaries, and frontiers perme-
ate colonial discourses, providing potent metaphors for distinctions between
races and for the imperial project itself. Such metaphors were especially significant to settler colonies, where, as Paul Carter notes, the frontier was "a per-
sistent figure of speech" imagined as "a line, a line continually pushed forward
(or back) by heroic frontiersmen, the pioneers. Inside the line is culture; beyond it, nature."[1] Colonial frontiers were as much temporal as geographical
boundaries, since distinctions between civilized and savage races were bound
up with concepts of evolutionary periods. In his study of time in anthropological thought, Johannes Fabian argues that during the colonial era "all living societies were irrevocably placed on a temporal slope"[2] with "advanced,"
"urbanized," and "modernized" cultures at the apex. Indigenous peoples occupied the lower realms of this scheme; indeed, they were frequently consigned to a space-time outside of history, being (so it was generally assumed)
without a history of their own and incapable of participating in the modern
era in which the nations of the New World invented themselves.

As colonial narratives of exploration, adventure, and settlement produced and reinforced the givens of Western cartography, alternative modes
of mapping the world—the spatio-temporal cartographies of Indigenous
peoples—were rendered invisible; as David Harvey says, "the 'imperial gaze'
mapped the world according to its own needs, wants, and desires, imposing
a map of the world in such a way as to suppress difference."[3] The imperial

Notes to chapter 6 on pages 244–46.

map of the world was deeply implicated in the expansion of western capitalism, whose relentless push towards new forms of production and new mar-
kets has continually reshaped the way space is used and represented, affect-
ing time-space relations, the material practices associated with production
and consumption, and processes of urbanization. Colonial frontiers were
never simply lines between races, no matter how strenuously colonial discourses sought to maintain racialized distinctions. Boundaries in modern
settler nations are even more indistinct, blurred by the mingling and interpenetration of identities that characterizes the contact zone; in many texts,
negotiations between cultures are mapped through narratives involving journeys and border crossings.

The last two decades have seen the production of a significant number of
texts (most, but not all, by Indigenous authors and illustrators) that thematize journeys undertaken by Indigenous children and young people, journeys previously invisible because they lay outside the schemata of colonial
narratives of settlement and adventure. There is, for instance, a steadily
growing body of autobiographical and fictional texts dealing with enforced
travel and narratives of escape involving children and adolescents removed
from their families and cultures under assimilationist policies in Australia,
Canada, and the United States, and sent to institutional settings such as orphanages and residential schools, or to domestic settings as foster children
or servants to white families.[4] Many such texts, like Beatrice Culleton Mo-
sioner's *In Search of April Raintree* (1983), Basil Johnston's *Indian School
Days* (1988), the Australian film *The Rabbit-Proof Fence*, and Glenyse Ward's
two autobiographies *Wandering Girl* (1988) and *Unna Ya Fullas* (1991), cater
to both adult and adolescent readerships. Others, like Chiori Santiago and Judith Lowry's *Home to Medicine Mountain* (1998), Shirley Sterling's *My Name
Is Seepeetza* (1992), and James Houston's *Drifting Snow* (1992), imply child audiences. These texts trace the boundaries of race, gender, and class that Indigenous characters traverse, and show the effects of such border-crossing
upon children's development as postcolonial subjects.

Houston's *Drifting Snow* traces a symptomatic story of border crossing in
which an Indigenous child is forced to travel far from her home and family
and is interpellated as a colonized subject. The subtitle of the novel is *An
Arctic Search*, and the search in question is undertaken by Elizabeth Queen,
an Inuk girl of around thirteen, who contracts tuberculosis in her infancy
and is sent from what is now the territory of Nunavut to a hospital in southern Canada and then to a boarding school, losing contact with her family
just as Kataujaq's mother disappears from her family in *Northern Lights: The
Soccer Trails* (discussed in chapter 5). Whereas *Northern Lights* deals with the
predicament of those left behind when loved ones are transported vast dis-

tances for medical treatment, *Drifting Snow* traces the physical and psychological journey of one who is first taken away, and later searches for her home.

Elizabeth's very name is an invention, based on the figure of Queen Elizabeth on Canadian banknotes, and her linguistic experience echoes the fracturing of her identity: she recalls only tiny snatches of Inuktitut, and, while her first language is English, she has learned to speak French and, in the hospital school, some Cree and Ojibwa. When she travels to Nesak Island off the Baffin Island coast to search for her family in the 1950s setting of the narrative, she is viewed through the focalizing perspective of Poota, the young son of the Kiawak family, whose members live a nomadic life and befriend Elizabeth during her stay on the island. To Poota, she is an anomaly, Inuk in appearance but with the paler skin of someone unaccustomed to the Arctic climate, lacking knowledge of language and culture, and wearing a nylon parka that marks her as coming from elsewhere. Elizabeth's plane flight from the south to the far north ushers in a psychological journey involving a series of boundaries that she must cross in order to become an Inuk subject. One such boundary involves the necessity of moving from a world where climate is controlled through central heating to a setting where people live with extremes of cold; thus, Elizabeth's first task is to learn how to make a caribou skin and woollen parka in the style used by young Inuit unmarried women, and her wearing of this parka symbolizes her induction into Inuit culture and into a different set of values and practices around relations between people and their environment.

A crucial mode of border crossing is constituted by Elizabeth's acquisition of language and protocols of speech behaviour. Thus, at first she asks to be called "Elizabeth," but when she learns that the Inuktitut form of the name is "Elizapee" she realizes that her status as an outsider will be reaffirmed if her name does not conform to Inuktitut language practices. When Elizapee eventually makes contact with her grandmother Sala, her discovery of her Inuktitut name "Apoutee" marks her entry to her family; and her final choice of name, Elizapee Apoutee, incorporates her former and new identities within her growing sense of becoming Inuk.

Like all journeys, Elizapee's removal from her family and her search for them traverse time as well as space. Colonial and postcolonial journeys are arguably more complex than most in the time-space relations they involve, partly because they are caught up in cultural differences around how time and space are conceptualized, and partly because of the rapidity with which colonization affected Indigenous populations and the drastic changes that ensued. As Doreen Massey observes, Western models of travel during colonization acknowledged that exploration or settlement involved temporal as well as spatial journeys, but travel in time was envisaged as a process through which "the West imagined itself going out and finding not contemporary stories but the past."[5] These notions of colonial travel represented space as an unproblematized surface of landscape and topographical features. Rather, as Massey argues, "The ravages of imperialism and the conquerings and co-optations of colonialism were not horizontal movements across a space that is a surface. They were engagements of previously separate trajectories. And it is the terms of that meeting that are the stuff of politics."[6] The 1950s setting of *Drifting Snow* is a time well removed from the colonial era but still deeply affected by colonial politics. Elizapee's removal from her family, represented within the novel as an analeptic account of her early life, exemplifies the production of colonized bodies: the child, taken from her mother's parka hood, bundled in a blanket, and carried by ship to a hospital in the south, has been detached from all connections to her home and transmuted into a colonized subject, renamed, institutionalized, and inducted into Western culture. At the same time, her family's search for her has been hindered by the fact that her records have been lost and she is thus effectively without identity. During the period when Elizapee has grown up in hospitals and schools, her family has moved from one camp to another before abandoning nomadic practices and settling in the town of Iqaluit, where her parents have found work.

When Elizapee finds her parents and grandmother, her journey thus accords precisely with Massey's description of "colonial conquerings and co-optations" that function as "engagements of previously separate trajectories"; in this case, both Elizapee and her parents have known the conjunction of coercion and agency characteristic of postcolonial experience before they meet in Iqaluit, and their meeting is inflected by the innumerable quotidian accommodations and choices that have brought them to the place and time of their encounter. The separation of Elizapee from her family has effected a rift constituted by the different spatio-temporal schemes that they have inhabited: while Elizapee and her parents can talk together about their lives once they are reunited, they have no lived experience in common; and as Elizapee has undertaken the process of shifting from Western to Inuit modes of life, her parents have sought to live as Inuit in a Western setting.

The politics of their meeting is merely sketched in *Drifting Snow*, its complexities too much for the narrative to bear. Elizapee's mother Mukitu and her father Namoni have lost hope that she is alive, and in their shock and disbelief they scarcely know how to respond to the sudden discovery of an adolescent daughter; for her part, Elizapee realizes that although she longs for warm relations with her parents, the lack of a history of shared experience and communication work against the possibility of such relations. When Elizapee makes the decision to leave Iqaluit and her newly discovered parents and

return to Nesak Island for the winter, her grandmother Sala, who has unwillingly moved with Elizapee's parents to Iqaluit, takes the opportunity to accompany her so as to "live the good country life again,"[7] and before entering
the winter tent of the Kiawak family, Sala sings the following song:

> Glorious it is
> when wandering time
> has come.
> Glorious it is
> to see the changing lands,
> the changing seasons.
> Glorious it is
> to be alive.[8]

This song is intended for "everyone to hear—perhaps even the spirits of the
ancient people from the past and other new ones from the future who had not
yet been born."[9] The significances of Elizapee's decision and the power of the
old song valorize nomadic life over the settled existence of Elizapee's parents
even as the narrative resists a facile identification of ancient practices with authenticity. Houston's reference to the audience of the song, who are imagined
as including the spirits of those who have died and of those to be born, and
who gather at a particular place to celebrate the commencement of winter,
constructs a spatio-temporal system that is built on seasonal and cyclic journeys and implicitly contrasted with the linear time scheme and the separation of time and place characteristic of Western culture.

Foucault's treatment of the strategy of surveillance in *Discipline and
Punish* (1979) outlines the use of the panopticon, Jeremy Bentham's design
for a prison divided into cells whose inhabitants could be observed from a
central vantage point. As I noted in chapter 5, surveillance was a central
strategy through which colonial powers possessed and ordered space and
human subjects. Such strategies were used to control and regulate the actions
of Indigenous children consigned to institutions such as residential schools
and orphanages. Conversely, in narratives of border crossing, Indigenous
children are frequently represented as evading surveillance and hence, even
if to a limited degree, recovering power and agency.

Like *Drifting Snow*, the picture book *Home to Medicine Mountain* traces
a journey symbolic of the recuperation of identities that are bound up with
a particular place and culture. In the 1930s, two young brothers, Stanley and
Benny Len, of the Mountain Maidu and Hamawi Pit-River people, are sent by
train from their home in the mountains of northern California to a residential school in Riverside in the south of the state. After several months, the
boys run away and ride the rails back to Yo-tim Yamne (Medicine Mountain) because the school does not provide funds for them to return home

FIGURE 13  Photograph from *Home
to Medicine Mountain*, by Chiori
Santiago and Judith Lowry. Copyright © 1998 by Judith Lowry.

for the summer. The narrative is framed by two peritextual references. In
the book's introduction, the illustrator Judith Lowry, who is Benny Len's
daughter, describes the residential school system, which, she says, was gov-
erned by "the idea that [Indian children] needed to unlearn their Indian
ways and live as the settlers did."[10] The material on the final page of the book
includes photographs of Stanley and Leonard (Benny Len) as elderly men,
standing between railroad tracks at Susanville, their childhood home, and the
place where they now live (fig. 13). Taken together, these pages insist not
merely on the historicity of the events of the narrative but on the capacity of
Indian people, metonymized by the figures of Stanley and Leonard, to resist
incorporation into the settler discourses represented by the boarding school.
*Home to Medicine Mountain* is thus as much about the present as about the
1930s in its treatment of the role of stories in identity formation, especially stories of resistance that model strategies for maintaining cultural and family
connections.

   The cultural boundaries crossed by Stanley and Benny Len when they
arrive at the boarding school are, like those traced in *Drifting Snow*, imbri-
cated within habitus and inscribed in language. The "hard, stiff leather
shoes"[11] that the children wear are contrasted with Benny Len's memories of
how the earth feels at home, "comforting beneath his feet,"[12] evoking a com-

parison between home, where people walk directly on the earth, and school, where shoes are worn to separate human bodies from the earth. Similarly, the habitus of the school, seen by Benny Len as one of "sharp edges, shiny surfaces and shouting bells" and where the children are taught to march in lines and perform sharp turns,[13] is at odds with "back home," where "people danced in circles to honor the earth."[14] Lowry's illustration of the children standing in line before the school (fig. 14) emphasizes the regularity and order of the scene, in which the children's clothing and posture play out their forced compliance. The blank windows of the school and the gaze of the two teachers construct a world where the children are controlled through constant surveillance.

Whereas Elizapee in *Drifting Snow* must relearn Inuktitut language in order to re-enter the conceptual world of the Inuit, the children at the residential school are banned from using their first languages or observing customary practices. The only refuge is the domain of dreams, in which Benny Len retrieves memories of his life at Medicine Mountain: the stories his grandmother tells him, the herbs she collects on Medicine Mountain, and the bear dance that celebrates the end of winter. The final illustration of *Home to Medicine Mountain* (fig. 15) shows Stanley, Benny Lee, and their grandmother seated around a fire in whose flames can be seen images of animals—bear, wolf, and deer. This illustration deftly reprises and overturns earlier images of the children within the school setting, with their sharp lines and homogenized figures. The circle of the fire, echoed in the spreading branches of the trees, is aligned with the circle of the grandmother's arm, within which Benny Len is securely enclosed. So reintegrated into the habitus of their culture, the boys again hear the stories that restore their sense of themselves as members of the community. The counter-discursive force of this illustration is qualified by a reminder, in the verbal narrative of the page facing it, that "the dominant dominates," as Terdiman puts it:[15]

> For the rest of the summer, and for many years after, Benny Len and Stanley told the story of their adventure on the train. They told it to their children and their grandchildren. Always, one of the children would ask: "Did you have to go back to the boarding school?"
> "Yes," Benny Len or Stanley would answer, remembering.
> They didn't mind the long journey so much after that. They were sure they would be back for the bear dance every year, because now they knew the way home.[16]

The vast distance between home and school has different significances following the boys' journey, because this geographical space, having once been crossed, is now assailable. What is implied by the peritextual information of

FIGURE 14 Illustration from *Home to Medicine Mountain*, by Chiori Santiago and Judith Lowry. Illustration copyright © 1998 by Judith Lowry.

the book's final page is that the boundaries between cultures are also assailable, as Benny Len and Stanley are described as having had "distinguished careers in the U.S. armed forces."[17] This information implies the boys' capacity to negotiate between concepts and institutions in a mixture and fusion of influences where subjectivities are formed both within and between cultures.

A striking feature of many narratives involving Indigenous children caught up in journeys occasioned by assimilationist policies is that signs of colonizing power are reconfigured as they take on positive meanings associated with the recuperation of Indigenous identities. Thus, while the train is a sign of industrialization and the reach of capitalism, it is also the means by which Stanley and Benny Len return to Medicine Mountain. Indeed, to Benny Len, it seems that the train wheels sing his name, the signifier of his selfhood: "Benny Len, Benny Len, Benny Len. He felt so free that he raised his arms to the sky. He felt as if he were flying."[18] A similar effect is evident in *The Rabbit-*

FIGURE 15  Illustration from *Home to Medicine Mountain*, by Chiori Santiago and Judith Lowry. Illustration copyright © 1998 by Judith Lowry.

*Proof Fence*, where the fence, a boundary established to divide rabbit-infested from rabbit-free land (and itself a signifier of the environmental degradation caused by introduced animals) becomes a sign of hope, since it leads three Aboriginal girls, Molly, Daisy, and Gracie, from the Moore River Native Settlement near Perth in Western Australia, through a journey of over 1,500 miles to their home in the desert community of Jigalong.

   *Drifting Snow, Home to Medicine Mountain,* and *The Rabbit-Proof Fence* deploy the motif of journeys away from institutional sites and toward family and homelands; these journeys are metonymic of Indigenous subjects reclaiming their cultural heritage. The Australian picture book *Down the Hole* (2000), by Edna Tantjingu Williams, Eileen Wani Wingfield, and Kunyi June-Anne McInerney, focuses rather on children's escape *into* country, a trajectory that accords with Aboriginal traditions in which one may be said to belong to one's country, and where, in the words of the poet and elder Bill Neidjie, "earth is my mother or my father."[19] The title of *Down the Hole* continues on the title page as *"up the tree, across the sandhills ... running from the State and Daisy Bates,"*[20] in an evocation of movement through country and beyond the reach of bureaucratic and institutional control. This is also a local and collective perspective of country, traced through first-person-plural narration that tells the story of Williams and Wingfield and treats them as figures representative of the mixed-race children affected by policies that sought to "breed out" Aboriginal ancestry by removing such children from their families.

The hole of the book's title, used by the children's parents to conceal them from the authorities, is one of many shafts and tunnels created by settlers mining for opals. In these holes, light-skinned children passed entire days, while their parents kept watch for "the State people"[21] and lowered food by ropes when it was safe to do so. The cover illustration of *Down the Hole* (fig. 16) shows a group of five children clinging together, placed within a circle of light as if discovered by the beam of a flashlight. The three older children in the illustration enfold the two younger ones in their arms, but this signifier of connectedness and support is disrupted by the searching eyes of the child second from right as she looks anxiously toward the source of light. Appropriating the shaft, created by the capitalist enterprise of mining, the children journey into the womb of the earth, which is at the same time their ancestral home and the source of individual and communal identities.

In *Down the Hole*, then, what is foregrounded is not the children's experience of border crossing but their refusal to do so, and a view of territory that has nothing in common with Western concepts of ownership and land usage but that refers back to ancient practices of journeys and rituals carried out according to the requirements of the Law. The very offhandedness of the narrative's reference to institutional life is metonymic of the narrators' refusal to enter the discursive domain of colonialism: "Yes, if they catch us fair kids, they put us in a home then—in Ooldea. I never lasted a month or two months in there. I was only in that home there for two weeks. And then I was **gone**!"[22] As they hide in holes and trees, and traverse sandhills, the children rely on country for protection, their bodily actions enacting relations between Aboriginal subjects and their country in which, to use the words of the anthropologist Deborah Bird Rose, "the person takes care of the country and the country takes care of the person."[23] Wingfield's autobiographical note at the end of the book relays the reciprocity of such interactions: in the country that protected her as a child Wingfield continues as an elder: "I'm ... travelling, keeping the culture going and looking after the country."[24]

FIGURE 16   Illustration from *Down the Hole*, by Edna Tantjingu Williams, Eileen Wani Wingfield, and Kunyi June-Anne McInerney. Illustration copyright © 2000 by Kunyi June-Anne McInerney, reproduced by permission of IAD Press.

## Cross-cultural Engagement in the Contact Zone

The texts I have discussed so far in this chapter focus on spatio-temporal journeys by Indigenous children who seek to recuperate or sustain connections with families, homes, and ancestral lands. There are many more texts where action occurs in liminal spaces where people from different cultures meet and interact. Texts by Indigenous authors often deploy as focalizing characters Indigenous children and adolescents who move between settings where Indigenous cultures are normative—such as reservations and reserves in North America and traditional communities in Australia—and settings such as schools and neighbourhoods where Indigenous and non-Indigenous characters meet. The movement of characters back and forth between these settings enables comparisons between cultures and examinations of the negotiations involved in cross-cultural friendships. Indigenous-authored texts that fall into this category are Lee Maracle's *Will's Garden* (2002), Betty Dorion's *Melanie Bluelake's Dream* (1995), Meme McDonald and Boori Monty

Pryor's *Njunjul the Sun* (2001),[25] Melissa Lucashenko's *Killing Darcy* (1998), Diane Silvey's *Raven's Flight* (2000), and Joseph Bruchac's *The Heart of a Chief* (1998) and *Eagle Song* (1997).

A few texts by non-Indigenous authors place Indigenous focalizing characters at the centre of contact-zone narratives, as is the case in James Moloney's *Dougy* (1993), Diana Kidd's *The Fat and Juicy Place* (1992), Ann Herbert Scott's *Brave as a Mountain Lion* (1996), and Deb Vanasse's *A Distant Enemy* (1997). More commonly, non-Indigenous authors focalize events through the perspectives of non-Indigenous characters whose assumptions and expectations are tested by encounters with Indigenous people. The following novels come from this category of texts: in Australia, Phillip Gwynne's two novels *Deadly Unna?* (1998) and *Nukkin Ya* (2000), James Moloney's *Angela* (1994), and Pat Lowe's *The Girl with No Name* (1994) and *Feeling the Heat* (2002); in New Zealand, Paula Boock's *Home Run* (1995) and William Taylor's *Beth and Bruno* (1992); in Canada, Andrea Spalding's *Finders Keepers* (1995) and Lesley Choyce's *Clearcut Danger* (1992); and in the United States, Marsha Qualey's *Revolutions of the Heart* (1993) and A.E. Cannon's *The Shadow Brothers* (1990).

The term "liminality" refers in postcolonial theory to the concept of a domain "in-between" cultures, languages, and subjectivities, where individual and group identities are formed. In his introduction to *The Location of Culture*, Homi Bhabha writes of an installation by the African American artist Renée Green at the Institute of Contemporary Art in New York, where Green used the museum space as a metaphor. Green says, "The stairwell became a liminal space, a pathway between the upper and lower areas, each of which was annotated with plaques referring to blackness and whiteness."[26] Bhabha applies this image to the liminal spaces of nations marked by histories of colonial and postcolonial migration:

> The stairwell as liminal space, in-between the designations of identity, becomes the process of symbolic interaction, the connective tissue that constructs the difference between upper and lower, black and white. The hither and thither of the stairwell, the temporal movement and passage that it allows, prevents identities at either end of it from settling into primordial polarities. This interstitial passage between fixed identifications opens up the possibility of a cultural hybridity that entertains difference without an assumed or imposed hierarchy.[27]

This image as Homi Bhabha applies it to postcolonial identities is an appealing one because it seems to promise a way of theorizing cross-cultural and interracial relations; but the concept of liminality is also problematic. First, the liminal spaces referred to by Bhabha seem to float in a conceptual scheme uninflected by the historical and cultural contexts in which they are located; second, "space" as an abstract concept may readily be viewed in terms of a location "in-between" cultures and ethnicities, colonized, and colonizers. However, when we consider the specificities of *place*—that is, lived-in and known locations marked by history, memory, and formations of power—it is clear that places are never neutral but are always informed by meanings that they gather from social practice and cultural discourses. In settler societies, place is imprinted with colonial histories and with Indigenous histories of life before colonization. A helpful metaphor here is the concept of place as palimpsest, a site on that "traces of successive inscriptions form the complex experience of place, which is itself historical."[28]

In many children's texts, school settings constitute a liminal space where differences of class, gender, sexuality, ethnicity, and race are played out. Schools are, of course, far from neutral zones and are deeply implicated in the political and cultural systems they serve, so that relations of power generally favour majority cultures. In the texts I discuss next, Lee Maracle's *Will's Garden* and Joseph Bruchac's *The Heart of a Chief*, Indigenous adolescents must negotiate differences of valuing, intersubjective relations, and styles of learning as they move back and forth between home and the liminal space of school. In the two novels with which I conclude the chapter, Pat Lowe's *Feeling the Heat* and Paula Boock's *Home Run*, non-Indigenous characters find themselves in settings coded as Indigenous and hence cross borders of race and class. In all four texts, relations between individuals are inflected by histories, positive and negative, of engagement between Indigenous and non-Indigenous people, and by the stories, memories, and expectations that inform the ways young characters envisage and experience intersubjective relations complicated by racial and cultural difference.

The presence of the past is especially significant in *Will's Garden*, which traces events occurring over a period just prior to Will's Becoming Man Ceremony. Leading up to this event, Will and his family produce gifts to distribute to guests; Will's contribution consists of beaded items (barrettes, bags, capes) that he creates in conjunction with his cousin Sarah. Will's personal preparation involves a process of reflection that culminates in the speech he delivers at the ceremony, when he gives thanks to those who have assisted him in his growth to manhood and outlines his sense of the self he undertakes to become. Over the same stretch of time, he works with other band members constructing a community centre on the Sto:loh reserve where he lives and he attends high school in the town.[29] The narrative thus criss-crosses between the settings of reserve and school, tracing Will's experience in the liminal space of the school and the "strategies for personal or communal self-hood" that it affords.

Will is both an engaging and a flawed first-person narrator, so that to a degree the narrative distances readers, encouraging a style of reading that weighs up Will's perceptions against other perspectives. Thus, at the beginning of the novel, his cousin Sarah offers him advice as to how to handle the taunts of "the jocks" with whom he plays football. Sarah suggests that he align himself with "the ones they don't want," who are, she says, "usually the thoughtful ones,"[30] unnoticed among the noisy, racist minority. Accordingly, at lunchtime Will sits with the school nerds, and when Joseph, one of the nerds, asks him why he chooses to associate himself with this unpopular group, he replies, "My cousin says you are thoughtful. I think her exact words were, nerds are thoughtful, for white people that is."[31] These are, in fact, not Sarah's exact words, and the gap between her more nuanced view and his propensity for homogenizing white culture undercuts Will's attempts to project a worldly and mature self.

Wit, one of the "geek clique"[32] with whom Will associates, is gay; moreover, while his racial origins are not evident in his appearance, he has a Squamish grandmother and is therefore "an almost Indian."[33] In the liminal space of the school, Will's developing friendship with Wit challenges the binaries (white/Native, straight/gay) that have to this point largely informed his view of the world; but when he takes the risk of inviting Wit to his home, he comes up against homophobic attitudes present within the Sto:loh setting, when an elder known by Will as "Buster-Christ-Jesus-almost-second-coming" recognizes Wit's sexuality and engages in a diatribe in which he "mentions the 'devil, evil and unnatural' in the same sentence."[34] Will's verbal challenge to Buster is an affront to Sto:loh practices of respect for elders, but it also represents his developing sense that becoming a Sto:loh man means more than merely conforming to an originary, predetermined identity. Thus, the garden of the book's title is a beaded cape on which Will represents his mother's rose trellis, a sign that he is not bound by stereotypical notions of masculinity—that is, Will intends to pursue interests traditionally associated with the feminine at the same time that he constructs himself as a Sto:loh man.

While Will's experiences both on the reserve and at school destabilize his ideas of fixed identities and sharp contrasts between Indigenous and non-Indigenous culture, he returns through a series of visions to his great-grandfather Lapogee, who as a young man worked in the road gangs of Asian, Indian, and white men who built highways through the Rockies. This was a transcultural space where men of different races negotiated exchanges of words and language systems: thus, Lapogee taught the white man Jimmy to speak grammatical English, Jimmy taught Lapogee to write, and the Indian men decided "not to talk so much, rather than shrink the language,"[35] in deference to the anxieties of the Chinese worker Charlie, who feared that he might forget Chinese if he spoke too much English. The cultural exchanges of this past setting are echoed in Will's experience at school, where he engages in a tentative process of negotiation with the nerds and the jocks. Homi Bhabha's description of how the past of colonialism is never really past is apposite to the dialogic interplay of past and present in *Will's Garden*: "the borderline work of culture ... renews the past, refiguring it as a contingent 'in-between' space, that innovates and interrupts the performance of the present."[36] Will's induction into cultural memory in his excursions into the past informs his developing appreciation of the possibility of respectful and informed cross-cultural relations in the present. The treatment of the past in *Will's Garden*, far from engaging in a nostalgic memorialization, intersects with and enriches Maracle's examination of postcolonial subjectivities. In Bhabha's terms, "the 'past-present' becomes part of the necessity, not the nostalgia, of living,"[37] since the "past-present" of Lapogee's life affords a model for living in the present.

Joseph, one of the nerd clique, asks his father to assist the Sto:loh by acting as site supervisor in their building project, and Joseph joins Will on the building site, where Will guides Joseph in regard to Sto:loh protocols of behaviour. This scenario allows a self-reflexive narrative mode, since Will narrates events at the same time that he scrutinizes the assumptions and values that drive him and that Joseph must learn consciously and painfully. Many of these assumptions and values are encoded in language, and it is when Joseph decodes a Sto:loh joke that he establishes his credentials as one who has begun to comprehend Sto:loh modes of thought and expression:

> "How are you getting home, Joseph?" Thomas sounds genuinely concerned. Somehow Joseph had kept up with our rage driven furious digging.... He half smiled at Thomas. He felt the tenderness in the words.
> "Don't worry. My dad is still here."
> "We might as well hang out 'til you leave. If I know my pop, we will be the last to go."
> "You want to work 'til then?" Joseph asks.
> "Are you kidding?" I reply with a little too much intensity.
> Joseph laughs. He caught us. It was his first crack at an Indian joke. He nailed us.[38]

This textual moment discloses both cultural difference and the complexities of cross-cultural engagement in an exchange incorporating Sto:loh humour. The juxtaposition of this episode with Will's vision of the transcultural space where Lapogee, Jimmy, and Charlie learned, painfully and slowly, to communicate across distances of language and culture, historicizes the contact zone by situating Will's developing friendship with Joseph against a backdrop of similar exchanges in the past. This strategy both resists a simplistic view of cross-cultural negotiation and affords an optimistic perspective on the contact zone.

Indigenous representations of settings such as reserves and reservations often struggle between disclosure and reticence. The tensions around such representations are clear in Joseph Bruchac's author's note in *The Heart of a Chief*: "I decided ... not to set this novel on a real reservation. Some of the issues in the book, such as casino gambling, leadership, and alcohol abuse, are too sensitive for me to do that. Instead, I have imagined a reservation where none currently exist...."[39] In addition to issues concerning the identification of actual places and people, contemporary Indigenous authors are often caught between agendas of celebrating and affirming Indigenous cultures, and depictions, especially in realistic texts, of the negative effects of colonialism, signalled by Bruchac in his references to "casino gambling ... and alcohol abuse."

In *The Heart of a Chief*, Bruchac uses the strategy of focusing on the interpersonal relations of a group of eleven-year-old children (including two Indian students, Chris and Katie) who work on a project concerning the use of Indian names for sporting teams. In this novel, as in *Will's Garden*, first-person narration is deployed to align readers with young narrators groping toward a sense of self. Many of the givens informing the beliefs and values of the protagonists of these two novels are at odds with the norms of white culture, so that non-Indigenous readers are positioned in quite complex ways, at once aligned with and distanced from the Indigenous characters central to the narratives.

The thematics of the group's discussions about the use of Indian names both foregrounds the cultural distance between Indian and non-Indian members and also structures shifts in understanding and empathy. In a key episode when the group's discussion moves to the meanings of Thanksgiving Day, Chris points out that Indian children attending schools where students dress in Indian costumes with "eagle feather head-dresses made of paper and cardboard"[40] feel alienated and insulted. One of the non-Indian children, Melissa, comments, "I don't think people mean to make Indians feel bad about Thanksgiving,"[41] a statement so revelatory about the invisibility of Indians within white culture that it enables Bruchac to demonstrate the power of those myths of nationhood that efface Indian experiences of colonization.

Bruchac's deployment of Indian expressive and narrative modes accords closely with Pratt's concept of transculturation. A telling instance of this occurs when Alicia, one of the children in the group, having learned about colonial history from the stories told by Chris and Katie, asks the question: "So do Indians hate us?"[42] The first-person narrative here incorporates an embedded story, one of several in the novel, as Chris draws on both his memory of particular stories and his sense of Penacook discursive practices whereby people respond to questions obliquely and through story. Chris tells about a Penacook man living next door to a white racist who burns his house down, destroys his cornfield, and shoots his dog. The Penacook man pursues the culprit and eventually tracks him down, and the story concludes with the following exchange:

> "Are you the one who burned my house, destroyed my cornfield, and shot my dog?" the Indian asked.
> The white guy was quaking in his boots, but he managed to answer. "I am," he said.
> "Well," said the Indian, "you better not let that happen again."[43]

The reaction of the group of children is depicted as follows: "I look around the table. At first everyone looks stunned. Then Katie starts to laugh and everyone else joins in."[44] The puzzlement of the children is used to evoke a sense of the strangeness of this story for its white hearers, the cultural difference it installs in its wry, understated humour, and its wider significations for an understanding of relations between Indian and non-Indian people.

In a telling sequence, a non-Indian character, Coach Takahashi, drives Chris home, visiting the Penacook reservation for the first time. In this situation, Chris is on his home territory and Coach Takahashi is out of his element, and Bruchac uses the episode to visualize the reservation through non-Penacook eyes as the two pass landmarks familiar to Chris but strange to the Coach: the ruin of a house that burned down years before; the shabby trailers and the "small, worn-looking houses";[45] the new building that houses the tribal headquarters; and the church that serves as a community meeting place. Chris's sense of being a stranger in the world of Rangerville Junior High is balanced by Coach Takahashi's awareness of the difference of Penacook culture, a difference that is also plain to Chris as he observes the Coach observing the reservation.

The novel's title, with its play on the word "chief," alludes to processes of identity formation that run parallel in the liminal space of the school and the home territory of the Pennacook reservation. At school, Chris and his friends conduct an oral presentation in which they argue that the school football team should change its name from the Rangerville Chiefs. At a tribal meeting on the reservation, Chris plays an active part in ensuring that a casino is built not on an island with deep symbolic and ceremonial significances, but on a site owned by Chris's family. The fact that Chris speaks on behalf of his absent father, Mito, who is undergoing treatment for alcoholism, is symbolic of both the weight of the past and the promise of Penacook survival. In *The Heart of a Chief*, then, as in *Will's Garden*, the liminal space of the school is a site of intercultural engagement where Indigenous subjects move through insecurity and fear to an enhanced sense of agency, while non-Indigenous readers are positioned both to engage with modes of Indigenous thought and language and also to view their own cultural givens as they are refracted through the perspectives of Indigenous characters.

Both Pat Lowe's *Feeling the Heat* and Paula Boock's *Home Run* trace the progress of non-Indigenous characters who align themselves with Indigenous culture: *Feeling the Heat*, a sequel to *The Girl with No Name* (1994), picks up the relationship between Matthew Scott, a white boy, and Frances Bulu, an Aboriginal girl, who had a close friendship as children and are reunited when Matthew returns from Perth to the country town where Frances lives; and in the New Zealand text *Home Run*, a Pakeha girl, Bryony, shifting with her family to a new city and school, befriends Ata, a Maori girl.

In *Feeling the Heat*, Matthew finds Frances living with her father, Ajax, in a house in the town. Without anyone actually inviting him, he finds that he is expected to stay, and is given a bed on the verandah. In Australian popular and literary traditions, verandahs are regarded as in-between spaces between inside and outside, private and public, and thus between culture and nature.[46] Matthew's location on the verandah places him outside Aboriginal culture, though adjacent to it; simultaneously, he places himself at odds with white culture in his preference for associating with Aborigines. His rediscovery of Frances is complicated by the interplay between his socialization in the dominant culture and his desire to engage with Frances, Ajax, and their extended family. Romantically attracted to Frances, Matthew discovers that she is pregnant and that the child's father is an Aboriginal man, Roy, who is married and has two children. Matthew's reflex reaction is to apply the sexual mores of his cultural conditioning to Frances's situation; however, Frances refuses to behave either as a wronged woman or a promiscuous one, the two possibilities that Matthew imagines must apply to her.

Lowe's use of dialogue in *Feeling the Heat* shows how language variance constructs cultural difference. Ashcroft notes that a key feature of cross-cultural textuality is that it "inscribe[s] *difference* and *absence* as a corollary of cultural identity,"[47] and indeed the language exchanged between Matthew and the Aboriginal characters foregrounds the distance between cultures "at the very moment in which it proposes to bring them together."[48] The following conversation occurs as Roy, Ajax, and Frances explain to Matthew that he is obliged to come to an arrangement with Roy, to whom Frances was given as a marriage partner at a young age (even though he subsequently formed a relationship with another woman):

Roy turned to Matthew. "I gotta fight you, give you belting with a boomerang." He didn't sound serious and Matthew took it that Roy was just explaining the rules.

"Why?" he asked.

"That's the law for blackfellas. When man take wife from 'nother bloke, that man gotta get punish."[49]

The terms "fight," "wife," and "punish" carry meanings both accessible and mysterious to Matthew—accessible because these are familiar terms, mysterious because they mean differently, referring to protocols that relate to laws of kinship, obligation, and justice, and are susceptible to adjustments of interpretation and practice. As the episode develops, Roy and Frances explain that Aboriginal law cannot be applied to *kartiya* (white people), first because *kartiya* have "weak heads" and cannot withstand traditional punishments, and also because to "belt a kartiya blackfella way"[50] would invite police intervention. Matthew can *understand* these laws—and indeed he seeks to do so—but this exchange and others like it confirm his sense of the gap between his cultural experience and that of Roy and Frances.

The novel's strategy of interspersing dialogue with Matthew's represented thought slows down the action, demonstrating that cultural exchange cannot be hurried but depends on mutuality and trust, and that it is reliant upon the capacity of participants to accept difference without recasting it into the familiar lineaments of their own experience of life and language. It is generally the case that when the narration of a novel is conducted in standard English and exchanges of dialogue incorporate non-standard forms—such as the Aboriginal English spoken by Frances and her family—the impression is that the English of the narration is normative and that of speakers of non-standard English a departure from the norm, a lesser, inferior form of English.[51] In *Feeling the Heat* Lowe's depiction of Aboriginal English departs from this pattern in two ways. First, the represented speech of Aboriginal characters is often expressive and revealing, far from the pidgin forms still sometimes used by authors unfamiliar with Aboriginal English; secondly, Lowe conveys through the speech of Aboriginal characters their struggle with English, their attempts at encoding in English meanings particular to Aboriginal culture.[52]

In *Feeling the Heat*, Matthew decides that the cultural differences between him and Frances are too profound to bridge, and he moves out of her house. On his way back to the cattle station where he works, he goes to a site that he visited often with Frances as a boy, where there are ancient rock paintings. In the silence of the scene, so hot that even the birds do not sing, he feels a sense of awe and also of familiarity with this known and remembered landscape. When he hitches a ride with a tradesman to travel the rest of the way to his workplace, the man asks him, "You live up here, then?" Matthew thought for a moment, then he turned his head towards the driver and looked him in the eye. "Yes," he said. "Yes, I do."[53] In this moment, he dares to claim the land as home, a home imprinted with the familiar yet strange cultural meanings of his Aboriginal family, and home because of its significances for him as a non-Aboriginal Australian. At the same time, he undertakes to live with the indeterminacy of his relationship with Frances and her family—thus, within a system of kinship relations in which he is both inside and outside, always *kartiya* but now admitted to a scheme of relations where he is placed, known, and named. This transformative moment may seem to gesture toward Bhabha's metaphor of the stairwell as liminal space, but it is grounded too in a strong consciousness of the inequities of power and influence in postcolonial settings. As I noted earlier, the notion of liminality goes only some distance as a metaphor for intercultural relations in the contact zone. The concept of hybridity, which hovers about Bhabha's formulation of the liminal, all too readily forecloses on differences between Western and non-Western conceptions of subjectivity.

In Paula Boock's *Home Run*, the narrative locates its white protagonist, Bryony Page, in a setting where she is "out of place." Bryony's parents have purchased the most luxurious house in Merimeri, a working-class area in Auckland, so that Bryony moves between the privileged, middle-class habitus of her home, and Merimeri High School, a coeducational school very different from the elite girls' school that she formerly attended. After her first, uncomfortable day at school, Bryony's father suggests that on the following day she should use Maori language as a greeting, and engage her fellow-students in conversation about Maori culture. When Bryony attempts this strategy, however, she discovers that her overtures are regarded as condescending, and the hostile reaction of the Maori students unsettles her faith in the judgement of her liberal father.

In an attempt to find acceptance at Merimeri, Bryony joins a group of girls who engage in shoplifting, daring one another to steal items of increasing value, and she is trapped in this cycle of rebellion along with her Maori friend, Ata Apirama. In *Home Run*, the school is less a liminal space than a dystopic setting where cultural difference is folded into distinctions of class. When Bryony visits Ata's home, Maori culture is represented through two axes of reference: the poverty of the Apirama family, and the warmth and cleanliness of their home. The snatches of Maori language used in this episode function as superficial markers of identity, but in other respects there is nothing in the text's treatment of Maori to suggest cultural difference. Rather, the text's representation reinvokes stereotypes in which people of lower socioeconomic status are divided between worthy and unworthy poor, with the Apirama family located in the former category.

While most of the novel is focalized through Bryony's perspective, in one episode we observe the action through Ata's eyes when she walks to Bryony's home, concerned that the latter has been arrested for shoplifting. Ata has not previously seen the large, comfortable house where Bryony lives with her parents, and her reactions gesture toward an internalization of dominant discourses concerning class, which inflect Ata's view of her own home and her recollections of Bryony's visit there. She reflects on the bright pink colour of the Apirama home: "It was painted a horrible pink, she knew that, but Auntie Pipi had got it for them cheap cheap and they couldn't say no."[54] Her mother's words, "Don't you be ashamed Atawhai, we do better than a lot of people, and we're hard-working and good-looking ... and our clothes are clean and we're honest...,"[55] propose a view of the social order where class distinctions are accepted as givens, with the worthy poor occupying their rightful place. Questions about the overrepresentation of Maori within the category of the poor, and about the impact of colonial history on the lives of contemporary Maori, are effaced through the text's assumptions about what is normal and natural. The novel hints at the existence of such questions as it relegates them to a domain outside the world of the novel, thus implying that individuals are incapable of actions that might remedy an unjust social order.

Bryony's home is out of place in its working-class suburb just as Bryony is out of place at Merimeri High School, and when her parents remove her from Merimeri and send her to a private girls' school, Peterson Girls' College, she is in effect restored to her proper class setting. Reflecting on the contrasts between sporting equipment at the two schools, Bryony is filled with regret: "something bigger must be wrong, something that meant there were schools like Merimeri and people who couldn't afford to go to schools like Peterson."[56] The novel's closure occurs when Bryony is reconciled with Ata and offers her a softball glove that she has received at her new school, marked with the school's name. Through this gesture Bryony attempts to redress what she regards as the "unfairness" of the imbalance of opportunity embodied in the contrasts between Peterson Girls' College and Merimeri High School, and Ata's refusal of the gift represents social disadvantage as inescapable: "You can't make it fair, not by giving me a softball glove, not by giving me anything."[57] When Bryony gives Ata her own, prized glove instead, the narrative falls back into notions of individual growth and progress that largely evade the questions about class and social inequality raised by comparisons between the opportunities available to Bryony and to Ata. In *Home Run*, Merimeri High School is not a liminal or transcultural space allowing interchange between cultures, but a domain inhabited by Maori and Pakeha characters who are excluded by virtue of their lower socioeconomic position from the more expansive possibilities open to Bryony and the students of Peterson Girls' College. In his essay "Biculturalism and Multiculturalism in New Zealand," Vince Marotta remarks that "it is not only the *maintenance*, but also the *transcendence* of boundaries that may deny and repress the identity of others."[58] In *Home Run*, it is possible to read the absence of reference to Maori culture in Boock's depiction of Ata and her family as a form of repression where racial difference is effaced by a homogenizing view of class distinctions.

The example of *Home Run* supports an observation I made at the beginning of my discussion of liminality: this concept, like the notions of hybridity with which it is connected, presents difficulties if it is understood as a space unmarked by relations of power and by histories of cross-cultural exchange. In *Home Run*, the in-between space where Ata and Bryony meet is curiously empty, uninflected by past events and the unsettling racial politics of New Zealand in the 1990s, so that it is not a liminal space at all, but rather an undifferentiated conceptual field where the category "Maori" is absorbed into a set of oppositions between privileged and disadvantaged New Zealanders. The other texts I have discussed in this section, particularly *Will's Garden*, locate their characters in liminal spaces where memories, imaginings, and stereotypes influence but do not determine the possibility of symbolic exchange across racial divides.

In *The Heart of a Chief*, *Will's Garden*, and *Feeling the Heat*, negotiations between Indigenous and non-Indigenous subjects are shown to embody—and to be embodied by—negotiations over language. The conversational exchanges that I have discussed, between Chris and his classmates in *The Heart of a Chief*, between Joseph and his Penacook friends in *Will's Garden*, and between Roy and Matthew in *Feeling the Heat*, involve Indigenous and non-Indigenous characters who, in the telling of a joke, a story, or an explanation about appropriate behaviour, experience the disorientation that arises from their sense that words mean differently across cultures, and that the way stories are structured and jokes told is determined and shaped by cultural practices. In *Will's Garden*, Joseph haltingly attempts Sto:loh-style humour, in the process demonstrating that he is capable not merely of working alongside his Sto:loh friends but of understanding their world view. In *Feeling the Heat*, Matthew is faced with the incommensurability of meaning when words that hold clear meanings for him—"fight," "wife," "punish," "law"—conjure up a plethora of cultural practices that are outside his apprehension. In these texts, readers are presented with models of intersubjectivity that promote the possibility of mutuality even in difference.

# 7 Politics and Place

"I not understand," Attean scowled. "How can man own land? Same as air. Land for all people to live on. For beaver and deer. Does deer own land?"
—Elizabeth George Speare, *The Sign of the Beaver*

In discussing *The Sign of the Beaver* and *Take the Long Path* in chapter 5, I touched on how these texts skirt, respectively, around questions concerning the colonial appropriation of land in the United States and negotiations over land ownership in contemporary New Zealand. In this chapter, I focus on the politics of spatiality, which are shaped by cultural traditions steeped in the ideologies, beliefs, and practices of imperialism, and specifically of British imperialism. Like other European powers, England regarded the New World as a source of vast wealth in the form of minerals, forests, and farming land; but imperial nations did not all desire the same things or engage in the same processes, and the histories of New Zealand, Australia, Canada, and the United States are marked by peculiarly English inflections. In *American Pentimento*, Patricia Seed distinguishes between the colonizing vision of England and that of Spain. The English, she says, "had conquered property, categorically denying the natives' true ownership of their land. Spaniards, on the other hand, had conquered people, allowing sedentary natives to retain their terrain in exchange for social humiliation. Thus regaining soil comes first on the agenda in aboriginal communities once dominated by England, whereas seeking human respect is central to contemporary aboriginal struggles in regions once controlled by Spain."[1] Seed argues that these contrasts can be explained neither by differences between the Indigenous peoples colonized by Spain and by England nor by the historical events associated with first encounters between colonizers

Notes to chapter 7 on pages 246–48.

and colonized and the meanings attributed to these encounters, but rather by deep-seated cultural traditions that informed colonial practices.

Fundamental to English legal traditions by the seventeenth century was the idea that land ownership was established by the labour invested in planting, fencing, and farming tracts of land, expressed in the saying "Possession is nine-tenths of the law." Moreover, the investment of capital in land, in the shape of labourers paid to work, was regarded as labour, in that one's money could be said to be at work. Native Americans who worked on their land, however, were not thereby entitled to own the land, since in the eyes of the colonizers their work did not constitute farming, nor did they give or receive money for labour.[2]

Territory not fenced off, planted with crops, or in other ways identified as cultivated was regarded as waste land, ideal for the resettlement of England's surplus population of labourers. The principle that "waste land" should be put to profitable use was employed to justify the seizure of vast tracts of Indigenous territories across English settler colonies, the most extreme expression being the concept of *terra nullius*, "uninhabited land," which was applied in Australia to the entire country until 1992, when the Australian High Court rejected this justification for the appropriation of Aboriginal land; nevertheless, as Richard Bartlett notes, "the rejection of *terra nullius* by the majority of the High Court was empty rhetoric and irrelevant to the existence of native title."[3] Although both *The Sign of the Beaver* and *Take the Long Path* set the British preoccupation with using "waste land" against Indigenous conceptions and values concerning ancestral territory, they treat settler values as normative, so that in *The Sign of the Beaver* Attean's question "How can man own land?" is a sign of otherness, of the incompatibility of Indian and settler world views, and of the inevitability of Indigenous dispossession.

The attitudes of Indigenous peoples to their ancestral lands were and are quite different from those of non-Indigenous settlers. Augie Fleras and Jean Elliott describe as follows how Indigenous peoples of Canada, the United States, and New Zealand regard their land:

> For aboriginal peoples, land possesses a sacred quality, rooted in an attachment to history, a sense of identity, and a perception of duty towards future generations. In this sense, land is not merely inherited from our ancestors: even more important, it is held in custody for our unborn children. Land and natural resources are not to be exploited and consumed in the pursuit of material gain; they must be protected and conserved. This collective reverence for land and spiritual rapport with it contrast sharply with the larger society's material conception of land as a commodity for individual ownership, consumption, and sale.[4]

While British colonizers across colonial sites found such attitudes to land unfathomable, they adopted different methods of installing British culture in new territories. Treaties were signed soon after British colonizers reached Canada and the United States, and in New Zealand the colony's founding document was the 1840 Treaty of Waitangi. Despite the fact that they afforded only limited protection against the appropriation of land, treaties at least established the idea that Indigenous peoples constituted "nations within" settler societies;[5] and discourses of treaty rights have been prominent in Indigenous activism in these nations since the 1960s. In Australia, in contrast, Indigenous people have never enjoyed treaty recognition; it was not until the 1970s that the Australian government began to address land rights and not until the 1990s that courts developed a common-law basis for such rights. Paul Havemann notes that in contemporary settler nations, a discursive shift is now occurring where "a new politics of identity and cultural recognition occupies the political stage, and newly heard claims are couched in the language of rights to self-determination."[6] These discourses (of identity, cultural recognition, and self-determination) are now clearly apparent in texts by Indigenous authors, whereas much writing by non-Indigenous authors continues to accept as normal the colonial appropriation and contemporary disadvantage experienced by Indigenous peoples.

### Unsettling Discoveries

In the New Zealand novel *Owl*, which I discussed in chapter 1, the Pakeha protagonist, Hamish, finds a carved stone in a cave. His act of removing it reactivates an ancient Maori legend that impinges on his life and shapes his relations with Tama, the Maori boy whose tribe has close connections with the place and its stories. Another novel I considered in chapter 1, *Take the Long Path*, involves the discovery of a whalebone club that connects a contemporary character with his ancestor, the warrior who owned the weapon; and in the Canadian text *False Face*, discussed in chapter 3, an ancient Mohawk mask found buried in a bog exercises occult power in the contemporary setting. In my discussion of historical novels and themes in chapter 4, I considered two texts—Felice Holman's *Real* (1997) and Lorraine Orman's *Cross Tides* (2004)—in which characters find human remains that testify to colonial atrocities. Such stories of discovery, or, more accurately, uncovering, have particular resonances for settler cultures.

The plot device of the buried object whose discovery triggers or completes a search is, of course, widespread across narrative modes (fiction, film, and computer games, for instance); but in the very many settler culture texts for children in which Indigenous objects or human remains are discovered by contemporary (usually non-Indigenous) characters, such discoveries inevitably involve stories about Indigenous people and cultures prior to colonization or during colonial times. The objects so uncovered are always *placed*, suggesting relations between the locations where they are found and the individuals connected with them; and they are informed by concepts, ideologies, and cultural tensions around colonization and land. So widespread is the use of this narrative motif by non-Indigenous authors that it constitutes a trope in settler society children's texts, deployed as a metaphor for the uncovering or acquisition of knowledge about colonial events and their contemporary consequences. In some texts, such as *Owl* and Andrea Spalding's *Finders Keepers* (1995), ancient objects are discovered by Indigenous and non-Indigenous children who are friends or allies; however, these narratives are commonly focalized by non-Indigenous characters through whose perspectives readers are positioned to view Indigenous characters as well as the ways intersubjective relations are inflected by cross-cultural negotiations. When, as in Gary Paulsen's *Canyons* (1990) and Martha Brooks's *Bone Dance* (1997), they incorporate focalization through the perspective of Indigenous characters, they tend to deploy narrative strategies that construct non-Indigenous cultural beliefs and practices as normative.

The cover blurb of *Canyons* announces that the book is "a thrilling story of a friendship that spans the canyons of time."[7] Even allowing for the hyperbolic expression of this discursive mode, the term "friendship" makes a large claim for a relationship that exists within the imagination of one character, a teenager called Brennan Cole who lives in El Paso. Brennan is a fourteen-year-old boy whose main joy lies in running: "He did not run from anything and did not run to anything, did not run for track nor did he run to stay in shape and lose weight. He ran to be with himself."[8] Through the first nine chapters, the narrative is focalized alternately by Brennan and by Coyote Runs, an Apache boy who takes part in a horse-stealing raid in 1864 and is tracked down and killed by soldiers from Fort Bliss.[9] Brennan senses the presence of Coyote Runs when he camps in the canyon where the boy was executed, and the remainder of the novel traces a sequence of events in which Coyote Runs, mysteriously present to Brennan as a voice speaking within his consciousness, directs Brennan to unearth his skull from behind the rock where it has rested since 1864 and to take it to a flat rock at the top of the bluff, the "medicine place"[10] where his spirit can be set free.

The raid on which Coyote Runs rides is his induction into manhood, and his death a cruel one at point-blank range. In the chapters focalized through his perspective, the narration achieves a distancing effect by constructing Coyote Runs as mistakenly believing in the efficacy of a vision that he experiences at his sacred place, which convinces him that bullets have no power to kill him. The gap between his world view and that of implied readers privileges Western values and perspectives and foregrounds the Apache boy's incapacity to comprehend the actions and motivations of the colonizers. This impression is heightened by the contrast between the language used in these chapters and that of the rest of the narration. For instance, Coyote Runs prays to the spirits to "ask for guidance and bravery to have a thick neck and be a man";[11] and his incomprehension of Western practices and artifacts is conveyed through strategies of defamiliarization, such as the description of his experience of attending a Quaker school where he learns to use "some symbols on a black stone written with a piece of white dirt."[12] Such language features construct Coyote Runs as a naïve and otherworldly figure and impart a sense of pathos and impending disaster.

While it reinvokes the figure of the "disappearing Indian" implacably clinging to ancient beliefs, the novel treats Brennan's dreams and visions, and his capacity to hear the voice of Coyote Runs, as innate and natural. When he enters the canyon, "something about the place took him, came into him and held his thoughts. Something he couldn't understand."[13] As he embarks on his quest to return Coyote Runs' skull to the sacred place, he receives guidance: "and he knew things then without knowing how it was he could know them."[14] He is directed, for instance, to push a stick ahead to seek small snakes on his path, and to drink water from yucca quills, and these actions locate him within the land as a native of the country. The ideological work that the novel carries out, then, is similar to that of many of the texts I have discussed in this book: it resides in its construction of the white boy who is effectively indigenous, an insider to Apache knowledge of the country, its dangers, and its sacred places.

The mountainous country where Brennan carries out his task of returning Coyote Runs' skull to his "medicine place" is said to have been "the last stronghold of the Apache nation."[15] The text depicts this terrain as empty of all signs of Indigenous life, a site used by non-Indigenous Americans seeking adventure and novelty, typified by the camping excursion in which Brennan participates. The emptiness and vastness of the canyons renders the area attractive as an antidote to life in metropolitan settings, and here Seed's discussion of "imperial nostalgia"[16] is pertinent. Seed describes how, at the end of the nineteenth century, "Americans...regretted the loss of what they understood themselves to be destroying, the vanishing American commons....Middle-class Americans wanted to spend time in uninhabited spaces, sometimes seeking such activity in highly structured forms, such as scouting."[17] The boys with whom Brennan goes camping are members of a church youth group, and they are both titillated and frightened by the stories of battles and ghosts told by Bill, the group leader. That is, the uninhabited space of mountains and desert is all the more attractive because it was once inhabited by a noble, now "vanished" people. Similarly, echoes of sacredness enhance the appeal of the "medicine place" where Brennan places the skull of Coyote Runs, and where the blackened colour of the limestone near the rock testifies to ancient Apache fires. Readers are positioned to align themselves with Brennan as he "saw the world" from the top of the bluff: the haze of El Paso, the splendor of the Organ Mountains and the white sands shining "so bright it seemed the desert had been washed and bleached and painted."[18] The text's emphasis on the antiquity of the "medicine place" and on the destruction of Apache culture represented by the murder of Coyote Runs seems to pay tribute to a vanished people, even as it normalizes the colonial appropriation of Apache land.

So closely does Brennan identify with Coyote Runs that in effect the subjectivities of the two teenagers merge. Whereas the raid that constituted Coyote Runs' entrée into manhood ended miserably with his execution, Brennan's quest to restore Coyote Runs' skull to the "medicine place" instantiates his transition from a state of aimlessness to an enhanced sense of agency, so mobilizing the familiar narrative pattern whereby non-Indigenous characters gain psychic strength from knowledge of or contact with Indigeneity. At the end of the novel, after Brennan places the skull on the rock, a sudden gust of wind "caught some dust from rock around the skull and took the dust in a swirling column up, up over the bluff, over the canyon, over Brennan and into the sky and gone, gone where the dream of the eagle had flown, gone for all of time, gone and the skull was just that, a skull, a bone, nothing more, empty, as Brennan was empty."[19] With its elevated language and sense of finality, it is difficult to read this moment, when Coyote Runs' spirit is liberated from his earthly remains, as anything but a metaphor for the expulsion of Indigeneity from the national imaginary. If Brennan feels himself to be empty, this is because the uncomfortable knowledge of Indigenous presence is expunged from his sense of self, restoring Brennan to an ordinary life untroubled by a close knowledge of Coyote Runs' short life and violent death. In this manner, the land is emptied of its associations with Indigenous cultures and the canyons and desert are rendered unproblematically "American." The contradictory discourses at work in this text are most evident in its closure, where the uncanny presence of Indigenous sacredness struggles with the text's insistence on the absence of Apache people and culture.

Like *Canyons*, Martha Brooks' *Bone Dance*, described by Perry Nodelman as "the archetypical Canadian novel for young people about the non-Aboriginal encounter with Aboriginality,"[20] also incorporates an episode in which human remains are uncovered. This incident is described analeptically through the perspective of one of the novel's two focalizing characters, Lonny, who as an eleven-year-old boy discovered a child's skull unearthed by a badger from Medicine Bluff, an ancient burial mound on the property where Lonny lives with his mother and his Métis stepfather, Pop LaFrenière. Directed by his parents to rebury the skull, Lonny and his friend Robert instead dig up the rest of the child's skeleton, and then the remains of an adult. Although they return the skeletons to the mound, the boys feel guilty about their actions, and when Lonny's mother dies suddenly two days later, he feels that "her death and their bad luck and the unearthing of those ancient skeletons were all entwined."[21]

This piece of land in rural Manitoba is of central importance as well to Alex, a Winnipeg girl whose father, Earl McKay, abandoned her and her mother when Alex was an infant. He has bought a parcel of land, including Medicine Bluff, from Lonny's stepfather, and when McKay dies he leaves this property to Alex, who discovers his death and her inheritance at the same time. Both Lonny and Alex are of Indigenous descent, since both Lonny's mother and Alex's are Indigenous. In addition, both enjoy close relationships with Indigenous characters: Lonny with Pop LaFrenière and Alex with her Cree grandfather, who long ago married her grandmother and adopted her mother. While the text goes to some lengths to establish these Indigenous connections, its treatment of place is curiously overwrought, reminiscent of Katz's *False Face* in its evocation of hostile spirits. Thus, after his mother's death, Lonny is oppressed by the "ghosts of the Ancients that lurked between the smells of burned toast and unwashed clothing and growing dust,"[22] and when Alex comes to claim the property, Lonny fears for her well-being and sleeps all night in his truck outside Earl McKay's cabin in case the spirits harm her.

In addition to these references to the dark and vengeful forces that inhabit the burial mound, the text draws on two other discursive strands to represent the significances of Medicine Bluff and the land around it: mainstream perspectives of private property, and New Ageism. One of Lonny's earliest memories of arriving at the LaFrenière property is that of his stepfather taking him to show him Medicine Bluff and impressing on him the antiquity of the site and the necessity of caring for it: "'[This land] was here before the earliest people. And most certainly it was here before the French and the English. *And* the Metis,' he said, indicating his own heart. 'It's old, Lonny. Old as time. So that's why we have to take care of it. It's our job. Our responsibility.'"[23] These references to custodianship and responsibility for the land are seemingly at odds with Pop LaFrenière's later decision to sell it off to various purchasers, including Earl McKay. However, the narrative's closure affords a resolution to this apparent breach of responsibility for the land through the romance between Lonny and Alex, which offers the possibility that Lonny may after all recover the LaFrenière property in partnership with Alex. What might seem to be a contest of values (Aboriginal custodianship against mainstream practices of buying and selling land) is thus deflected by way of a conventional romantic ending.

New Age discourses permeate the text in several forms, one of which is the many visions and dreams that Lonny and Alex experience and that are described in language that often hovers on the edge of bathos: "And a sudden image spun wildly in, crashing powerfully against [Alex's] heart. A bone-shaped lake with the hill of her dreams rising above. Grandpa and Old Raven Man fishing at the rocky shoreline. Grandpa's fish breaks the surface.... It's the mother of all fishes, full of God and terrifying magic."[24] Loaded with metaphorical language and references to heightened emotions, such passages suggest what Diana Brydon calls "the Disney simulacrum,"[25] a likeness of spiritual or mystical experience that reduces to a flattened and commodified version of Indigenous sacredness. Another New Age effect in *Bone Dance* is that Aboriginal cultural expressions such as fasting and prayer are represented as universally available and efficacious. Thus, in the letter that Earl McKay writes for Alex's seventeenth birthday, and which she receives after his death, he describes his experience of sitting for three days, wrapped in a blanket, on the top of a "hill that used to be a vision-quest place for the Plains Indians."[26] He sees a vision of "Indian people dressed in ghost shirts"[27] and is inspired to dance with them. Transformed by this experience, he realizes that "They'd got rid of one more white man by giving me the vision of an Indian."

Brooks' deployment of New Age discourses in *Bone Dance* construes as universalized and homogenized the specific and particular associations that connect places, narratives, and traditions in Aboriginal cultures. When Earl McKay is endowed with "the vision of an Indian," he resolves to change his life: he purchases the LaFrenière property, builds a cabin, and writes a will. The novel's ideologies are here exposed in all their convolutedness: Earl McKay, having become a white indigene, has purchased an ancient and sacred site for his (Indigenous) daughter, thereby disrupting Métis connections with the land in a manner that is justified by the romance between Lonny and Alex, whose implied "happy ever after" sweeps aside thoughts of ancestry, memory, and rights to land. If, as Nodelman says, *Bone Dance* is an "archetypical" work thematizing relations between Aboriginal and non-Aboriginal cultures, it is also a novel whose homogenization of difference undermines its ostensible agenda of respect for Indigenous beliefs and spirituality.

## Place, Embodiment, Memory: Other Perspectives

The texts I have discussed so far, which incorporate the trope of discovery of colonial objects, accept (even if uneasily) the belief, central to British imperialism, that the appropriation of Indigenous territories and the dispossession of Indigenous peoples were unavoidable consequences of colonization and hence signs of progress. As Seed notes, "regaining soil comes first on the agenda in aboriginal communities once dominated by England,"[28] and although children's texts by Indigenous authors do not often directly thematize contemporary struggles for land rights, they are preoccupied with the cultural meanings of place and their significances for Indigenous identity formation. Whereas the trope of discovery is common in texts by non-Indigenous authors, Indigenous authors are far more likely to draw upon discourses and episodes involving storytelling, especially where adults pass on memories and traditional knowledge to children. While the non-Indigenous texts I have just discussed seek to explain, justify, or interrogate colonial stories, Indigenous texts incorporate stories where colonized people are not tragic victims, like Coyote Runs in *Canyons*, but ancestors, members of clans and communities, and thus people connected by descent and place with the contemporary characters of these texts.

Pat Lowe and Jimmy Pike's *Desert Cowboy* (2000) writes back to colonial first-contact texts, which invariably privilege the perspectives of white children observing Aborigines represented as primitives or savages. The focalizing character in *Desert Cowboy* is Yinti, a young boy whose family is among the last of the Walmajarri people of the Great Sandy Desert in Western Australia to leave their ancestral homelands in order to live and work on the cattle stations established when Aboriginal homelands were appropriated by settlers. *Desert Cowboy* is the product of collaboration between Pike, who contributed illustrations, and the non-Aboriginal author Pat Lowe, who produced the verbal narrative, which works as a series of discrete stories following the course of Yinti's life as he meets white people for the first time and works on cattle stations owned and managed by white employers.

The narrative defamiliarizes settler practices by representing them from the point of view of Aboriginal people. For instance, a story about kangaroo-hunting begins with these words: "The kartiya people at Wynyard Station didn't like kangaroos. They didn't hunt them and eat their meat. Instead they ate the meat of their own sheep."[29] It seems to Yinti extraordinarily wasteful to take the trouble of introducing animals only to slaughter them, when there are abundant native animals to be used as food. Whereas Paulsen's strategy of defamiliarization in *Canyons* constructs Coyote Runs as other to the colonizers, Lowe's use of the same technique, in a narrative located within Walmajarri culture, exposes how colonizers are captives of their preconceptions, misrecognizing as "waste land" territory whose resources have enabled the Walmajarri to live in their desert country for many thousands of years.

Two episodes in *Desert Cowboy* deal with colonial violence and its effects on Aboriginal subjects. Yinti, employed as a stockman on a sheep station remote from his homelands, is working alongside other Aborigines when he observes a red-hued hill that rears out of the plains.[30] His companion, Danny, warns him against visiting this place:

> "That's a bad place, boy," [Danny] said.... "Lot of black people were killed over there."
> "What for?" asked Yinti. Danny shrugged.
> "Might be they were spearing cattle. Might be for nothing. Kartiya used to kill a lot of blackfellas in the early days."[31]

Danny's bald and evasive telling refers to but does not explain this incident of colonial violence. Deborah Bird Rose, describing her experience of living with the Yarralin people in the Northern Territory, explains that "verbal learning, although it may seem straightforward, is often opaque to the newcomer,"[32] since to understand one story one needs to be familiar with others, and with broader social processes. In *Desert Cowboy*, Yinti is observed undergoing such verbal learning, which must be informed by the reading of country and of the physical traces of the past.

Soon after he has been warned off visiting the site of the massacre, Yinti is commissioned to kill a rogue bull and is given a gun for this purpose. Having carried out this task, he visits the hill he noticed earlier. As he reads the contours of the land, he can tell that people once dug for water at a waterhole that is now dried up. On the red sand are white fragments, neither wood nor stone, and when Yinti picks some up he realizes that they are shards of bone. He replaces them on the sand so as not to disturb the site, and returns to the homestead. The next story relates to Yinti's discovery, though in an indirect and allusive way. Here, Yinti returns to the homestead with the manager's gun. It is dark and he looks inside the house to where the manager and his wife sit at the kitchen table after their meal. Yinti lifts the gun to his shoulder and aims first at the manager, then at his wife. He stands for a long time in this posture, but does not press the trigger. Then he lowers the rifle, hangs it in the rack, and returns to the camp.

Beneath the deceptive simplicity of this sequence lies a set of complex meanings encompassing colonial relations: the need for reticence in referring to events like the massacre, the connections between the past and the present, and questions of retribution and compensation. Similarly, Pike's illustration of the homestead story (fig. 17), with its emphasis on the figure of Yinti

FIGURE 17  Illustration from *Desert Cowboy*, by Pat Lowe and Jimmy Pike. Illustration copyright © 2000 by Jimmy Pike, reproduced by permission of Magabala Books.

and the possibilities open to him, locates the key players against a ground suggesting country, the site of personal and collective identity, but a version of
country in which the homestead, the windmill, the farm shed, and the util-
ity iconically represent the pastoral industry and refer to the colonial appropriation that transformed country into bundles of land owned by white
people. The juxtaposition of narratives insists that the homestead story
should be read in the light of the previous episode; hence, while the land
may now be occupied by settlers, it bears the signs of Aboriginal bodies, both
in what it reveals to Yinti about the practices of people in the past, and in the
fragments of bone that testify to the massacre. In this way, *Desert Cowboy*
affirms the tenacity of Aboriginal knowledge of and attachment to country
in a nation where dispossession is still the experience of most Indigenous
people.

Whereas *Desert Cowboy* is a first-contact narrative told through an Indigenous perspective, Shirley Sterling's *My Name Is Seepeetza* (1992) follows the
progress of an Indigenous subject whose experience of assimilation is inflected by colonial histories stretching back through several generations.
The protagonist of this text is known both as Seepeetza, the name that her
family call her, and also as Martha Stone, the name she is obliged to use in the
Kalamak Indian Residential School (KIRS) in British Columbia, which, as a status Indian, she is obliged to attend from the age of five.[33] These two names,
splitting the narrator into two versions of the self, symbolize the psychological and physical violence of a regime whose aim, in the words of Bonita
Lawrence, was to "effect the total assimilation of Native people into the body
politic of Canadian society, through policies of removing children from their
parents and societies, suppressing their language, and systematically negat-
ing the value of Native cultures."[34] At KIRS, Seepeetza is stripped of all associations with home and family: she loses her name, her hair is cut, and she is
stripped, washed, and clothed in garments that are identical with those of all
the other girls at the school.

Seepeetza has three escape routes to alleviate her homesickness and
loneliness: the school library, where she can immerse herself in reading; the
secret journal in which she writes for a year, from September 1958 to August
1959; and dreams and memories of home. It is the third of these that concerns
me here, because Sterling's narrative, criss-crossing between Seepeetza's
life at school and her memories of home, powerfully evokes the politics of
place. Within the framing narrative of the journal, multiple stories of places
and their meanings construct a world where white privilege is paramount. An
episode at the beginning of the narrative will illustrate what I mean. Seepeetza
reflects on the dangers of keeping a journal in a world where letters to families are censored and children punished for negative comments about the

school: "I might get the strap, or worse. Last year some boys ran away from school because one of the priests was doing something bad to them. The boys were caught and whipped. They had their heads shaved and they had to wear dresses and kneel in the dining room and watch everybody eat. They only had bread and water to eat for a week. Everybody was supposed to laugh at them and make fun of them but nobody did."[35] To twelve-year-old Seepeetza, the boys' ordeal is a warning about the impossibility of escape from the school and what it represents. The sexual abuse from which the boys have sought to escape occurs at the school, so that the public humiliation and deprivation of food is a minor aspect of their punishment. In the school the authority of the nuns and priests is supreme; nevertheless, even in the dining room where the withdrawal or supply of food, constitutes a major means of control, the children have a sliver of resistance available to them: they refuse to mock the boys as they are supposed to.

Many episodes in the novel juxtapose memories and dreams with accounts of school routines, punishments, or labour. Thus, when Seepeetza shucks corn after school, she escapes in memory to times when she has carried out the same task for her mother; set to mop the floors, she recalls horse-riding early in the morning; left by herself because she has chickenpox, the unaccustomed quiet reminds her of the quiet of the forest. Her memories are suffused with imaginings of places, family, and the routines of her community. While Seepeetza's life and that of her family has been shaped and regulated by colonization, her community maintains its attachment to land and to the cultural practices associated with particular sites. At the end of summer, when Seepeetza and her community go berry-picking in the mountains, the adults "discuss serious business;"[36] the elders instruct children on where and how to gather berries; at the campfire, people exchange stories. Such communal activities teach Seepeetza that "there is something really special about being mountain people. It's a feeling like you know who you are, and you know each other. You belong to the mountains."[37]

These narratives of collective survival are offset by references to the impact of colonization and its imbrication with place. Seepeetza's father is a rancher, supporting his family on his hundred-acre holding and thus living out the Canadian ideal of private property and individual labour; yet his own experiences of residential schooling and army service periodically spill over into alcoholic violence, and the family are obliged to leave their home and sleep in the hills when Seepeetza's father "yells and throws dishes around or anything he can get his hands on."[38] Toward the end of the novel, Seepeetza records her father's words as she and her sister Missy prepare, unwillingly, to return to school: "'It's going to get crowded in the valley in a few years,' he said. 'People will be building houses all around the ranch. Ranching won't pay much anymore. You kids want to get yourselves an education. Get a job. That way you'll be okay.'"[39] That the family's access to land and livelihood is provisional and limited is evident in these words; nevertheless, the ranch, the mountain where they pick berries together with their relatives, and the river where their father catches fish are sites redolent with personal and cultural meanings. The politics of *My Name Is Seepeetza*, like those of Lowe and Pike's account of the massacre in *Desert Cowboy*, centre on land and its personal and cultural meanings. In both these texts, land is storied with narratives about people and spirits and about their relations with place.

I turn now to two picture books: *How the Indians Bought the Farm* (1996), authored by Craig Kee Strete and Michelle Netten Chacon and illustrated by Francisco Mora, and Allen Say's *Home of the Brave* (2002), which more explicitly address the meanings of place for colonized and marginalized people. *How the Indians Bought the Farm* interrogates the agendas of privatization that dominated federal government policies in the United States in the 1980s during the terms of Ronald Reagan and George Bush.[40] In *Home of the Brave*, Say uses the structuring organization of a journey to expose the strategies of repression that enable the nation to forget the stories of two groups of dispossessed children: Japanese-American children incarcerated during the Second World War and Native American children removed from their families and communities and placed in Indian schools.

In *How the Indians Bought the Farm*, a government official comes to visit "a great Indian chief and his great Indian wife," who "lived on the homeland of their people,"[41] and tells them that they must move to a farm where they are obliged to raise farm animals: sheep, pigs, and cows. The chief and his wife are perturbed by this command, since they cannot afford to purchase farm animals. However, when the chief travels by canoe down the river, he encounters three animals who agree to accompany him in exchange for food and shelter: a moose, a beaver, and a bear. Delighted with their new home, the animals invite their friends to join them. A week later, the government official arrives with a number of "men dressed in green uniforms"[42] to investigate the number of animals at the farm. In the darkness of the barn, the chief, and his wife present the bears and beavers as sheep and pigs. When the official asks to see their cows, the chief stamps on the ground, signalling to the moose herd, which stampedes toward them:

> The government man's face was whiter than his white papers.
> "Here they come," said the great Indian wife. Suddenly, big brown shapes came running out of the forest.
> "They are really mad," said the great Indian chief.
> "As mad as can be," agreed his wife. "They might trample our barn down. Or worse."

"Do you believe us now?" asked the great Indian chief.

But the government man was gone, leaving only his tracks behind.[43]

In its fantasy about the triumph of cleverness over officialdom, this text evokes the many Native American stories in which apparently powerless figures are shown to wield power. While it thus builds on stories that are founded in Native American principles of ecological balance and respect for all creatures, the narrative of *How the Indians Bought the Farm* also engages in ironic play with stereotypes and with colonial and assimilationist agendas. In particular, it evokes the discourse of treaties in which honorific titles such as "Great White Father" and "Great Indian Chief" were used to mask the deceptiveness and cynicism that often characterized the United States' actions in relation to treaty violations, and in this way *How the Indians Bought the Farm* accords with traditions of Native American activism that have deployed treaty discourses for political purposes since the 1960s.[44]

Just as British colonists regarded communal ownership of land by Indigenous nations as an affront to individualism, so this view resurfaced during the Reagan and Bush years, when it constituted a dominant theme in relations between government and Native American nations. *How the Indians Bought the Farm* parodies federal policies as they are enacted by the "government man," who orders the "great Indian chief" and his "great Indian wife" to become individual property holders and to engage in activities the government recognizes as farming. The veneer of respect suggested by treaty discourse in "great Indian chief," "great Indian wife," and "Great White Father" is set against verbal exchanges that expose the real agenda of the "government man"—that the Indians will fail in the task he has set them and that "the government" will appropriate their farm:

> "If you are to keep this farm we gave you, you must raise sheep and pigs and cows," said the government man. "Lots of them."
>
> "We don't have any sheep or pigs or cows," said the great Indian chief.
>
> "We don't have any money to buy sheep, pigs, or cows," said the great Indian wife.
>
> "That's not my problem," said the man. "But you will be in big trouble if you don't get some."[45]

This text derives its subversive edge from its strategy of positioning readers to cheer on the great Indian chief and his great Indian wife against the bullying tactics of the government officials. The final illustration (fig. 18) shows the chief and his wife surrounded by their animals, in a vignette of domestic calm that draws on the conceit of collusion between the Indians and the animals to signal a model of resistance based on collective and communitarian action.

FIGURE 18  Illustration from *How the Indians Bought the Farm*, by Craig Kee Strete, Michele Netten Chacon, and Francisco Mora. Illustration copyright © 1996 by Francisco X. Mora, reproduced by permission of Francisco X. Mora.

Allen Say's *Home of the Brave* explores the processes of national myth-making that construct the United States as "home" while children within the nation are wrenched away from homes and families: the Native American children sent to Indian schools from 1879 (when the Carlisle Indian School was established) until the 1960s; and the children who constituted around half of the 120,000 Japanese Americans, most of them American citizens, rounded up and relocated in concentration camps in remote sites across the United States from 1941 to 1944. In her essay "Resisting Reconciliation," Jane Jacobs suggests that while resistance is often understood in terms of an oppositional politics, there is another way of thinking of this concept: "the psychoanalytic … understanding of resistance as a patient's refusal to move to a point which will enable healing to occur. Resistance, in this context, is a form of defence against the anxiety which might be produced by recognising some repressed 'truth' or confronting the repressed emotional traces of a past trauma."[46] Say depicts the nation's repression of trauma in *Home of the Brave* through the figure of an unnamed man of Japanese appearance who undertakes a dangerous journey into the murky spaces of the nation's history. His kayak is swept through a gorge, down a waterfall, and into an underground river, after which he climbs up a shaft and finds himself in a desert where he sees two children with luggage labels around their necks. He cannot make out the writing on these labels—or, to read his actions psychoanalytically, he resists knowing what is painful to know, for the landscapes, buildings, and actions of the narrative gesture toward psychic processes. With the two children, he struggles through a dust storm, and at length the three come to "a row of buildings made of wood and tarpaper."[47] When he enters one of these houses, the man sees on the floor a luggage label like those around the children's necks, and he finds that it bears his own name; later, he finds another label carrying his mother's name; still later, he remembers that he was named after his mother's father.

These moments of self-recognition constitute the turning point of the narrative, because they represent a shift from the wilful forgetting constituted by repression, to an acknowledgement of the past as present in the lived experience of the children and their descendants. When the protagonist turns from the house, he finds himself facing "a group of children…like one large body with many eyes," who cry, "Take us home!"[48] (fig. 19). Suddenly a loudspeaker booms out, "Get back inside!" and when "two watchtowers [loom] in the darkening sky,"[49] the children run away. Following an exhausted sleep, the man wakes to see that he is lying by the side of a river, where children are standing by his kayak; but these are not the same as the Japanese American children of the earlier scene. These are Native American children who tell him, "You're in our camp"[50] (fig. 20). Here Say connects the two groups of objectified child others—the interned Japanese American children and the many thousands of Native American children institutionalized in the name of assimilation.

Say's audacious coupling of two marginalized groups suggests a complex set of ideas around spatiality. I have suggested that the protagonist's journey is a metaphor for the recovery of memories repressed by formulations of the nation as home; but the desert and mountain landscapes through which the protagonist journeys are multivalent signs. While the land has been *taken over* for purposes of segregation and institutionalization, it has also been *taken from* its Indigenous owners as part of the colonial seizure of territory; moreover, the generations of Native American children relocated to Indian schools have been *taken away* from homelands and families. *Home of*

FIGURE 19  Illustration from *Home of the Brave*, by Allen Say. Reprinted by permission of Houghton Mifflin Company. All rights reserved.

*the Brave* does not promote the facile notion that "we are all victims"—that is, that marginalized populations are alike in their experiences of loss and disruption. Rather, the discovery (or recovery) of memories about the incarceration of Japanese American children triggers memories about the Indian schools and their long-lasting effects, and about the older dislocations of colonialism. In this way, Say signals that the nation in its very foundation has constituted "home" at the expense of its excluded, who have been

FIGURE 20  Illustration from *Home of the Brave*, by Allen Say. Reprinted by permission of Houghton Mifflin Company.

wrenched from their homes and homelands in the interests of the national culture.

The luggage labels that the children wear, that fix them as objects of the State's strategies of naming and of surveillance, are reconfigured in a transformative moment at the end of the narrative when the man flings them into the air:

Suddenly the cloud of nametags seemed to turn into a great flock of birds. The man and the children watched until they disappeared over the mountains.

"They went home," said a child.

"Yes, they went home," the man said.

And the children nodded.[51]

The statement "They went home" is culturally dense and loaded with emotion. As it is used here it is also imbued with doubt and uncertainty because Say's allegory of repression suggests that the nation is not and cannot be "home" until its displaced children are psychologically and psychically at home. The book's title, *Home of the Brave*, conjures up the words "home of the free" in "The Star-Spangled Banner," itself an expression of patriotism that represses all but the most positive and celebratory formulations of nationhood. While *How the Indians Bought the Farm* uses spatiality parodically and *Home of the Brave* to encode repressed memories, both texts are deeply subversive, exposing the contempt for marginalized and non-white others that has all too often shaped government policies and processes in settler cultures.

### Place, Race, Gender, Class: Intersections of Power

As I noted previously, Indigenous peoples in New Zealand, Australia, Canada, and the United States share a bundle of depressing statistics relating to economic and cultural disadvantage, including lower life expectancy than non-Indigenous populations, poorer health, and higher rates of incarceration and suicide. Just as non-Indigenous representations of Indigenous people tend to cluster around a narrow range of character types, so also the settings in which such characters are located are limited, the most common being rural or remote locations (especially in the case of elders and sage-figures) and impoverished urban areas (in representations of children and young people "torn" between cultures).

A relatively common intersection of race and class in these texts depicts Indigenous characters who are rescued from poverty and inducted into middle-class settings that may be ostensibly neutral as to race but are in fact normatively white.[52] Thus, the Native ancestry that marks Willow, in Jean Little's *Willow and Twig* (2000), as "100-percent native"[53] is an inert aspect of her identity, because her sense of self turns on her relationship with her grandmother, who legally adopts Willow and her brother after they are abandoned by their mother and installs them in a white, middle-class habitus. Another common representational pattern, evident in James Moloney's novels *Dougy* (1993) and *Gracey* (1994), focuses on questions of authenticity, implying that when Indigenous characters attain middle-class privilege by moving out of poverty, they suffer a diminution of Indigenous identity. As Augie Fleras notes, "White settler discourse preferred to define indigenous groups as a 'problem people' in need of control or solution in the 'national interests.'"[54] It follows, then, that Indigenous people who are active in achieving their own solutions can appear to transgress these colonialist norms, which are ultimately concerned with maintaining power.

A noticeable feature of contemporary Indigenous texts is that even though they commonly locate characters in settings marked by poverty, they tend not to focus on the negative effects of factors such as substandard housing, lack of food, or insufficient money, but rather on the agency characters exercise and on values associated specifically with Indigenous traditions. This is as true of texts where characters live in urban settings as those where settings are coded as Indigenous, such as communities on reserves or traditional land. I am uncomfortably aware as I make this point that it may be construed as arguing that Indigenous authors do not position their Indigenous readers as aspirants to middle-class privilege; rather, that they advocate the maintenance of class systems where non-Indigenous people occupy the lower echelons. Or it may seem that I am arguing that Indigenous populations are constituted as homogenous groups in class terms. My reading of Indigenous texts is somewhat different from such formulations of class and Indigeneity. I find that these texts are concerned above all with communitarian ideals, rather than with liberal humanist principles that advocate the growth of individual identity, the dominant concern of most children's literature. Self-actualization as it is represented in mainstream children's texts often incorporates a shift out of poverty, or from a lower-class habitus to one marked by access to cultural signs such as books and classical music. The Indigenous texts I will now examine depart from these patterns, effacing notions of class difference by insisting on the agency of their characters and on their capacity to imagine uses for resources that might otherwise be misrecognized as worthless.

The picture book *Flour Sack Flora* (2001), written by Deborah Delaronde and illustrated by Gary Chartrand, is symptomatic of the many Indigenous texts that represent identities forged through the intersecting effects of race, class, and gender. Flora is a young girl who lives in the 1950s in a Métis community "a long way from the nearest town,"[55] and the narrative traces her quest for a new dress so that she will be able to travel to the town with her parents in order to shop for supplies. Like Cynthia Leitich Smith's *Jingle Dancer*,[56] *Flour Sack Flora* centres on relationships of support and obligation among girls and women. Just as Jenna in *Jingle Dancer* visits female relatives and friends to gather the jingles that her grandmother sews on her dress for the approaching powwow, so Flora calls upon women in her community: her grandmother, Marta of Kookoo Marta's Second Hand Store, and her grandmother's friends Emily, Gladys, and Mary, each of whom contributes to the creation of the dress that Flora proudly wears when she accompanies her parents to town.

*Flour Sack Flora* emphasizes the creativity with which the community produces a beautiful dress for Flora out of unpromising materials: the "flour sack" of the title, the unbleached cotton sacks in which bulk flour was purchased; the worn leather jacket out of which Kookoo Marta makes a white leather purse embroidered with a beaded red flower; the second-hand shoes that Flora's father polishes; the embroidery thread that Mary supplies; the lace provided by Gladys; the ribbon from Emily; and the cranberry dye that Grandma uses to transform the dress from cream to red. In each case, referring to Métis practices of barter, Flora repays the giver with a prized object of her own. As Paul DePasquale and Doris Wolf note, the value that Grandma and her friends place on Flora's dress reveals how "the Métis community depicted here, in spite of its implied isolation, is always affected by the white colonizer's world."[57] In particular, the flour sack that becomes Flora's dress evokes the impact of industrialization on Métis communities, and affirms the ingenuity of Grandma and her friends as they painstakingly make it over as a dress fit to be worn by Flora on her first visit to town; but the dress itself accords with the norms of white culture.

While the narrative of *Flour Sack Flora* is rich in references to female traditions of embroidery, beadwork, and dressmaking in Métis culture,[58] Deborah Delaronde's illustrations also foreground products and household items that hold iconic status, such as the Singer treadle sewing machine, the wood-fired stove used to dye Flora's dress, and proprietary brands of flour: Robin Hood and Five Roses.[59] Several of the book's illustrations locate Flora and her grandmother against windows through which can be seen components of the landscape: lake, trees, sky, and ground. Here (fig. 21), for instance, Grandma's sewing machine partially obscures a scene of lake, sky, and fishing boat seen through the window, while Flora rummages for buttons in a box of old clothes. The division between inside and outside here suggests a split between masculine and feminine domains, just as the sparse simplicity of the room is offset by the scene outside.

A poignant aspect of the narrative is that Flora's *rite de passage* involves her transition from the inside world of girls and women to the town, an outside space that is both dangerous and desirable, where Métis culture is marginal to social and commercial processes. In addition to the primary story of Flora's dress, the narrative refers to multiple histories of negotiation between cultures, and to the concessions and compromises necessary to colonized

As Grandma sewed, Flora looked through a box of old clothes until she found the prettiest buttons for her dress. She snipped them off and placed them in a bowl. They would be sewn down the back of the dress.

FIGURE 21  Illustration from *Flour Sack Flora*, by Deborah Delaronde and Gary Chartrand. Illustration copyright © 2001 by Gary Chartrand. Reprinted by permission of Pemmican Publications.

people. These histories are signalled by the household items that feature in the illustrations, by the women's memories of their own first trips to town, and by Flora's parents' insistence that she should not wear her moccasins with her new dress, an indication that she must discard signs of Métis culture that might bring shame on her community and family. Although Delaronde's illustrations are readable in relation to the lower-class habitus suggested by Grandma's frugality and simplicity of life, the narrative refuses notions of disadvantage or lack by insisting on the countervailing strengths of Flora and her community.

A strikingly similar ideological thrust is evident in two picture books by the Maori author Patricia Grace, *The Kuia and the Spider* (1981), illustrated by Robyn Kahukiwa, and *The Trolley* (1993), illustrated by Kerry Gemmill; and in Cynthia Leitich Smith's *Indian Shoes* (2002), a novel for younger readers. *The Kuia and the Spider* is set in a Maori village where the *kuia* lives, weaving mats and baskets out of flax.[60] She conducts a debate with her companion the spider, concerning which of the two is the more skillful weaver, and this debate modulates into a competition that reaches its climax when the *kuia*'s ten grandchildren come to stay with her, while the spider's grandchildren visit him in his web. Finally, the two agree to continue living together: "And they argued and argued and argued for the rest of their lives."[61]

Kahukiwa's illustrations powerfully evoke relations between place and culture. In the scene where the spider challenges the *kuia* by calling out "Hey old woman, my weaving is better than yours,"[62] the illustration (fig. 22) connects inside to outside by way of the window, through which beach, hills, and sky can be seen, and the open door, which shows a part of the *kuia*'s garden. As in *Flour Sack Flora*, a wood-burning stove refers to the interplay of Indigenous and Western materiality played out in the lives of these elderly women; but here, signs of Maori traditions are evident in the flax drying on shelves next to the door, the carved gourd on the mantelpiece, and the flax baskets and mats that the *kuia* has woven. By the time her grandchildren come to stay, the *kuia* has woven their names into the kits (baskets) that she gives them; they sit on the mats she has woven, singing, and talking; and at night they sleep on the sleeping-mats she has prepared (fig. 23). Just as the women of Flora's community induct her into Métis selfhood through sustaining traditions and practices, so in *The Kuia and the Spider* the *kuia* incorporates her grandchildren into a Maori habitus; and again, the signs of working-class life evident in the *kuia*'s home are effaced by her skilled use of natural resources and by the amplitude of these resources.

In *The Trolley*, Gemmill's illustrations locate characters in the urban setting of a working-class Maori family comprising Tania and her daughter and son, Miria and Hoani. Tania cannot afford to buy Christmas presents, and she

One day the spider called out to the kuia,
'Hey old woman,
my weaving is better than yours.'

FIGURE 22 Illustration from *The Kuia and the Spider*, by Patricia Grace and Robyn Kahukiwa. Illustration copyright © 1981 by Robyn Kahukiwa, reproduced by permission of Robyn Kahukiwa.

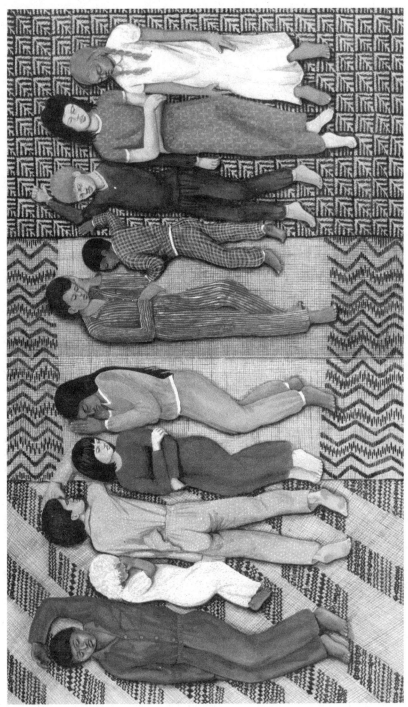

FIGURE 23  Illustration from *The Kuia and the Spider*, by Patricia Grace and Robyn Kahukiwa. Illustration copyright © 1981 by Robyn Kahukiwa, reproduced by permission of Robyn Kahukiwa.

FIGURE 24 Illustration from *The Trolley*, by Patricia Grace and Kerry Gemmill. Illustration copyright © 1993 by Kerry Gemmill, reproduced by permission of Kerry Gemmill.

conceives the idea of making Miria and Hoani a trolley out of discarded items: the wheels from an old pram,[63] pieces of wood from the woodstack, an old skipping rope from the toybox, and a wooden box for a seat. The text does not pursue the personal history that has led Tania to single parenthood and poverty, but foregrounds her ingenuity and the responses of the polyglot, multicultural community in which she lives with her children. Worried that the trolley will not be able to compete with the new bicycles and skateboards that the other children have received, Tania waits anxiously to see how Miria and Hoani respond to her gift; but very soon the entire neighbourhood of children are clamouring to ride on the trolley, and in the book's final illustration (fig. 24), they are gathering materials to construct another trolley. Implicit in this representation of a New Zealand urban habitus is the ideal of the nation as a community constituted by the energies and capacities of its Maori and Pakeha members, prominent among them Tania's regard for imagination and for tradition—the homemade trolley, which triggers memories of her own childhood, affords as much pleasure as the bicycles and skateboards that the other children have received for Christmas.

Cynthia Leitich Smith's *Indian Shoes* is an episodic novel whose focus is the relationship between a Cherokee-Seminole boy, Ray Halfmoon, and his grandfather, with whom Ray lives following the death of his parents. While Ray and Grampa live in Chicago, their extended family live in Oklahoma, which Grampa regards as home. In the first chapter of the novel, Grampa reluctantly faces the fact that his pickup has finally broken down, so that he and Ray will be unable to travel to Oklahoma for Christmas. In Murphy Family Antiques, Ray and Grampa notice a pair of moccasins labeled as "Seminole Moccasins from Oklahoma" and priced at $50. While Flora's moccasins, in *Flour Sack Flora*, are "too Aboriginal" to be respectable footwear for Flora's first visit to town, the moccasins in Murphy Family Antiques are offered for sale as kitsch or exotic mementos. When Ray decides to cheer Grampa up by buying him the moccasins with his savings and visits the shop to make his best offer, he finds himself in competition with a woman customer who asks the shop owner, "Do you know if these are real? ... Native American worn and Native American made?"[64] The spectre of authenticity shadows these questions, which hinge on a narrow definition of "real."

Like the picture books I have discussed in this section, the narrative of *Indian Shoes* hinges on a demonstration of ingenuity that enables an Indigenous character to transcend limitations of opportunity or resources. Ray approaches the woman who has bought the moccasins and offers to trade them: "'Wanna trade?' he asked the lady. 'I've got some Indian shoes you could use. Beats me who made 'em, but they're for-sure Indian worn.'"[65]

The woman agrees, and Ray exchanges his worn high-tops for the moccasins, which he gives to Grampa:

> When the wind whispered against the brick bungalow that night, Grampa slid his feet into the moccasins. "These really take me back," he said. "They feel like home."
>
> Come Tuesday morning, at the high school four blocks away, the librarian placed a pair of beat-up hightops with neon orange shoelaces in her Native American books display. She propped a laser-printed card to the right of the toes. The card read:

> Traded from Ray Halfmoon
> Cherokee-Seminole Hightops
> Not Indian Made, but Indian Worn
> (Guaranteed)

Like the handmade objects central to *Flour Sack Flora, Jingle Dancer, The Kuia and the Spider,* and *The Trolley,* the moccasins that Ray obtains for

Grampa testify to individual agency, cultural traditions, and significant places; they are incorporated into transactions of reciprocity and affection between adults and children; and they are evocative of relations between Indigenous people and settler cultures. Smith evokes binaries that commonly structure notions of Indianness—authentic against inauthentic; traditional against modern; nature against culture—and deconstructs them in her depiction of Ray's playful negotiation with the librarian, when his reality as a Cherokee-Seminole subject confers "authenticity" on his highstops, which are "for-sure Indian worn." Simultaneously, the "real" moccasins that were displayed in Murphy Family Antiques as mere exhibits, trophies of the past, are re-endowed with the significances of lived experience when they are worn by Grampa.

It is above all in their approach to the ownership and use of land that Indigenous texts for children depart from most non-Indigenous writing. Whereas among non-Indigenous populations the importance placed on Indigenous rights to land fluctuates according to its impact on settler political economies, for Indigenous authors, land—its ownership, its histories, and its significances—is always a crucial component of narratives. Nevertheless, even a text such as *Canyons*, which presents an attenuated and reductive version of Apache culture and its connections to place, projects unease about Indigenous sacredness onto the mountains, canyons, and desert settings described in the novel. The other novels I have referred to in this chapter— *Owl*, *The Sign of the Beaver*, *False Face*, *Take the Long Path*, *Bone Dance*— evince lively tensions about the uncanny presence of Indigenous cultures and people in landscapes where settler cultures have taken root.

These Indigenous texts do not engage in open polemics concerning land and the rights of Indigenous people, but adopt the subtler and more effective strategy of unsettling the assumptions and preconceptions of dominant cultures by accepting as normal the assumptions, values, and world views of Indigenous characters. In *Desert Cowboy*, Jimmy's gesture of returning the fragments of bone to the earth where people have been massacred is both unreadable and eloquent in its assertion about Aboriginal bodies and their relationship to country. Deborah Delaronde's insistence on the interplay of histories and cultures in the settings of *Flour Sack Flora* and Patricia Grace and Robyn Kahukiwa's celebration of Maori traditions of weaving and oratory in *The Kuia and the Spider* embodies place with memories, cultural practices, and knowledges. In his essay "The Local and the Global," Stuart Hall suggests that the illusory uniformity of globalization can be exploded by what he calls "the rediscovery of ethnicity," when "the moment of the rediscovery of a place, of a past, of one's roots, of one's context, is a necessary moment of enunciation. The margins could not speak up without first grounding themselves somewhere."[66] The Indigenous texts I have discussed in this chapter go further than this, since even as they acknowledge the depredations of colonialism, they do not claim rediscovery so much as survival, continuity, and presence.

# 8 Allegories of Place and Race

> Hello, says one of the men in silly clothes with red hair
> all over his head. I am Christopher Columbus. I am sailing
> the ocean blue looking for India. Have you seen it?
> Forget India, says Coyote. Let's play ball.
>                    —Thomas King and William Kent Monkman,
>                                        *A Coyote Columbus Story*

Within postcolonial literary studies, allegory has generally been regarded as a key form of counter-discourse, a strategy by which
colonialist versions of history and dominant modes of representation are
contested and resisted. Stephen Slemon was one of the first theorists to recognize the power of postcolonial allegory, observing that, within postcolonial
literatures, "Allegory becomes a site upon which post-colonial cultures seek
to contest and subvert colonialist appropriation through the production of
a literary, and specifically anti-imperialist, figurative opposition or textual
*counter-discourse*."[1] Bill Ashcroft points out that "fundamentally, all historical writing is allegorical" because "narrativity reproduces, metonymically, the
teleological progression of the history it 'records.'"[2] Postcolonial allegory is,
then, a particularly potent mode of historical revision, since it lays bare the
tropes, figures, and teleologies on which dominant versions of history are
built. In this chapter I discuss children's texts that treat historical and contemporary sociopolitical processes and outcomes by way of metaphor and allegory. These texts are, however, not all equally counter-discursive. Rather,
their treatments of colonial and postcolonial issues track a continuum between militant, open, and critical approaches, and those whose figurative
effects fold into the dominant representational practices of colonialism.

The most openly and self-consciously allegorical works for children,
Thomas King and William Kent Monkman's *A Coyote Columbus Story* and
Gavin Bishop's *The House That Jack Built*, are picture books by Indigenous
authors and artists, a fact that suggests that the dialogical form of the picture

Notes to chapter 8 on pages 248–50.

book is particularly well suited to the layered and ironic treatments of colonial discourse evident in these texts. In *A Coyote Columbus Story*, the trickster Coyote is at the centre of a narrative that begins as follows: "It was Coyote who fixed up this world, you know. She is the one who did it. She made rainbows and flowers and clouds and rivers. And she made prune juice and afternoon naps and toe-nail polish and television commercials. Some of these things were pretty good, and some of these things were foolish. But what she loved to do best was to play ball."[3] When Coyote changes the rules of the ballgame and "doesn't watch what she is making up out of her head,"[4] Christopher Columbus and "those Columbus people" arrive, intent on plunder. In this way, King's narrative attributes contingency, haphazardness, and ulterior motivations to a sequence of historical events generally represented within dominant discourses as inevitable and heroic.

In *A Forest of Time*, Peter Nabokov outlines the "motivations and practices through which American Indians have remembered their diverse pasts."[5] One such practice is to invest traditional stories with counter-discursive meanings. Nabokov notes that these stories are often about "randy animal tricksters who get their comeuppance and yet straggle on to entertain us for another day,"[6] and are "couched in seemingly apolitical, amusing forms, and featuring culture heroes, evil monsters, and other familiar characters whose fantastic antics seem outside historical time."[7] In line with these narrative practices, Thomas King's Coyote shows how not to behave toward the colonizers. She is slow to recognize Columbus's mercantile and selfish interests, and she misreads his intentions of selling human beings into slavery: "When Coyote hears this bad idea, she starts to laugh. Who would buy human beings, she says, and she laughs some more."[8] The human beings are indeed enslaved and sold "to rich people like baseball players and dentists and babysitters and parents,"[9] whereupon Coyote makes the empty promise that she will "take Christopher Columbus back."[10]

Coyote is a black joke precisely because she does not appreciate that the advent of Columbus represents a cataclysmic and irreversible change to a world previously ordered and balanced. In line with the subversive stories described by Nabokov, she "enacts a new set of unwelcome cultural actions and values that have been introduced by alien historical actors,"[11] showing herself up as a bad judge of character and a foolish optimist. The figure of Coyote thus simultaneously refers to colonial imaginings of docile and collusive Native Americans, and demonstrates the deleterious effects of collusion on Native American subjects. More than this, *A Coyote Columbus Story* produces what Edouard Glissant refers to as "a prophetic vision of the past,"[12] conflating the past with the present. The illustration in which Coyote's friends are auctioned off (fig. 25) depicts the "baseball players and dentists and

FIGURE 25  Illustration from *A Coyote Columbus Story*, by Thomas King and William Kent Monkman. Illustration copyright © 1992 by William Kent Monkman, reproduced by permission of Douglas & McIntyre.

babysitters and parents"[13] who gather to buy the human beings Columbus has transported to Spain. Seated in his convertible, Columbus resembles a sleazy entrepreneur, transforming the auction into spectacle by observing it through his side-view mirror. The diagonal axis that links his self-satisfied smile with the group of Native American slaves at the top left of the picture leads the reader's eye to the sign "Imported," which descries the slaves as mere items for consumption. However, the contemporary references of the illustration— the fluffy dice hanging from the rear-view mirror of Columbus's car, the zero on the back of the baseball player, and the clothes of the bidders—fuse these past events with the present, where Indigenous cultures and peoples continue to experience commodification and exploitation through neocolonial processes and regimes.

Similarly, Gavin Bishop's *The House That Jack Built* both undermines the teleologies of colonial history and enforces the sense that the past is not over and finished. The figure of Jack, the Everyman settler, stands for colonial teleologies of change and progress. The destruction of his home and business represents the larger destruction of which Bishop's narrative is a part: dismantling of triumphalistic stories of settler success and exposing them as fictions. An alternative teleology is proposed in Bishop's account of the intervention of the god of war, Tumatauenga, who calls on the Maori to resist the environmental and cultural destruction effected by colonization. It is especially in the endpapers of *The House That Jack Built* (fig. 26) that Bishop brings together the past and the present of New Zealand postcolonialism. Between the European settler and the Maori warrior is the god of war, his warlike posture echoed by that of *Te Tangata Whenua* (the people of the land, or Maori), so that the book's closure suggests that the struggle over place and identity is by no means over. These are uncomfortable significances for contemporary audiences, since they contradict political discourses that imply that New Zealand's development as a bicultural society is merely a matter of peaceful coexistence.

While the two texts I have just discussed work unequivocally as allegory, there are many other children's texts that to a lesser extent involve allegorical treatments of colonialism. These lesser allegories feature most often in non-literary and popular modes including "family" films and various styles of speculative fiction. I next focus on three groups of texts whose narratives involve encounters between humans and strange or alien figures. The first group comprises texts in which children engage with alien beings who visit earth; the second group consists of science fiction involving humans who seek to establish planetary colonies; and the third group comprises postdisaster novels in which humans seek to produce new societies in lands ravaged by ecological disasters and warfare. The narratives of these texts

FIGURE 26   From *The House That Jack Built*, by Gavin Bishop (www.gavinbishop.com), reproduced by permission of Scholastic New Zealand Limited.

resemble other postcolonial writing for children in that they locate their characters in contact zones where cultures meet and where individuals from these cultures seek to communicate with one another across racial and cultural difference.

In all three narrative types, strategies of defamiliarization similar to those deployed in historical fiction produce effects whereby readers are positioned either to read place and its meanings either through the perspectives of alien others or to imagine familiar settings differently. The interface between place and identity, which is such a prominent component of postcolonial writing for children, hinges in these texts on encounters between figures whose views of place reflect and refract colonial discourses. Like most texts produced by non-Indigenous authors, they tend, with the exception of Brian Caswell's *Deucalion*, to focalize phenomena and events through the perspective of human characters whose views of the other are treated as normative.

### The Alien at Home

It is primarily through representations of aliens and alien worlds that speculative fiction engages with ethnic and cultural difference. Joan Gordon points out that alien contact novels place readers "on the borderland between the familiar and the alien,"[14] where they cannot but be cognizant of the ways in which humans perceive and deal with their others. Many critics have observed that "bad" aliens in Hollywood films such as the *Alien* series, *Independence Day*, and *Mars Attacks* function as metaphors for the dangers that cultural and ethnic diversity present to the safety and security of the United States,[15] especially in periods marked by a conservative backlash against immigration and multiculturalism. The dangerous aliens of these films attack national institutions and destabilize border control and social order, but they also suggest anxieties about an intermingling and mixture of cultures and ethnicities, thus reinscribing colonial fears regarding miscegenation. However, when aliens infiltrate or otherwise find their way into domestic and national settings coded as realistic, rather different meanings are generated, hinging on conceptions of home and nation. In *Shape-Shifting: Images of Native Americans in Recent Popular Fiction* (2000), Andrew Macdonald, Gina Macdonald, and Mary Ann Sheridan argue that colonial encounters between settlers and Native Americans constitute a typology of encounters with difference, so that "embedded in every alien story is the seed of a Native American story,"[16] whether one of savagery, abduction, romance, or friendship. Another way of formulating this relationship is to say that alien stories are allegories of colonization.

In this section, I consider positive representations of alien figures in three texts from the United States, New Zealand, and Australia—the film *E.T. the Extra-Terrestrial* (1982), Margaret Mahy's *Aliens in the Family* (1986), and Gillian Rubinstein's *Beyond the Labyrinth* (1988), respectively—in which creatures from other planets befriend child protagonists in realistically drawn family settings. In her essay "E.T. Go Home: Indigeneity, Multiculturalism and 'Homeland' in Contemporary Science Fiction Cinema," Helen Addison-Smith argues that the aliens in films such as *E.T.*, *Close Encounters of the Third Kind*, *Contact*, and *Cocoon* manifest a mode of otherness that is "biological" and that draws on the "rhetorics of human cultural difference that have historically involved the reification of the alien through biology as race."[17] Addison-Smith's analysis links these positive depictions of aliens with a representational mode that has characterized romantic depictions of Indigenous peoples as childlike figures whose principal function is to enhance the well-being of non-Indigenous citizens of settler societies.

The friendly, harmless aliens of *E.T.*, *Aliens in the Family*, and *Beyond the Labyrinth* are cut off from their planetary homes: E.T. is mistakenly left on Earth by his spacecraft while gathering botanical samples; Bond, the alien in Mahy's *Aliens in the Family*, is a neophyte scientist sent to New Zealand on the "old, original planet"[18] to gather information for the "inventory" developed by his teachers on the planet of Galgonqua; and in Rubinstein's *Beyond the Labyrinth*, Cal, an alien anthropologist, is stranded in an Australian coastal town. In all three cases, aliens come from cultures with "advanced" systems of science and communication, so that on face value it might seem that the narratives of these texts reverse colonial processes, with figures coded as Indigenous depicted as technologically sophisticated in comparison with the "primitive" capacities of humans. However, this seeming reversal is undercut by the fact that, far from being protected by imperial connections (as were explorers and colonists), E.T., Bond, and Cal are isolated figures, dependent on the friendship of humans. The regimes of power and control at play in these narratives favour humans over aliens, adults over children, and (in the case of *E.T.*) government forces over individuals. Moreover, the categories "child" and "adult" are unstable in regard to alien figures, since while E.T. is of indeterminate age and Rubinstein's Cal is an adult, both are represented in ways that emphasize their relative powerlessness in relation to adult society, and their "natural" affiliations with child characters. Whereas "bad" aliens are definitively other to humans, "good" aliens such as E.T., Bond, and Cal are both "like us" and "less than us," in ways that echo representations of Indigeneity within settler society mythologies and in many children's texts.

Spielberg's treatment of the character of E.T. develops the "alien-child" association by showing E.T. engaged in actions evocative of children testing out adult behaviours, and by foregrounding the psychic links that exist between E.T. and Elliott, the younger boy in the family. Thus, the scene where E.T. drinks cans of Coors beer from the refrigerator while he is alone in the family home emphasizes the comical effects of his intoxication as viewers are positioned to observe his actions from a vantage point around a child's height—that is, through Elliott's eyes. This connection is enforced by cross-cutting back and forth between the kitchen and the classroom, where Elliott's teacher is instructing his class in administering chloroform to frogs in preparation for dissection. When E.T. drinks the beer, Elliott burps loudly; when E.T. lurches about the kitchen and collides with the counter, Elliott exhibits signs of intoxication; and when E.T. passes out on the floor, Elliott sinks down in his chair, falling to the floor beneath his desk. A scene featuring a ten-year-old child drinking beer to the point of intoxication would be taboo for a family film; however, by showing Elliott's drunkenness to be the result of his identification with E.T. and by treating E.T.'s behaviour as "normal" for an alien, the film contrives to distance its audience from E.T.'s actions and to play up the comedic features of the sequence. Indigenous people were frequently represented in colonial discourses as childlike and naïve,[19] and the film's treatment of E.T. in this episode folds this association into a conventional contrast between the child-Indigene (spontaneous, driven by curiosity, lacking control) and the implied ideal of the European adult as rational and controlled.

While E.T. is spectacularly different from Elliott and his family, Bond and Cal are capable of passing as humans. In both cases, their colour distinguishes them from the whiteness of the children who befriend them. The slightly built, dark-complexioned Cal has been sent to Australia in order to study an Aboriginal tribe, the Narrangga, who turn out to be extinct; and one of the narrative's ironies is that Cal is frequently mistaken for an Aboriginal child and subjected to reflex racism by several of the novel's white characters. In *Aliens in the Family*, Bond's appearance too connects him with Indigenous culture: while his face is fair and his hair blond, he has gill flaps that enable him to breathe in earth's atmosphere and that look like "black and scarlet lace tattooed onto his skin between the base of his ears and his throat,"[20] a description suggestive of Maori traditions of facial and bodily ornamentation. More than this, Bond wears "an ancient sliver of jade,"[21] which he was given by his father and that links him with the New Zealand nephrite jade (*pounamu*) prized by Maori artists and carved as pendants and decorative objects.

In all three texts, the families into which aliens are incorporated are divided and unhappy. In *E.T.*, the children's father has abandoned the family and "gone to Mexico with Sally," as Elliott reminds his mother in a tense moment during the opening scenes of the film. Elliott himself is bullied by friends of his elder brother Michael, and he is an isolated and dispirited figure. *Aliens in the Family* also features a family that has undergone the stresses of divorce: twelve-year-old Jake is visiting her divorced father for the first time since his marriage to Philippa, whose first husband abandoned her, leaving her with two children, Lewis and Dora; the three children are uneasily conscious of the fragility of family alliances. In *Beyond the Labyrinth*, twelve-year-old Vicky has been sent from Africa by her parents and is an unwilling visitor at the home of the Trethewans, family friends in Australia with whom she stays before she attends boarding school. Fourteen-year-old Brenton Trethewan, obsessed by images of nuclear war, is deeply alienated from his family and especially from his father and brother, who despise him for his lack of adherence to masculinist ideals of toughness and competitiveness. The three families are thus riven by tensions and characterized by a sense of not being *at home*.

The most crucial functions of alien characters in these texts are to restore equilibrium among characters formerly at odds with one another and to enhance characters' sense of security and well-being. In *E.T.*, the older boys who formerly teased Elliott become his allies, flying on their BMX bicycles in convoy with E.T. and witnessing his safe delivery to the mother ship. In the final scene of the film, Elliott's mother is accompanied by Keys, one of the government agents who have been conducting surveillance of the family. In addition to this promise of a new father-figure, Elliott is "healed" through an exchange of promises whereby he and E.T. pledge that each will forever be present to the other. *Beyond the Labyrinth* offers its readers alternative endings in the style of "Choose your own adventure" narratives: in the first, Cal and Brenton are spirited away to Galgonqua; in the second, Cal dies while being treated in hospital, and Brenton, healed of his sense of psychic unease, concludes that "he may be going to live to grow up after all,"[22] resolving to become a scientist, perhaps an anthropologist. The ideological directions of the novel, and particularly its drive toward a positive resolution for Brenton, favour the second ending, in which Brenton's self-realization derives from his encounter with Cal. Again, in *Aliens in the Family*, family divisions are healed when Bond is restored to his home planet: Jake is reconciled with her stepsister Dora, and the tensions of the blended family are alleviated through humour and honesty.

While E.T., Bond, and Cal are all "higher intelligences," what they offer humans is a gift of affect rather than of cognition, since they leave characters *feeling* happier and wiser rather than *knowing* more about the universe. Spielberg's reliance on religious symbolism has frequently been observed by critics,[23] among them Vivian Sobchack, who notes that *E.T.* "gives its little alien a 'faith healing' finger matched only in special affect by his 'heartlight' (even further sentimentalized in an immensely popular Neil Diamond song)."[24] *Aliens in the Family* and *Beyond the Labyrinth* are produced in New Zealand and Australia, societies more secular than the United States; these narratives do not draw on religious symbolism but rather on settler culture traditions of looking to Indigenous cultures for ancient spiritualities that afford depth and transcendence, and thus provide a balance to the rational, materialistic values of dominant groups. While these texts invoke soft versions of science fiction, their distrust of hard sciences is nowhere more apparent than in the scenes in both *E.T.* and *Beyond the Labyrinth* where medical science jeopardizes the very survival of alien beings and threatens to transform them into objects. In *Beyond the Labyrinth*, Brenton's anxious prediction "It'd be just like in *E.T.*" claims as its pre-text the scenes in *E.T.* where the alien is, as Brenton says, made "into some kind of specimen."[25]

If the children in these texts are to benefit from their engagement with aliens, the aliens must leave them—or, in the case of the second (valorized) ending of *Beyond the Labyrinth*—must die as Cal does, "far from home among primitive people who killed her by trying to save her life."[26] Indeed, E.T., Cal, and Bond cannot survive away from their homes and desire nothing more than to return, the intensity of this desire encapsulated in E.T.'s repeated "E.T. phone home." That Indigenous peoples were destined to disappear because of their incapacity to adjust to (superior) white cultures was a common expectation and desire of colonizers in settler nations, and contemporary representations continue on the whole to evade the alterity of Indigenous cultures by relegating them to the margins of national life. The departure of E.T. and Bond and the death of Cal can be read in the light of these cultural norms, since their return to their distant homes obviates the troublesome necessity that the white children they befriend should engage with cultural (and racial) difference. As Jake says of Bond at the end of *Aliens in the Family*, "he didn't need to stay any longer,"[27] because, like E.T. and Cal, he has performed his task of providing meaning, hope, and a kind of spirituality to "alienated" children and families who are now "at home" in the worlds they inhabit.

Commenting on mainstream science fiction films including *E.T.*, Sobchack reads their representations of friendly aliens who are "just like us"[28] in the light of Foucault's distinction between relations of resemblance and of similitude. Foucault says:

Resemblance has a "model," an original element that orders and hierarchizes the increasingly less faithful copies that can be struck from it. Resemblance presupposes a primary reference that prescribes and classes. The similar develops in series that have neither beginning nor end, that can be followed in one direction as easily as in another, that obey no hierarchy, but propagate themselves from small differences among small differences. Resemblance serves representation, which rules over it; similitude serves repetition, which ranges across it. Resemblance predicates itself upon a model it must return to and reveal; similitude circulates the similacrum as an indefinite and reversible relation of the similar to the similar.[29]

Sobchack notes that in films such as *Close Encounters*, *E.T.*, and *Starman*, alien figures are "predicated upon and subordinated to a human model, and their 'faithlessness' as copies is ironically and conservatively an idealization of that model."[30] Seen in this light, E.T.'s comical drunkenness can be seen to gesture toward an ideal of human behaviour in which rationality wins out over bodily self-indulgence; and his obsessive desire to "phone home" points to and validates human desires for stability and familiarity while also, ironically, engendering a distrust of the new. Similarly, in *Aliens in the Family* and *Beyond the Labyrinth*, Bond and Cal manifest a reverence for technology that is undercut by the humanist values proposed by the texts, so that in the end both are seen to "return to and reveal" qualities, such as empathy and loyalty, that characterize human characters proposed as admirable. By constructing alien characters who, in Foucault's terms, manifest relations of resemblance to humans, these texts idealize humanness; specifically, they promote whiteness as the default model of humanness. If, as I have argued, their friendly aliens can be read as allegories of Indigeneity, then *E.T.*, *Aliens in the Family*, and *Beyond the Labyrinth* demonstrate that the proper function of the alien-as-Indigene is to maintain colonial hierarchies within fictions that claim that "they" are "just like us."

## Entering Alien Spaces

In his essay "Aliens, Alien Nations, and Alienation in American Political Economy and Popular Culture," Ronnie D. Lipschutz concludes that science fiction is "never really about the future or strange, new worlds where 'no one has gone before.' It is about us and the world in which we live."[31] The novels that I now consider hinge on "us and the world in which we live" by rewriting colonial histories through narratives of planetary colonization. Of particular interest here is how these texts represent the processes and ideologies whereby autochthonous inhabitants are transformed into colonized populations. Geoffrey Whitehall suggests that in science fiction "what is said is less interesting than how the beyond is used,"[32] and part of my emphasis in this section is to consider the extent to which "the beyond" is used allegorically in order to unsettle the teleologies of European history.

Texts thematizing the establishment of planetary colonies generally involve journeys necessitated by overcrowding, conflict, or environmental disasters on Earth. Across science fiction for children, most narratives of colonization, such as Pamela Sargent's *Earthseed* (1983), H.M. Hoover's *Another Heaven, Another Earth* (1983), Paul Collins's *The Earthborn* (2003), and Monica Hughes's trilogy, *The Keeper of the Isis Light* (1980), *The Guardian of Isis* (1981), and *The Isis Pedlar* (1982), trace journeys of colonization to planets uninhabited by intelligent life forms. In such narratives, storylines generally revolve around conflicting or opposing models of how new societies should organize themselves.

The texts I focus on—Monica Hughes's *The Golden Aquarians* (1995), Mary Caraker's *The Faces of Ceti* (1991), and Brian Caswell's *Deucalion* (1995)— deal with journeys where colonists encounter alien beings on planets where humans seek to establish settlements. While these texts have in common a bundle of science fiction *nova*,[33] including space travel and telepathic communication, their representations of colonization are inflected by particular settler culture histories. For instance, *The Faces of Ceti* compares two colonizing groups from the starship *Columbia*—those who settle on the earth-like planet Arcadia under their despotic leader Carlos Vega, and the smaller group that settles on Ceti One and aims at constructing an ideal society. One of Vega's strategies of control over his subjugated group of colonizers is his invention of the "Cosmic Plan,"[34] a set of principles and rules that he attributes to a divine revelation; these rules involve strict hierarchies based on essentialist constructions of gender and race. Caraker's characterization of the Arcadians problematizes colonial discourses particular to the United States— namely, of manifest destiny and Puritanism, as well as contemporary debates concerning the increasing influence of the fundamentalist right—and engages in strategies of defamiliarization that draw attention to the contingent, constructed nature of those discourses. In particular, the text's exposure of Vega's opportunistic exploitation of religious discourses writes back to notions of divine guidance and intervention in the founding of the United States.

All three texts are crucially preoccupied with human subjects and their relations with alien species: the Elokoi of *Deucalion*, the hlur of *The Faces of Ceti*, and the eponymous Aquarians of *The Golden Aquarians*. In the Earth colonies of Deucalion, Ceti, and Aqua, colonizers appropriate territory, plunder resources, and destabilize Indigenous cultures. While *The Faces of Ceti* and

*The Golden Aquarians* trace events on planets newly colonized by humans, *Deucalion*—the most complex of the three texts—deals with the events leading to "The Deucalion Revolution," when the colonial rule that has operated for a century is brought to an end through an alliance between Elokoi and second-generation Deucalions. Like the texts discussed in chapters 5 and 6, the narratives of these novels hinge on the interdependence of identity and place and on notions of home.

A crucial aspect of all three novels is the contrast between the symbolic systems of humans and of aliens. The hlur, the Elokoi, and the Aquarians engage in telepathic communication and are thus free of the restrictions of time and distance that affect humans. In *The Faces of Ceti* and *The Golden Aquarians*, certain human children—those open to the possibility of alternative ways of thinking and being—are inducted into telepathic communication and hence into the conceptual worlds of hlur and Aquarians. However, both texts are cautious about the extent to which humans can readily enter into the cultures of these others. In *The Faces of Ceti*, Jenny, the young girl most apt at telepathy, finds herself unable to communicate with her hlur friend Tela after an episode when Tela witnesses an angry confrontation between two colonizers, so averse are the hlur to violence. The misapprehensions and frustrations that characterize attempts at communication between the hlur and the Cetians instantiate the gulf between the two races; and the narrative is curiously pessimistic about the possibility of closer and more empathetic relations. Thus, when Jenny weeps at the loss of her friendship with Tela, her older sister Maya, the novel's protagonist, "could offer Jenny little true comfort.... It didn't bode well for future relations."[35] In *The Golden Aquarians*, the children Walt and Solveig are telepathically endowed with images of an approaching tidal wave that threatens to kill the colonists unless they leave Aqua; but when the two escape with the other colonists, their relations with the Aquarians do not allow ongoing communication, modulating into memories destined to fade over time.

In *Deucalion*, the only humans capable of engaging in telepathic communication with Elokoi are the "Icarus children," the group of human–Elokoi hybrids produced following genetic experimentation in the early days of the colony. In contrast, even the most informed and sympathetic humans struggle to comprehend the complexities of Elokoi communication and culture. A key distinction between humans and Elokoi is that whereas humans constantly prevaricate and exaggerate for political and personal gain, Elokoi are, by virtue of their practices of telepathy, unable to dissemble; nor can they understand why humans should invest energy and intelligence in lying about what they feel and know. This quality constitutes the most telling threat to the corrupt and cynical regime of Dimitri Gaston, the president of Deucalion, who realizes that a population of citizens who "could read every one of your thoughts and knew your every move in advance and all your guiltiest secrets"[36] constitutes the most potent threat to illegitimate power. That these three novels so insistently represent adult humans as incapable of engaging in telepathic communication with aliens underscores the sense that colonizing groups have routinely underestimated and undervalued Indigenous cultures. The corollary of this idea is that Indigenous cultures, like the hlur, the Elokoi, and the Aquarians, possess deep knowledge and traditions, that they carefully guard from colonial incursions.

Attachment to place is the most crucial component of alien identities in the three novels. The givens of British colonialism play out in the actions of colonizers who misrecognize "empty space" as useless, and who in the absence of signifiers such as walls, cities, and buildings assume that planetary spaces are open to conquest and exploitation.[37] However, the texts differ markedly in the extent to which they interrogate colonial practices: whereas *The Faces of Ceti* treats the conquest of space and the creation of a new world as normal and natural, *The Golden Aquarians* and in particular *Deucalion* offer much sharper critiques of imperialism.

In *The Faces of Ceti*, episodes where colonizers name Indigenous species enforce distinctions between "bad" and "good" colonizers: the Arcadians and the Cetians. The Arcadians attribute the name "Yeti" to the native species living on the planet, although they know that the creatures' own word for themselves is "Grokuk."[38] In contrast, the name "hlur" used by the Cetians is based on the "soft warbling sounds"[39] that the hlur make. Yeti, like so many of the names that colonists gave various nations of Native Americans,[40] carries derogatory meanings—specifically, of mythical savagery and bestiality—whereas the name "hlur" functions as a metonym for the more respectful treatment of the hlur by the Cetians.

The propensity of this text to construct oppositional relations between Ceti and Arcadia and between good and bad colonizers extends to its treatment of alien species. The "good" hlur with whom the Cetians form an alliance are compared with the marsh hlur who engage in hostile behaviour, and (more markedly) with the Yeti of Arcadia, who attack the Arcadian settlers, killing six hundred of them and torturing captives. The text's explanation for these actions is that the Arcadians have failed to negotiate properly with the Yeti: Sandor, the Cetian leader, remarks querulously, in a reprise of the many instances in colonial discourses where Indigenous populations are regarded as problems or obstacles to progress, "It's not easy to coexist peacefully with a native species."[41] By limiting its interrogation of colonization to matters of communication and interpersonal relations, *The Faces of Ceti* is oblivious to the larger principles on which its narrative is based: the assumptions that the colonists' desire for territory is enough to justify their appropriation of large swathes of Ceti, and that the planet's resources are available for them to plunder. As soon as the colonists arrive on Ceti, they take over land for crops and proceed to harvest native plants, and their initial failures at farming are attributed to their slowness in seeking hlur assistance, while the appropriation of hlur territory is treated as normal.

A key achievement of the Cetians is their construction of a city, Halvar, whose design includes a "rec centre,"[42] a communal dining hall, hospital, and central plaza, with towers and "a row of Doric columns."[43] Toward the end of the novel, the narrative gestures toward the possibility that hlur have rights to territory, when they seek an agreement that the colonizers will abandon their iron mine in the mountains. Reluctantly, and because "after all, we *are* the invaders,"[44] Sandor acquiesces to this request, while leaving open the possibility of "development" at a later stage. The unexamined tensions of the text occasionally surface, as in Maya's reflection: "She had thought of herself as a Cetian, and now she realized how wrong she had been. Her references were all to old Earth—memories, history, literature—not of this world.... Perhaps [the children of the community] would be Cetians someday, but now only the hlur deserved the name, and it was a shock for her to acknowledge it."[45] Such moments of ambivalence and doubt jostle against the larger concepts that the text accepts without question. As the narrative's description of the new city of Halvar suggests, with its recreation centre, plaza, and columns, the ideal that the text proposes is that the new society should replicate a late-twentieth-century version of the ideal city that resembles nothing so much as a shopping mall. Indigenous species—the marsh hlur and the Yeti—who resist the colonizers' projects are "bad," and alterity is valued only insofar as it reflects positively upon humans by demonstrating the colonizers' capacity for tolerance and patience.

While *The Faces of Ceti* virtually disregards the appropriation of territory that is fundamental to colonialism, Monica Hughes's *The Golden Aquarians* focuses on environmental questions within a dystopian portrayal of planetary imperialism. Walt, the young protagonist, leaves his home in Lethbridge, Alberta, to visit his father, who heads a terraforming agency currently conducting its business on the planet Aqua. The fact that the Federation has forbidden terraforming on all but uninhabited planets implies that such wholesale refashioning of planetary worlds will inevitably be detrimental to any Indigenous inhabitants, and the struggle between Walt and his father hinges on the contrast between Walt's readiness to accept that the Aquarians are sentient and intelligent beings, and his father's anthropocentric insistence on the primacy of humans.

Walt imagines at first that his father's work involves going to "horrible and unlivable planets" and shaping them into "places more comfortable for Earth colonists to live in."[46] The narrative positions readers to reassess this view of technological achievement, and concludes with the evacuation of the Aquarian colonists just in time to avoid their destruction in one of the cyclic tidal waves that are essential to the ecology of the planet and its inhabitants. The novel's negative view of terraforming is underscored by its treatment of the psychological trajectory of the colonel, Walt's father, who descends into a madness triggered by the failure of his program on Aqua, sails off in a canoe in a crazed attempt to fight the tidal wave, and is saved by the Aquarians. The magnanimity of the Aquarians, who are unfailingly generous even toward those who have sought to destroy their planet, echoes romantic representations of Indigenous figures such as Pocahontas, who are exceptional because of their openness to colonizers. A related effect of romanticization is evident in the way in which both *The Faces of Ceti* and *The Golden Aquarians* invest child characters with the capacity to imagine life beyond human experience and to empathize with alien others, while adults are, in general, oblivious or hostile to the claims of non-human beings.

The imperial project as Hughes represents it in *The Golden Aquarians* is a masculine enterprise, characterized by the machismo of the colonel and his terraforming troops, for whom the fact that the reconstruction of planets involves the destruction of ecological systems is no more than an unfortunate side effect. The children of the terraformers replicate the masculinist, competitive culture of their fathers, with the result that Walt is victimized by the other boys, who have grown up on the planets where their parents work under the colonel's direction. His teacher tells him, "Even humans who left Earth for other planets a generation or more ago regard it as home in a special way. So [the other boys] envy you for actually having lived there."[47] While the human inhabitants of Aqua long to return to Earth, the Aquarians, an amphibious species possessing higher intelligence, desire above all to preserve their watery home.

The Federation that produces rules and protocols for the terraforming projects carried out by Walt's father is a faceless and nameless body; moreover, because the Aquarians are clearly an alien species (green-skinned, golden-eyed, froglike), and because they are always viewed through Walt's limited perspective, their motives and way of life remain mysterious and other to those of humans. For these reasons, the novel's treatment of colonization is subsumed into a focus on environmental degradation and a technophobic account of human intervention in planetary settings. In Brian Caswell's *Deucalion*, in contrast, historicized, and politicized implications are built into the narrative, not least because, unlike the other texts that I have discussed in this section, narrative agency is attributed to Indigenous characters who function as focalizers. By setting the perspectives of the Elokoi figures Cael, Saebi, Rael, and Saani against those of other characters in the novel's multifocalized narrative, Caswell builds up a complex picture of the discourses of colonialism, resistance, science, and politics, which intersect in the sociopolitical world of the novel. In its positive treatment of relations between Elokoi and second- and third-generation Deucalions, the novel reflects a post-Mabo mood of optimism[48] concerning reconciliation between Indigenous and non-Indigenous Australians.

An account of Deucalion's history is interpolated into the narrative by way of excerpts from the works of the (fictive) historian A.J.L Tolhurst, whose description of the colony's founding evokes the hyperbolic claims by which British citizens were persuaded to emigrate to the colonies: "It has been claimed that it was the high expectations of the early colonists, as much as their xenophobic attitudes, that led to the destruction of the native Elokoi population. Coming as they did from underprivileged and mainly urban backgrounds, the early colonists had absorbed the enlistment propaganda: *Land of your own. Full employment in a booming environment. No pollution, no ruling class. Build a new life with hard work.*"[49] This account of the utopian beginnings of the colony is undercut by Tolhurst's analysis of the new ruling class (constituted by self-made politicians, officials, and representatives of the exploration companies bent on plundering the colony's resources) and of the colonists' treatment of the Elokoi—"small and non-violent, and with a telepathic ability that was just alien enough to suggest a possible threat"[50]—whom they hunt, kill, and force onto Reserves.

One of the Elokoi focalizers, Cael, is an artist who has been chosen by the Ancestors to produce cave paintings that trace Elokoi history during and after the colonization of Deucalion. Another, Saebi, is a Teller whose task it is to learn and transmit the ancient songs, Dreams, and stories of the Elokoi. In its portrayal of the Elokoi as valuing goods such as songs, paintings, and stories over material objects that signify status and wealth, the narrative alludes to the practices and values of Australian Aboriginal cultures, just as the actions of the first colonists on Deucalion refer to the "killing years" from 1788 to the 1920s, during which the Indigenous population of Australia plummeted from around a million to about 60,000.[51] Daryl, one of the main characters, is of Aboriginal ancestry, and the narrative traces his developing awareness of the parallels between Aboriginal and Elokoi experiences of colonization.

The novel's imagining of new (postcolonial) world orders centres on the group of children and young adults, the "Icarus kids," whose genetic mix endows them with Elokoi and human characteristics. When the Grants

Council on Earth decides that the existence of these hybrid beings (endowed with telepathy as well as human characteristics) has the potential to desta-bilize systems of power, the Icarus children are marked for death, euphemisti-cally referred to as "termination." However, the elite group of scientists who have been responsible for the Icarus project determine to rescue the children, who are sent to a remote island in Deucalion's island sea. Of the twelve or so focalizing characters in the novel, a key figure is Jane, a gifted young genet-ics researcher and herself one of the Icarus children. When she unearths in-formation on the Icarus project she comes to the attention of Dimitri Gaston, who assassinated his main rival and rigged the election to become the pres-ident of Deucalion. Gaston is obsessed by the fear that Elokoi-humans might access his thoughts and expose his election as a fraud, and he orders his in-telligence agents to discover and kill Jane and the rest of the Icarus children.

This narrative strand, which takes the form of a psycho-political thriller, intersects with another strand tracing the progress of Elokoi self-determi-nation. The teller Saebi receives a "True-dream,"[52] a song endowed on her by the Ancestors, which predicts that the Elokoi will embark on a long journey from the Reserves where they have been imprisoned, to their ancestral lands on the shores of the inland sea at the centre of Deucalion. However, this ter-ritory is now the property of the Deucalion Mining Corporation, an instru-mentality of Old Earth's Ruling Council, a fact that Gaston emphasizes when he meets with the Elokoi representatives who seek to tell him of their inten-tions to undertake their journey. The narrative then traces the development of a political movement that brings together Elokoi and native-born Deu-calions, especially young people who do not harbour the colonial attitudes of Old Earthers toward the nation's Indigenous inhabitants.

In its depiction of the last days of Gaston's reign, *Deucalion* presents a model of political action where progressive groups join forces. The 90,000 members of the various clans and groups of Elokoi, summoned by Saebi, gather outside the Presidential Complex in a silent but eloquent protest. At the same time, young Deucalions place posters around the city in support of the Elokoi, questioning the legitimacy of Gaston's presidency. In a pointed ref-erence to the influence of new technologies, Caswell introduces Internet as an independent network eager to break a story that will gain them ground with their rivals. Briefed by sympathizers of the Elokoi, Internet's chief re-porter charges Gaston with oppressing the Elokoi, acting as a stooge for Old Earth's Ruling Council, and corruptly influencing the outcome of the election. Faced with a barrage of accusation and proof, Gaston resigns, the Elokoi em-bark on their Trek, and Deucalion enters a phase of democratic government. This imagining of sociopolitical processes that redress the wrongs of colonial-ism thus advocates a productive alliance of Indigenous and settler citizens capable of influencing the direction of the body politic. The novel's allegory undermines colonial teleologies in that it rejects narratives of progress and refuses to accept as inevitable the ascendancy of European culture in a settler society.

The three texts I have considered here vary widely in their use of "the beyond." Hughes's treatment of Aqua emphasizes the radical difference between the planet's ecological systems and those of earth, and the incommensurability of meaning that is evident when humans (even the most well intentioned and sympathetic) seek to communicate with the Aquarians. As an allegory of colonization, this text produces an analogy between the anthropocentrism of the terraformers and the Eurocentrism of settlers in the New World, and between the environmental damage caused on Aqua and that in the colonies of imperial powers on Earth. While *The Faces of Ceti* contrasts "good" with "bad" versions of colonization, it accepts as a given the principles of British colonization: "the beyond" is available to humans as a resource; its Indigenous inhabitants are treated, on the whole, as obstacles to progress. *Deucalion* is the only text of the three to imagine a utopian "beyond" where the negatives of colonial history in Australia are addressed through collaborative political action incorporating Indigenous and non-Indigenous inhabitants. At the same time, Caswell's vision of a transformed Australia is deeply ironical in that the Indigenous inhabitants of contemporary Australia continue to experience discrimination and injustice.

## Home and Homeland in Post-Disaster Fiction

The post-disaster texts I discuss in this section rehearse colonial histories and their consequences or implications in societies that have emerged following catastrophic environmental events. While they are set in dystopic worlds, they also construct young protagonists capable of breaking free from the conditioned, reflex ideologies of colonialism in order to shape new societies and relationships. To some extent, then, they accord with the dominant narrative schemata of adolescent and young adult literature, in which young characters are seen to progress toward enhanced capacities for self-realization and empathy with others. However, these conventional psychological trajectories are modified by their location in post-disaster settings that allude to the complex and resistant tensions that characterize settler societies.

My discussion centres on Australian and New Zealand texts: Victor Kelleher's *Red Heart* (2001), and Jack Lasenby's *Travellers Quartet*, comprising *Because We Were the Travellers* (1997), *Taur* (1998), *The Shaman and the Droll* (1999), and *Kalik* (2001). Kelleher's *Red Heart* is set in a post-greenhouse Australia, and Lasenby's novels in a New Zealand where global warming and pollution have destroyed the city of Orklun (Auckland, in the north of the country), and scattered tribes of humans eke out precarious lives. The oppressive regime that dominates the setting of *Red Heart* combines the old hierarchies of imperialism with contemporary neoliberal politics, while the *Travellers Quartet* novels feature societies preoccupied with survival and internecine struggles between rival groups. The narratives of these texts are structured by journeys where protagonists seek homes and homelands that offer them safety, agency, and collective purpose.

Raffaella Baccolini says of dystopia that it "is usually located in a negatively deformed future of our own world. In this respect, it clearly appears as a critique of history—of the history shaping the society of the dystopian writer in particular."[53] In *Red Heart* and the *Travellers Quartet*, Kelleher and Lasenby blame discourses of individualism, growth, and progress for the catastrophic environmental events that have all but destroyed the landscapes of Australia and New Zealand in the settings of the novels. In the Australia of *Red Heart*, floods caused by climate change have ruined the farm where the protagonist, Nat Marles, lives with his family. The harsh political climate of the new post-disaster society is dominated by the Company, an organization that owns half of the continent, having loaned money to struggling farmers and then foreclosed on their failed farms. While the Company is modelled on the neoliberal politics of the conservative government in power in Australia at the time the novel was published, its values and practices are also shown to sustain the trajectory of colonization, resulting in a neocolonial order where the corporation assimilates and controls the lives, property, and bodies of citizens.

When his family is threatened with eviction by representatives of the Company, Nat leaves home to seek help from his uncle, Jack Curtis, who is indebted to Nat's parents because three years prior to the time of the narrative they provided him with funds to engage in an expedition up the Darling River, which runs from Victoria to northern New South Wales. During these three years, Jack Curtis has established a "heartland" where he presides over an empire funded by extortion and violence. The pre-text of *Red Heart* is Joseph Conrad's *Heart of Darkness*, with Nat's journey up the Darling echoing Marlow's voyage into Africa, and Jack Curtis's "heartland" evoking Kurtz's outpost in the heart of the Congo. In *Heart of Darkness*, Conrad represents Marlow's journey as a movement back into time, in line with the evolutionary notion of civilization popular in late Victorian England. In *Red Heart*, Nat's journey up the Darling involves a return to the past of colonialism as he enters the neocolonial regime that is misrecognized as a new world by the desperate and oppressed inhabitants of Jack Curtis's empire. The Company and Jack Curtis's heartland thus represent two sides of the coin of empire: the

Company as a callous, impersonal body that imposes its own logic of profit and loss on those unfortunate enough to come under its control; and Curtis's New Jerusalem, where he plays at colonial ruler, dispensing favours and punishments to members of the group known as the Tribe, young people, principally from wealthy families, who regard him as their saviour and who distinguish themselves from the "Pigs," the "Feral Nation" of homeless young people who are exploited by Curtis as "hewers of wood and drawers of water."[54]

A striking characteristic of Curtis's version of colonialism is that it is heavily reliant on white imaginings of Aboriginality while utterly ignorant of Aboriginal cultures and histories. The members of the Tribe darken their skin by ingesting hormones, paint their faces, engage in rituals invented by Curtis, and believe in an ersatz system of "big-time spirits. The ones that call the shots."[55] Curtis, however, maintains his hegemony by insisting on his status as the great white ruler, although he is wasted with H-fever, a tropical disease endemic to the region. The "real" Aboriginal figure in the narrative is Clarrie, a young woman who pilots an old paddle-steamer, the *Phoenix*, along the Darling, and who despises members of the Tribe for their appropriation of Indigeneity. When Curtis sinks into the last stages of fever, the leaders of the Tribe decide to follow what they call "the old way,"[56] a combination of Christian rites of transubstantiation and "savage" rituals of cannibalism, which will involve the ceremonial consumption of Curtis's body.

The resolution of the narrative involves a sequence in which Nat escapes from the heartland with his Pig friends Irene and Pete and the young Indigenous woman Clarrie. The four rescue Jack Curtis from the Tribe, but he is unable to contemplate a life in which he is no longer a colonial potentate, and he suicides by throwing himself into the river where he is snatched by crocodiles. When they reach the relative safety of "down river," Nat and his friends decide to pool the gold that Clarrie has appropriated from the former owner of the *Phoenix* in order to outfit the boat and ply their trade along the Darling, secure in the knowledge that as the waters continue to rise, the river will be the only means of carrying freight and passengers. This alignment of different ethnicities—Nat, the "whitey," Irene and Pete, members of the Feral Nation, and the Indigenous Clarrie—reimagines colonial history by constructing a coalition of individuals reliant on trust and friendship rather than on the antagonistic and hierarchical relations that informed colonial relations and enabled Jack Curtis to maintain his power. A limitation of the utopian future that Kelleher promotes in the closure of *Red Heart* is that it perpetuates hierarchies, deterministically consigning Curtis's former followers, the homogenized members of the Tribe, to a hopeless future: Clarrie remarks of the Tribe that "They're yesterday's people. Followers, not leaders. They always were. If y'ask me, they'll just drift off into the outback, or take to fightin' amongst themselves."[57] That is, the prosperity of the few will be at the expense of those they exclude.

Conceptions of Indigeneity are crucial to the ideologies of *Red Heart*, in that Clarrie represents the moral centre of the narrative. It is she who determines that Nat, Irene, and Pete are worth saving from the Tribe, she who engineers their escape, she who imagines the enterprise in which they engage at the end of the novel. While Jack Curtis claims ownership of the Darling River and its environs ("*My* Jerusalem! Mine by right of conquest ... to do with as I please"),[58] Clarrie invokes countless generations of ancestors in her insistence that she is at home in the country by virtue of her unique relationship to place and history. She distinguishes herself from the Pigs who only *appear* to be indigenous: "This skin colour of mine didn't come from no bottle. It came from way back";[59] and when Nat asks her if she feels lost in the dystopic world of "upriver," she retorts, "This is my country. How can you feel lost in your own home?"[60] Although Clarrie's dominance among the group of young entrepreneurs at the end of the novel constitutes a homage to Indigenous knowledge and heritage, she is something of a token figure: her connections to clan and place are compromised by environmental destruction, and her depiction echoes colonial narratives involving "good" Indigenous figures whose function it is to support settler enterprises. Thus, the novel's rewriting of history does not extend to an interrogation of colonial teleologies.

Like *Red Heart*, the setting of Lasenby's *Travellers Quartet* is a landscape recognizable yet deformed as the result of environmental degradation and human greed. Names such as "Orklun" (Auckland), "Hammerton" (Hamilton), "Elton" (Wellington), "Towmranoo" (Taumaranui), and "Lake Top" (Lake Taupo) encode a world in which only scraps and fragments of the past survive in memory and stories. The four novels trace the quest of the protagonist, Ish, for home, security, and family, against a background of tribal warfare over resources and territory. Ish is a member of the tribe of Travellers, a group who journey to the south in summer, to take advantage of fresh grass for their animals, and to the north in winter. That the necessity of travelling has been forced on the Travellers and is not their "natural" or preferred mode of life is evident in the fact that Ish, the first-person narrator in all four novels, longs above all for a secure and settled life such as he observes when he meets the Metal People who live in the utopian setting of Hawk Cliffs. While such utopian settings are generally vulnerable in post-disaster fiction, they shape narratives by providing models of sociality and happiness to which characters are seen to aspire. It is significant, then, that the utopian space of which Ish dreams resembles a settler lifestyle. At the end of *Kalik*, the last book of the quartet, Ish and the group of children with whom he travels imagine the dimensions and characteristics of "home": "Sometimes we sang as we travelled. Sometimes we talked of what we must do when we found our place: grow a crop of potatoes, plant our winter wheat, store food and herbs. Clip the wool and hair from the sheep and goats. Weave for another trip to the Cold Hills. And learn to read and write."[61] That is, Ish and the children desire nothing more than a pastoral life evocative of those myths of New Zealand nationhood that revolve around the settling and taming of the land by British settlers, and activities such as planting, harvesting, shearing, and the production of woollen fabrics. The inclusion of "learn to read and write" among this repertoire of desirable achievements suggests that Western practices of literacy and education are of fundamental importance as signs of civilization and knowledge.

If, as I have suggested, settler society constitutes the utopian ideal of the *Travellers Quartet*, the warring and aggressive tribes that seek to destroy or destabilize the Travellers' progress toward the acquisition of a homeland evoke aspects of Maori culture as they were represented in the colonial period and as they resurface at intervals in New Zealand culture.[62] Ish has a crippled leg, the result of an injury at birth, and in *Because We Were the Travellers*, he is abandoned by his tribe after the death of his father. Together with an old woman, Hagar, who is left behind because she is no longer of use, Ish follows the Travellers at a distance, until the tribe is ambushed by the fearsome Falcon Men, who murder the tribe's men and children and take their young women captive. The Falcon Men are "dark, their eyes black, fierce,"[63] but skin colour is only one marker of otherness in the *Travellers Quartet*. Rather, a bundle of cultural practices and ideologies distinguishes the Quartet's savage others from Ish and his allies.

The Salt Men who are Ish's most obdurate enemies are fierce and ruthless fighters, although in this respect they are no different from other tribes—or for that matter Ish himself—since in the world of the quartet it is normal to fight and kill for survival. In *Taur*, the second novel of the quartet, Ish takes a pounamu (nephrite jade) fish-shaped ornament from the neck of Tara, the young woman whom he had hoped to marry, after she is killed by the Salt Men. This stone turns out to have powerful religious associations for the Salt Men and their leader, Squint-face, who fanatically pursues Ish in order to recapture it. The Salt Men are marked as other by their practice of taking slaves, whom they treat as chattels, and by their deployment of females as decoys: a Salt Woman, Sodomah, seduces Ish to gain power over him. However, the feature that most clearly marks the Salt Men as other is their practice of cannibalism. In *The Shaman and the Droll*, Ish asks the question, "What was it made a Salt Man?" Answering his own question, he observes, "They are killers and eaters of people."[64] As Peter Hulme has noted, anthropophagy was a constant marker of savagery in colonial discourse, as "cannibalism marked the world beyond European knowledge";[65] and it is an enduring and powerful trope in contemporary literary and popular texts.

At issue here is not the question of whether Maori and other peoples engaged in cannibalism in precolonial and colonial times, so much as the uses to which discourses of cannibalism are put. In the *Travellers Quartet*, the fact that the Salt Men are cannibals places them in a category separate from other tribes, their savagery constituting a warning about the depravity to which post-disaster humans might sink. The Maori scholar Powhiri Wharemarama Rika-Heke notes that, in contemporary New Zealand, "terms such as 'backward,' 'cruel,' 'barbaric,' 'cannibalistic,' 'primitive' are immediately suggestive, everywhere, of the indigene and based on the dominant model of power—and interest—between the supposed inferiority of the native and the putative superiority of white society."[66] A similar cluster of terms defines the Salt Men, pointing to Ish as the ideal against which they are compared. In *Kalik*, the children who together with Ish form the utopian colony promised at the end of the quartet are Salt Children, whom Ish rescues from slavery with the Headland People. That these children are capable of "rising above" their savage origins is to Ish's credit rather than their own, since it is Ish who trains and teaches them, rewarding them by transforming them, finally, into settlers.

If the interrogation of history is a characteristic of postcolonial allegory, the *Travellers Quartet* novels are highly selective as to what constitutes history. To foreground the wastefulness and environmental carelessness of the late twentieth century is a relatively safe narrative move, especially in texts directed toward New Zealand readers powerfully conscious of ecological issues and their implications for the prosperity of the nation. The celebration of settler culture that dominates the closure of Lasenby's quartet relies on a strategic silence concerning colonial relations, a silence entirely consistent with national mythologies that cover over difference and conflict and lay claim to a civil society built on "a partnership of equals" between Maori and Pakeha.[67] New Zealand scholar Stephen Turner says of Pakeha conceptions of nationhood that "the denial of cultural difference [is] the determining factor in the construction of New Zealand history,"[68] and in this light the assimilation of the Salt Children at the end of the quartet can be read as an allegory of the incorporation of Maori within the dominant culture.

I began this chapter by noting that speculative fiction offers allegorical versions of historical and contemporary sociopolitical processes and outcomes. The fictions I have discussed frequently draw on particular, identifiable histories and settings to ground their imaginings of future worlds, but they are heterogeneous in the extent to which they resist the teleologies, tropes, and figures of colonial discourse. Merely to invent new worlds or new societies does not effect a reorientation of values: in the space colonization narrative of *The Faces of Ceti*, as in Lasenby's post-disaster *Travellers Quartet*, settlers manifest those same preoccupations with making profit out of "empty space" that informed colonialism and maintain their currency in modern settler cultures; and in *E.T.*, *Aliens in the Family*, and *Beyond the Labyrinth*, the figure of the friendly alien is folded into that of the helpful Indigene. It is nevertheless the case that several of the texts I have discussed in this chapter engage in far more trenchant critiques of colonial history than do the realist historical novels I discussed in chapter 4. The counter-discursive effects of postcolonial allegory are powerfully evident in *A Coyote Columbus Story* and *The House That Jack Built*, as well as in Monica Hughes's assault on Eurocentrism in *The Golden Aquarians* and Brian Caswell's idealistic view of a transformed Australia in *Deucalion*.

# 9 Conclusion

... and here I am today.
—Edna Tantjingu, Eileen Wani Wingfield, and-
Kunyi June-Anne McInerney, *Down the Hole*

I conclude this comparative study of settler society texts with a sense of the subtle, complicated relations of difference and likeness that I have tried to sketch. If I seek to compare cultures and texts, I am reminded of tensions and inconsistencies within particular national literatures; if I write about one context and its textual production for children, I am drawn to parallels with other literatures. My approach does not lend itself to lists of "good" and "bad" texts, or to a league table of national literatures. Believing that texts evade the intentions of their producers and that they are produced as much by cultural discourses as by authors, I read them to identify the discursive formations and the ideologies that inform them. In particular, I read them as postcolonial texts, looking to their rhetorics, fantasies, implications, and ideologies.

The fact that draws together the diverse body of texts I have considered is that of colonialism—specifically, the practices and regimes of colonization carried out in the name of British imperialism. As Patricia Seed notes (see chapter 7), the British conceived imperialism primarily in terms of the conquest of property, so that discourses of place and of identity interpenetrate each other in this body of settler culture texts. I began by anticipating that I would discover in children's texts evidence of unease and of unsettledness, since these texts position readers as citizens of nations marked by the violence of colonization.

To be sure, many of the texts I have discussed exhibit various degrees and styles of postcolonial anxiety. However, the discursive regimes of nations play out differently in literatures for children. Many texts from the

Notes to Conclusion on page 251.

United States—perhaps because of the long interval between British colonization and contemporary textual production, or perhaps because the assault on Native American populations was so successful—bear out Ghassan Hage's description of "the 'colonial *fait accompli*' confidence that permeates the ... national culture of the United States"[1] and that manifests in imaginings of Indigeneity so shaped by traditions of representation stretching back to colonial times that they are almost impervious to contestation.

In both Canada and Australia, Indigenous peoples constitute a rather higher proportion of the overall population than in the United States, and political and public discourses allude more regularly to relations between Indigenous and non-Indigenous citizens.[2] In Canadian as in New Zealand texts, narratives structured by questions about who owns particular tracts and parcels of land speak to the long histories of treaty negotiations in these cultures. In Australia, in contrast, where the land was, until the landmark Mabo High Court decision of 1992, regarded as *terra nullius* (nobody's land) prior to invasion, children's texts thematizing Indigeneity tend to foreground the possibilities of and the impediments to reconciliation between Indigenous and non-Indigenous populations. New Zealand children's literature affords a fascinating contrast with Australian and Canadian literatures, since despite—or perhaps because of—the high proportion of Maori in the population, relatively few texts have involved historicized and politicized treatments of Maori–Pakeha relations or Maori experience, although since the 1970s political action by Maori has been a leitmotif of New Zealand life.

It will almost certainly be asserted about this book that I prefer Indigenous to non-Indigenous texts, dealing in more severe terms with the latter than the former. My reading of a large number of Indigenous and non-Indigenous texts leads me to believe that non-Indigenous texts are much more likely than Indigenous texts to recycle the unquestioned assumptions of dominant cultures and their ingrained beliefs and convictions about Indigenous peoples and cultures. In particular, non-Indigenous texts are often oblivious to the historical and symbolic processes that have privileged whiteness as a normative mode of being. I come to this conclusion not because I subscribe to the idea that only members of minority cultures are entitled to write about their cultures, practices, and traditions, but because I see in many non-Indigenous texts from the United States, Canada, New Zealand, and Australia the bland assumption that "we" know what "they" are like, and that "they" are, after all, not very difficult to know.

While much of this book is taken up with readings of texts, I am much more concerned to produce a theory of postcolonial children's literature that embodies models of reading and analysis than merely to offer interpretations of particular texts. Leaving aside the perennially troublesome implications of the "post" in "postcolonial," I argue that the field of postcolonial studies has much to contribute to children's literature, which is above all concerned with enculturating children as members of societies and nations. I have emphasized postcolonial readings of Indigenous texts because I believe that these texts require different kinds of reading from those appropriate to mainstream texts—otherwise, they are too readily regarded as lesser versions of majority textuality. Indigenous texts deserve to be read in the light of the cultures in which they are produced, and with due attention to their difference from Western texts, rather than from within the assumptions of Western culture and textual practices. The Australian picture book *Down the Hole*, which I discuss in chapter 6, ends with the words "and here I am today."[3] Indeed, Indigenous cultures are "here ... today" in the United States, Canada, Australia, and New Zealand, having survived the assaults of colonization and assimilation. This book is motivated by my conviction that children's texts by Indigenous and non-Indigenous producers who afford diverse, self-conscious, and informed representations of Indigenous cultures comprise a crucial intervention in processes of decolonization across settler societies.

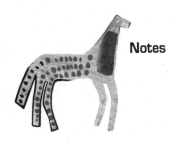

# Notes

## Introduction [pp. 1–16]

1  Lynne Cheney and Robin Preiss Glasser, *America: A Patriotic Primer* (New York and London: Simon and Schuster, 2002), 22.

2  Ibid., 38; my emphasis.

3  Ibid., 23.

4  Ibid., 33.

5  Throughout this book, I use the term "other" to refer to the strategies whereby non-Indigenous inhabitants of settler societies define themselves in relation to Indigenous peoples treated as different and as inferior. This usage of "other" should be distinguished from Lacan's formulation of the Other (the *grande-autre*), in whose gaze the subject attains selfhood. For a discussion of the distinction between other and Other in postcolonial theory, see Bill Ashcroft, Gareth Griffiths, and Helen Tiffin, *Post-Colonial Studies: The Key Concepts* (London and New York: Routledge, 2000), 169–73.

6  For a discussion of McKnickle's approach to Indigenous and American history, see Chadwick Allen, *Blood Narrative: Indigenous Identity in American Indian and Maori Literary and Activist Texts* (Durham and London: Duke University Press, 2002), 94–102.

7  Dolores Janiewski, "Gendering, Racializing and Classifying: Settler Colonization in the United States, 1590–1990," in *Unsettling Settler Societies: Articulations of Gender, Race, Ethnicity and Class*, ed. D. Stasiulis and N. Yuval-Davis (London: Sage Publications, 1995), 132. See also Deborah L. Madsen, "Beyond the Commonwealth: Post-Colonialism and American Literature," in *Post-Colonial Literatures: Expanding the Canon*, ed. D.L. Madsen (London: Pluto Press, 1999), 1–13; and Susie O'Brien, "The Place of America in an Era of Postcolonial Imperialism," *Ariel* 29.2 (1998), 159–83.

8  Peter Hulme, "Including America," *Ariel* 26.1 (1995), 120.

9  See Leela Gandhi, *Postcolonial Theory: A Critical Introduction* (St. Leonards, NSW: Allen and Unwin, 1998), 9–17.

10  Graham Huggan, *Territorial Disputes: Maps and Mapping Strategies in Contemporary Canadian and Australian Fiction* (Toronto and London: University of Toronto Press, 1994), xiii.

11  Cheney and Glasser, *America: A Patriotic Primer*, 6.

12  See, for instance, Daiva Stasiulis and Nira Yuval-Davis, eds., *Unsettling Settler Societies: Articulations of Gender, Race, Ethnicity and Class* (London: Sage Publications, 1995); John Docker and Gerhard Fischer, eds., *Race, Colour and Identity in Australia and New Zealand* (Sydney: University of New South Wales Press, 2000); Patrick Wolfe, *Settler Colonialism and the Transformation of Anthropology* (London and New York: Cassell, 1999); Lynette Russell, ed., *Colonial Frontiers: Indigenous–European Encounters in Settler Societies* (Manchester and New York: Manchester University Press, 2001); and Tom Griffiths and Libby Robin, eds., *Ecology and Empire: Environmental History of Settler Societies* (Edinburgh: Keele University Press, 1997).

13  Greg Dening, *Mr Bligh's Bad Language: Passion, Power and Theatre on the Bounty* (Cambridge and New York: Cambridge University Press, 1992), 178.

14  Quoted in Gillian Whitlock, "A 'White-Souled State': Across the South with Lady Barker," in *Text, Theory, Space: Land, Literature and History in South Africa and Australia*, ed. K. Darian-Smith, L. Gunner, and S. Nuttall (London and New York: Routledge, 1996), 68.

15  W.H. New, "Colonial Literatures," in *New National and Post-Colonial Literatures: An Introduction*, ed. B. King (Oxford, UK: Oxford University Press, 1996), 103.

16  Since the 1982 Constitution, the Aboriginal peoples of Canada have been defined as North American Indians, Métis (people of mixed Indian and European ancestry), and Inuit. The United States census identifies Native American people as comprising American Indian, Eskimo, and Aleut populations.

17  I use the terms "non-Indigenous" and "white" to refer to people other than Indigenous, and "Western" when I refer to the body of texts, and traditions informed by the ideologies and practices of Western cultures. In discussions of particular texts, I will use the terms they deploy; thus, for instance, I use the term "Indians" in discussing Elizabeth George Speare's *The Sign of the Beaver* because this is how the novel refers to Native Americans.

18  For instance, Michelle Pagni Stewart "Judging Authors by the Color of Their Skin? Quality Native American Children's Literature," *Melus* 27.2 (2002), 179–96; Debbie Reese, "'Mom, Look! It's George, and He's a *TV* Indian!'" *Horn Book Magazine* 74 (1998), 636–38; Melissa Kay Thompson, "A Sea of Good Intentions: Native Americans in Books for Children," *Lion and the Unicorn* 25.3 (2001), 353–74; and Joyce Bainbridge and Brenda Wolodko, "Canadian Picture Books: Shaping and Reflecting National Identity," *Bookbird* 40.2 (2002), 21–27.

19  See Ashcroft, Griffiths, and Tiffin, *Post-Colonial Studies*, 6–8, for a discussion of African–American and postcolonial studies.

20  See Kathryn Castle, *Britannia's Children: Reading Colonisation Through Children's Books and Magazines* (Manchester: Manchester University Press, 1996); and Jeffrey Richards, ed., *Imperialism and Juvenile Literature* (Manchester, UK: Manchester University Press, 1989).

21  Bill Ashcroft, *Post-Colonial Transformation* (London and New York: Routledge, 2001), 7.

22  Dipesh Chakravarty, "Postcoloniality and the Artifice of History: Who Speaks for 'Indian' Pasts?" *Representations* 32 (1992), 1–26.

23  See, for instance, Anne McClintock, *Imperial Leather: Race, Gender and Sexuality in the Colonial Contest* (New York: Routledge, 1995), 10–11.

24  Ashcroft, *Post-Colonial Transformation*, 13.

25  Augie Fleras, "Politicising Indigeneity: Ethno-Politics in White Settler Dominions," in *Indigenous Peoples' Rights in Australia, Canada, and New Zealand*, ed. P. Havemann (Toronto: Oxford University Press, 1992), 191–92.

26  Marcia Langton, "*Well I Heard It on the Radio and I Saw It on the Television.*" (Woolloomooloo, NSW: Australian Film Commission, 1993), 33.

27  Daniel Francis, *The Imaginary Indian: The Image of the Indian in Canadian Culture* (Vancouver, BC: Arsenal Pulp Press, 1992), 5.

28  Similar representational patterns occur in other novels, such as Lynda Durrant's *The Beaded Moccasins: The Story of Mary Campbell* (New York: Clarion, 1998), and Jan Hudson's *Sweetgrass* (Edmonton, AB: Tree Frog Press, 1984).

29  For a discussion of the interplay of gender and genre, see John Stephens, "Gender, Genre and Children's Literature," *Signal* 79 (1996), 17–30.

30  Diane Matcheck, *The Sacrifice* (New York: Farrar, Straus, Giroux, 1998), 47.

31  Ibid., 193.

32  Ibid., 194.

33  Ibid., 196.

34  Langton, "*Well I Heard It on the Radio,*" 27.

35  Ibid., 27.

36  Joseph Bruchac, *Eagle Song* (New York: Dial, 1997), 19.

37  The term "country" in Aboriginal English, and increasingly in Australian English, refers to land to which Aboriginal people belong through kinship relations and cultural practices. Relationships between various Aboriginal groups and tracts of land were established during the Dreaming, when the ancestors walked about the land shaping its features and creating the Law that determined how people should behave and how they should relate to other humans, to country, and to its flora and fauna.

38  Pat Lowe and Jimmy Pike, *Jilji: Life in the Great Sandy Desert* (Broome, WA: Magabala Books, 1990), n.p.

39  See Clare Bradford, "The End of Empire? Colonial and Postcolonial Journeys in Children's Books," *Children's Literature* 29 (2001), 196–218.

40  The defining text on this topic is John Stephens, *Language and Ideology in Children's Literature* (London and New York: Longman, 1992).

41  See Clare Bradford, *Reading Race* (Carlton South, VIC: 2001), 49–54; 127–30; 145–48.

42  Cited in Donnarae MacCann, "Editor's Introduction: Racism and Antiracism: Forty Years of Theories and Debates," *Lion and the Unicorn* 25.3 (2001), 342.

43  Ashcroft, *Post-Colonial Transformation*, 59.

44  Ibid., 60.

45  Patricia Linton, "Ethical Reading and Resistant Texts," in *Post-Colonial Literatures: Expanding the Canon*, ed. D.L. Madsen (London: Pluto Press, 1999), 42.

46  Ibid., 32.

47  Ibid., 43.

**Part One: "When Languages Collide": Resistance and Repression**
**1: Language, Resistance, and Subjectivity** [pp. 19–43]

1  Ngugi wa Thiong'o, *Decolonising the Mind: The Politics of Language in African Literature* (London: James Currey, 1986), 16.

2  Mary Louise Pratt, *Imperial Eyes: Travel Writing and Transculturation* (London and New York: Routledge, 1992), 4.

3  Jeannette Armstrong, "Threads of Old Memory," in *Breathtracks* (Stratford, ON: Williams-Wallace/Theytus Books, 1991), 61.

4  Homi Bhabha, "Of Mimicry and Man," in *The Location of Culture* (London and New York: Routledge, 1994), 89.

5  Renato Rosaldo, *Culture and Truth: The Remaking of Social Analysis* (Boston, MA: Beacon Press, 1993), 68–87.

6  George Littlechild, *This Land Is My Land* (Emeryville, CA: Children's Book Press), 20.

7  Ibid., 20.

8  Curtis, Edward S., *Edward S. Curtis's The North American Indian: Photographic Images*, Item 4 of 40, http://memory.loc.gov/cgi-bin/query/D?curt:3:./temp/~ammem_rjoi:: (accessed 3 April 2007).

9  Littlechild, *This Land Is My Land*, 20.

10  See Francis, *The Imaginary Indian*, 39–42.

11  See Bill Ashcroft, Gareth Griffiths, and Helen Tiffin, *The Empire Writes Back: Theory and Practice in Post-Colonial Literatures* (London and New York: Routledge, 1989), 168–69; Stephen Slemon, "Monuments of Empire: Allegory/Counter-Discourse/Post-Colonial Writing," *Kunapipi* 9.3 (1987), 1–16; Ashcroft, *Post-Colonial Transformation*, 32–35.

12  Michel Foucault, *Power/Knowledge: Selected Interviews and Other Writings 1972–1977* (Brighton, UK: Harvest Press, 1980), 114.

13  See Ashcroft, Griffiths, and Tiffin, *The Empire Writes Back*, 38–77.

14  Richard Terdiman, *Discourse/Counter-Discourse: The Theory and Practice of Symbolic Resistance in Nineteenth-Century France* (Ithaca and London: Cornell University Press, 1985), 61.

15  Pierre Bourdieu, *Outline of a Theory of Practice* (Cambridge and London: Cambridge University Press, 1977), 79.

16  Terdiman, *Discourse/Counter-Discourse*, 64.

17  John Stephens, *Language and Ideology in Children's Fiction*, 41.

18  Ibid., Terdiman, *Discourse/Counter-Discourse*, 149.

19  The *Papunya Book* was published by a mainstream publishing company, Allen and Unwin, through collaboration between members of the Papunya School Publishing Committee and non-Indigenous people, including school principal Diane de Vere, designer Ken Searle, and writer Nadia Wheatley.

20  Terdiman, *Discourse/Counter-Discourse*, 76.

21  While there are many desert languages, the Aboriginal language used in the *Papunya Book* is Luritja.

22  The word *ngurra* means "traditional country; homelands."

23  *Papunya School Book of Country and History* (Crows Nest, NSW: Allen and Unwin, 2001), 10.

24  Terdiman, *Discourse/Counter-Discourse*, 252.

25  Ibid., 246.

26  For discussions of postmodernist strategies and picture books, see Clare Bradford, "The Picture Book: Some Postmodern Tensions," *Papers: Explorations into Chil-*

*dren's Literature* 4.3 (1993), 10–14; Robyn McCallum, "Very Advanced Texts: Metafictions and Experimental Work," in *Understanding Children's Literature*, ed. P. Hunt (London and New York: Routledge, 1999), 138–50; Roberta Seelinger Trites, "Manifold Narratives: Metafiction and Ideology in Picture Books," *Children's Literature in Education* 25.4 (1994): 225–42.

27  Paul Goble, *Iktomi Loses His Eyes: A Plains Indian Story* (New York: Orchard Books, 1999), 2.

28  Ibid., 7.

29  Ibid., 5.

30  Peter Nabokov, *A Forest of Time: American Indian Ways of History* (Cambridge and New York: Cambridge University Press, 2002), 109.

31  Ibid., 110.

32  Terdiman, *Discourse/Counter-Discourse*, 254.

33  Ibid., 244.

34  *Lord of the Flies* was not written for a child audience, but is one of those texts adopted by child readers and incorporated into school libraries and literacy programs. For a discussion of *Silver's Revenge* and *Lord of the Flies*, see John Stephens and Robyn McCallum, *Retelling Stories, Framing Culture: Traditional Story and Metanarratives in Children's Literature* (New York and London: Garland Publishing, 1998), 267–91.

35  *The Sign of the Beaver* was awarded a Newbery Honor Citation, the Scott O'Dell Award for Historical Fiction, and the Christopher Award; in 1989, Elizabeth George Speare was awarded the Laura Ingalls Wilder Award for her children's books, including *The Sign of the Beaver*.

36  Joseph Bruchac, *The Heart of a Chief* (New York: Penguin, 1998), 19.

37  Ibid., 19.

38  Ibid., 20.

39  Ibid., 20.

40  Ibid., 20.

41  Ibid., 20.

42  For discussions of *In Search of April Raintree*, see Margery Fee, "Deploying Identity in the Face of Racism," in critical ed. of *In Search of April Raintree* by Beatrice Culleton Mosionier, ed. Cheryl Suzack (Winnipeg, MB: Portage and Main Press/Peguis, 1999), 211–26; Helen Hoy, "'Nothing But the "Truth"': Discursive Transparency in Beatrice Culleton," in critical ed. of *In Search of April Raintree* by Beatrice Culleton Mosionier, ed. Cheryl Suzack (Winnipeg, MB: Portage and Main Press/Peguis, 1999), 273–93; Peter Cumming, "'The Only Dirty Book': The Rape of April Raintree," in critical ed. of *In Search of April Raintree* by Beatrice Culleton Mosionier, ed. Cheryl Suzack (Winnipeg, MB: Portage and Main Press/Peguis, 1999), 307–22.

43  Beatrice Culleton Mosionier, *In Search of April Raintree*, critical ed., ed. Cheryl Suzack (Winnipeg, MB: Portage and Main Press/Peguis, 1999), 53.

44  Ibid., 54.

45  Ibid., 87.

46  Ibid., 76.

47  Terdiman, *Discourse/Counter-Discourse*, 185.

48  ANZAC biscuits (ANZAC is an abbreviation for the Australian and New Zealand Army Corps) are made without milk or eggs and were sent to Australian troops serving in the First World War. *The Magic Pudding* (1918), by Norman Lindsay, and *Snugglepot and Cuddlepie* (1918), by May Gibbs, are regarded as iconic Australian texts.

49  Anita Heiss, *Who Am I? The Diary of Mary Talence Sydney 1937* (Lindfield, NSW: Scholastic, 2001), 57.

50  Louis Althusser, *Essays on Ideology* (London: Verso, 1984).

51  Jacques Lacan, *Ecrits: A Selection*, trans. Bruce Fink in collaboration with Héloïse Fink and Russell Grigg (New York: W.W. Norton, 2002).

52  Foucault, *Power/Knowledge*.

53  Of the authors of these texts, Smith and Pryor are Indigenous. Smith is a "mixed blood, enrolled member of the Muscogee (Creek) Nation." See Cynthia Leitich Smith, *Rain Is Not My Indian Name* (New York: HarperCollins, 2001), n.p. Pryor is an Australian Aboriginal writer of Kunggandji and Birra-gubba descent, who writes in partnership with a non-Indigenous Australian, Meme McDonald. *Njunjul the Sun* features the same protagonist as McDonald and Pryor's earlier works, *My Girragundji* (1998) and *The Binna Binna Man* (1999).

54  Smith, *Rain Is Not My Indian Name*, 12.

55  Ibid., 17.

56  Ibid., 33.

57  Ibid., 20.

58  Ibid., 48.

59  Ibid., 48.

60  Ibid., 122.

61  Joanna Orwin, *Owl* (Dunedin, NZ: Longacre Press, 2001), 31.

62  Issues relating to land ownership have dominated New Zealand politics since the 1970s, when Maori embarked on political action to reinvoke the Treaty of Waitangi of 1840, which had to that point been largely ignored.

63  Orwin, *Owl*, 139.

64  Ibid., 87.

65  Ibid., 127.

66  Ibid., 220.

67  Ibid., 220.

68  Meme McDonald and Boori Monty Pryor, *Njunjul the Sun* (Crows Nest, NSW: Allen and Unwin, 2002), 9.

69  Ibid., 14. "The big smoke" is an Australian vernacular expression for cities as opposed to "the bush," or rural and (especially) remote regions.

70  Ibid., 26.

71  Ibid., 10.

72  Ibid., 20.

73  Ibid., 43.

74  Ibid., 62.

75  Ibid., 63.

76  Ibid., 83.

77  Ibid., 144.

78  Brian Doyle, *Spud Sweetgrass* (Toronto: Groundwood, 1992), 11.

79  Ibid., 11.

80  Ibid., 24.

81  Ibid., 51.

82  Ibid., 107.

83  Ibid., 117.

85  Ibid., 111.

85  Ashcroft, *Post-Colonial Transformation*, 4.

## 2: Indigenous Texts and Publishers [pp. 45–69]

1  Jingles are cone-shaped and made of metal. They are sewn onto dresses worn by girls and women performing jingle dances at powwows in Canada and the United States.

2  Cynthia Leitich Smith, Cornelius Van Wright, and Ying-Hwa Hu, *Jingle Dancer* (New York: William Morrow, 2000), 32.

3  Ibid., 6, 15.

4  Cynthia Leitich Smith, "A Different Drum: Native American Writing," *Horn Book Magazine* 78 (2002), 410.

5  Ibid., 409.

6  Ibid., 409.

7  Bill Neidjie, *Story about Feeling* (Broome, Western Australia: Magabala, 1989), 118.

8  Linda Tuhiwai Smith, *Decolonizing Methodologies: Research and Indigenous Peoples* (Dunedin, NZ: University of Otago Press, 1999), 19.

9  Terdiman, *Discourse/Counter-Discourse*, 149.

10  For discussions of Indigenous publishing for children in Canada, see Paul De-Pasquale and Doris Wolf, "A Select Bibliography of Canadian Picture Books for Children by Aboriginal Writers," *Canadian Children's Literature* 115/116 (2004), 144–59; and Paul DePasquale and Doris Wolf, "Home and Native Land: A Study of Canadian Aboriginal Picture Books by Aboriginal Authors," in *Home Words: Discourses of Children's Literature in Canada*, ed. Mavis Reimer (Waterloo, ON: Wilfrid Laurier University Press, forthcoming).

11  Kusugak explains at the beginning of *Hide and Sneak* that Ijiraqs "help [children] hide" so that they are never found again. See Michael Arvaarluk Kusugak and Vladyana Krykorka, *Hide and Sneak* (Toronto: Annick Press, 1992), 3.

12  Meme McDonald is a non-Indigenous author who writes in partnership with the Aboriginal author Boori Pryor.

13  Stephen Muecke, Introduction, in Paddy Roe, *Gularabulu: Stories from the West Kimberley*, ed. Stephen Muecke (Fremantle, Western Australia: Fremantle Arts Centre Press, 1983), vii.

14  See Stephen Muecke, *Textual Spaces: Aboriginality and Cultural Studies* (Kensington: New South Wales University Press, 1992), 65–66.

15  Joseph Bruchac, "Storytelling and the Sacred: On the Uses of Native American Stories," in *Through Indian Eyes: The Native Experience in Books for Children*, ed. Beverly Slapin and Doris Seale (Berkeley, CA: Oyate, 1998), 64–69.

16  For a discussion of the issues involved as they relate to Australian Aboriginal traditional narratives, see Clare Bradford, "'Oh How Different!': Regimes of Knowledge in Aboriginal Texts for Children," *Lion and the Unicorn* 27.2 (2003), 199–217.

17  Greg Young-Ing, "Aboriginal Text in Context," in *(Ad)dressing Our Words: Aboriginal Perspectives on Aboriginal Literatures*, ed. A.G. Ruffo (Penticton, BC: Theytus, 2001), 236.

18  Graham McKay, *The Land Still Speaks* (Canberra: Australian Government Publishing Service, 1996), 3.

19  The standard source of information on languages and their status is the SIL Ethnologue, which lists all known living languages. See Societas Internationalis Limnologiae (SIL), "Ethnologue: Languages of the World," http://www.ethnologue.com. In March 2004, the Ethnologue lists 217 Indigenous languages in Canada and the United States, of which 83 are nearly extinct, being spoken only by a few elderly speakers.

20  Bonnie Murray and Sheldon Dawson, trans. Rita Flamand, *Li Minoush* (Winnipeg, MB: Pemmican, 2001), 31.

21  Bill Ashcroft, *Post-Colonial Transformation*, 47.
22  Emma LaRocque, "Preface, or Here Are Our Voices—Who Will Hear?" in *Writing the Circle: Native Women of Western Canada*, ed. Jeanne Perreault and Sylvia Vance (Edmonton, AB: NeWest Publishers, 1990), xxvi.
23  Ibid., xxvi.
24  Tomson Highway and Brian Deines, *Caríbou Song: Atíhko Níkamon* (Toronto: HarperCollins, 2001), 7.
25  Ashcroft, *Post-Colonial Transformation*, 75.
26  Highway and Deines, *Caríbou Song*, 8.
27  Ibid., 13.
28  Ibid., 22.
29  Ibid., 25.
30  Neal McLeod, "Coming Home Through Stories," in *(Ad)dressing Our Words: Aboriginal Perspectives on Aboriginal Literature*, ed. Armand Garnet Ruffo (Penticton, BC: Theytus, 2001), 20.
31  Highway and Deines, *Caríbou Song*, 27.
32  Craig S. Womack, *Red on Red: Native American Literary Separatism* (Minneapolis, MN: University of Minnesota Press, 1999), 229–31.
33  Jace Weaver, *That the People Might Live: Native American Literatures and Native American Community* (New York and Oxford: Oxford University Press, 1997), xiii.
34  Ibid., 161.
35  Ashcroft, *Post-Colonial Transformation*, 72.
36  Young-Ing, "Aboriginal Text in Context," 236.
37  Mudrooroo, *The Indigenous Literature of Australia: Milli Milli Wangka* (South Melbourne, VIC: Hyland House, 1997), 190.
38  Bob Randall and Kunyi June-Anne McInerney, *Tracker Tjugingji* (Alice Springs, NT: IAD, 2003), 2–3.
39  Terdiman, *Discourse/Counter-Discourse*, 210.
40  While most desert people had moved to missions, settlements, or cattle stations by the 1960s, the outstation movement has seen many return to their traditional lands since the 1980s, to gather food, maintain traditional practices, and introduce children to country.
41  Ashcroft, *Post-Colonial Transformation*, 63.
42  Randall and McInerney, *Tracker Tjugingji*, 4.
43  Ibid., 30.
44  Ibid., 31.
45  Muecke, *Textual Spaces*, 167.
46  Quoted in LaRocque, "Preface, or Here Are Our Voices—Who Will Hear?" xxvi.
47  Bruchac's retelling of the Abenaki version of this story appears in the collection *Skins: Contemporary Indigenous Writing* (Cape Croker Reserve, ON, and Alice Springs, NT: Kegedonce Press and IAD Press/Jukurrpa Books, 2000), 65–72.
48  Joseph Bruchac, *Skeleton Man* (New York: HarperCollins Publishers, 2001), 1.
49  Ibid., 3.
50  Ibid., 6.
51  Ibid., 62.
52  Womack, *Red on Red*, 250.
53  Bruchac, *Skeleton Man*, 47–48.
54  Vine Deloria, "Ethnoscience and Indian Realities," in *Spirit and Reason: The Vine Deloria, Jr., Reader*, ed. B. Deloria, K. Foehner, and S. Scinta (Golden, CO: Fulcrum Publishing, 1999), 67.
55  Bruchac, *Skeleton Man*, 86.

56  Ibid., 39.

57  See Bradford, *Reading Race*, 183–90; Clare Bradford, "Transformative Fictions: Post-colonial Encounters in Australian Texts," *Children's Literature Association Quarterly* 28.4 (2003–2004), 195–202.

58  Womack, *Red on Red*, 15.

59  Bruchac, *Skeleton Man*, 112.

60  Ibid., 113.

61  Daisy Utemorrah and Pat Torres, *Do Not Go Around the Edges* (Broome, WA: Magabala Books, 1990), 24–25.

62  Ibid., 23.

63  Ibid., 25.

64  Ibid., 25.

65  Ian Anderson, "Black Bit, White Bit," in *Blacklines: Contemporary Critical Writing by Indigenous Australians*, ed. Michele Grossman, introd. Ian Anderson, Michele Grossman, Marcia Langton, and Aileen Moreton-Robinson (Carlton, VIC: Melbourne University Publishing, 2003), 46–47.

## 3: White Imaginings [pp. 71–96]

1  Linda Alcoff, "The Problem of Speaking for Others," *Cultural Critique* 20 (Winter 1991), 9.

2  Ibid., 26.

3  Hilary E. Wyss, "Captivity and Conversion," *American Indian Quarterly* 23.3–4 (1999), 63.

4  Michael Dodson, "The End in the Beginning: Re(de)finding Aboriginality," in *Blacklines: Contemporary Critical Writing by Indigenous Australians*, ed. Michele Grossman (Carlton, VIC: Melbourne University Press, 2003), 37.

5  Stephens, *Language and Ideology*, 26–27.

6  Ibid., 57.

7  S. Elizabeth Bird, "Introduction: Constructing the Indian, 1830s–1990s," in *Dressing in Feathers: The Construction of the Indian in American Popular Culture*, ed. S.E. Bird (New York: Westview Press, 1996), 1.

8  Betsy Sharkey, "Beyond Teepees and Totem Poles," rev. of *Pocahontas*, *New York Times*, 11 June 1995, sec. 2.1, 22.

9  Kent A. Ono and Derek T. Buescher, "Deciphering Pocahontas: Unpackaging the Commodification of a Native American Woman," *Critical Studies in Media Communication* 18.1 (2001), 34.

10  For discussions of this trope in colonial discourses see, for instance, Sara Mills, *Discourses of Difference: An Analysis of Women's Travel Writing and Colonialism* (London and New York: Routledge, 1991), 47–63; and Ashcroft, Griffiths, and Tiffin, *Post-Colonial Studies*.

11  Pauline Turner Strong, "Animated Indians: Critique and Contradiction in Commodified Children's Culture," *Cultural Anthropology* 11.3 (1996), 416.

12  Ibid., 416.

13  Edward Said, *Orientalism* (London: Routledge and Kegan Paul, 1978), 20.

14  See, for instance, Gandhi, *Postcolonial Theory*, 64–80; Mills, *Discourses of Difference*, 47–63.

15  Homi Bhabha, "The Other Question: Stereotype, Discrimination and the Discourse of Colonialism," in *The Location of Culture* (London and New York: Routledge, 1994), 81–82.

16  See Bradford, *Reading Race*, 49–56; 27–130; 145–48, for discussions of Wrightson's work.

17  Patricia Wrightson, "Ever Since My Accident: Aboriginal Folklore and Australian Fantasy," *Horn Book* 56.6 (1980), 612.

18  Ibid., 612.

19  Ibid., 615.

20  Pat Torres, "Interested in Writing about Indigenous Australians?" *Australian Author* 26.3 (1994), 25.

21  Wrightson, "Ever Since My Accident," 615–16.

22  Paul Goble, *Hau Kola—Hello Friend* (Katonah, NY: Richard C. Owen, 1994), 27.

23  Paul Goble, *Adopted by the Eagles: A Plains Indian Story of Friendship and Treachery* (New York: Simon and Schuster, 1994), 5.

24  Goble, *Adopted by the Eagles*, 7.

25  Paul Goble, *Iktomi and the Coyote: A Plains Indian Story* (New York: Orchard Books, 1998), 2.

26  Said, *Orientalism*, 20.

27  Julian Rice, *Black Elk's Story: Distinguishing Its Lakota Purpose* (Albuquerque: University of New Mexico Press, 1991), x.

28  See, for instance, *Borrowed Power: Essays on Cultural Appropriation*, ed. Bruce Ziff and Pratima V. Rao (New Brunswick, NJ: Rutgers University Press, 1997); *Blacklines: Contemporary Critical Writing by Indigenous Australians*, ed. Michele Grossman (Carlton, VIC: Melbourne University Press, 2003); Anita M. Heiss, *Dhuuluu-Yala To Talk Straight: Publishing Indigenous Literature* (Canberra: Aboriginal Studies Press, 2003); Rosemary J. Coombe, *The Cultural Life of Intellectual Properties: Authorship, Appropriation and the Law* (New York: Routledge, Chapman and Hall, 1998); and Francis Pound, *The Space Between: Pakeha Use of Maori Motifs in Modernist New Zealand Art* (Auckland, NZ: Workshop Press, 1994).

29  Jon C. Stott, *Native Americans in Children's Literature* (Phoenix, AZ: Oryx Press, 1995), 27–28.

30  Doris Seale, "Parting Words: The Works of Paul Goble," *MultiCultural Review* 10 (March 2001), 119.

31  Ibid., 119.

32  Paul Goble, *The Legend of the White Buffalo Woman* (Washington, DC: National Geographic Society, 1998), 5.

33  Ibid., 5.

34  Ibid., 28.

35  Patricia Wrightson, *The Ice Is Coming* (London: Hutchinson, 1977), 11.

36  Ibid., 12.

37  Joseph Campbell, *The Hero with a Thousand Faces* (London: Abacus, 1975 [1949]), 71.

38  Ibid., 299.

39  Ibid., 37.

40  Maurice Saxby, *The Proof of the Puddin': Australian Children's Literature 1970–1990* (Sydney, NSW: Ashton Scholastic, 1993), 533.

41  Hetti Perkins, "Seeing and Seaming: Contemporary Aboriginal Art," in *Blacklines: Contemporary Critical Writing by Indigenous Australians*, ed. Michele Grossman (Melbourne University Press, Carlton, 2003), 101.

42  From its publication, *False Face* attracted both praise and criticism for its representation of Iroquois culture. See Roderick McGillis, "'And the Celt Knew the Indian': Knowingness, Postcolonialism, Children's Literature," in *Voices of the Other: Children's Literature and the Postcolonial Context*, ed. R. McGillis (New York: Garland,

1999), 227–33, for a discussion of Katz's appropriation of Native American traditions and of the contradictions of the novel's reception. In his essay "At Home on Native Land: A Non-Aboriginal Canadian Scholar Discusses Aboriginality and Property
in Canadian Double-Focalized Novels for Young Adults," in *Home Words: Discourses
of Children's Literature in Canada*, ed. Mavis Reimer (Waterloo, ON: Wilfrid Laurier
University Press, forthcoming), Perry Nodelman presents a telling account of critical and scholarly readings of the text, including how his own perspectives have
shifted since 1987.

43  Welwyn Wilton Katz, *False Face* (Toronto: Groundwood Books/Douglas and McIntyre, 1987), 38.

44  Ibid., 154.

45  Ibid., 18.

46  Ibid., 25.

47  Ibid., 105.

48  Ibid., 147.

49  While the first section of the narrative describes what appears to be a precolonial setting, the Sioux of *Moonstick* ride horses, which places the narrative in the eigh-
teenth century following the acquisition of horses by Plains nations, and hence in
the early colonial period.

50  Eve Bunting and John Sandford, *Moonstick: The Seasons of the Sioux* (New York:
Joanna Cotler Books, 1997), 3.

51  Ibid., 26.

52  Ibid., 29.

53  Ibid., 31.

54  Bruchac, *Heart of a Chief*, 23.

55  Ibid., 24.

56  Deborah Root, "'White Indians': Appropriation and the Politics of Display," in *Borrowed Power: Essays on Cultural Appropriation*, ed. Bruce Ziff and Pratima V. Rao
(New Brunswick, NJ: Rutgers University Press, 1997), 227.

57  Ibid., 228.

58  Ibid., 231.

59  Ibid., 229.

60  Stewart, "Judging Authors by the Color of Their Skin?" 192.

61  Sharon Creech, *Walk Two Moons* (New York: HarperCollins Publishers, 1994), 15–16.

62  Ibid., 56.

63  Ibid., 57.

64  Ibid. 57.

65  Ibid., 58.

66  Ibid., 58.

67  Ibid., 109.

68  Ibid., 110.

69  See Olive Patricia Dickason, *Canada's First Nations: A History of Founding Peoples
from Earliest Times* (Don Mills, ON: Oxford University Press, 2002), 323–41.

70  For a thorough discussion of New Age appropriations of Native American cultures,
see Lisa Aldred, "Plastic Shamans and Astroturf Sun Dances: New Age Commercialization of Native American Spirituality," *American Indian Quarterly* 24.3 (2000):
329–53.

71  Patricia Seed, *American Pentimento: The Invention of Indians and the Pursuit of
Riches* (Minneapolis: University of Minnesota Press, 2001), 173.

72  Dodson, "The End in the Beginning," 37.

73  See Bradford, *Reading Race*, 56–60, for a discussion of such representations.

74  Katz, *False Face*, 18.
75  Deborah Savage, *Flight of the Albatross* (New York: Houghton Mifflin, 1989), 48.
76  Ibid., 198.
77  Ibid., 203.

## 4: Telling the Past [pp. 97–119]

1   Ashcroft, *Post-Colonial Transformation*, 112.
2   Said, *Orientalism*, 272.
3   Gandhi, *Postcolonial Theory*, 171.
4   See, for instance, several of the essays in *After the Imperial Turn: Thinking With and Through the Nation*, ed. Antoinette Burton (Durham and London: Duke University Press, 2003).
5   Minoru Hokari, "Images of Australian Colonialism: Interpretations of the Colonial Landscape by an Aboriginal Historian," *Senri Ethnological Studies* 60 (2002), 157.
6   Hokari, "Images of Australian Colonialism," 158.
7   Minoru Hokari, "Maintaining History: The Gurindji People's 'Truthful Histories,'" *Cultural Survival Quarterly* 26.2 (2002), 1. http://www.culturalsurvival.org/publications/csq (accessed 6 March 2005).
8   Minoru Hokari, "Localised History: 'Dangerous' Histories from the Gurindji Country," *Locality* (Autumn 2002), 4.
9   Ashcroft, *Post-Colonial Transformation*, 101.
10  For a summary of critical debates concerning some of the *Dear America* novels and other historical fiction from the United States, see Melissa Kay Thompson, "A Sea of Good Intentions," 353–72.
11  *Papunya School Book*, 2.
12  Claire Smith, *Country, Kin and Culture: Survival of an Australian Aboriginal Community* (Kent Town, SA: Wakefield Press, 2004), 3.
13  Michael Arvaarluk Kusugak and Vladyana Langer Krykorka, *Arctic Stories* (Toronto: Annick Press, 1998), 28.
14  See Rhonda Claes and Deborah Clifton, "Institutional Child Abuse: Needs and Expectations for Redress of Victims of Abuse at Native Residential Schools," Law Commission of Canada/Commission du droit du Canada, http://www.lcc.gc.ca/research_project/98-_child_abuse-en.asp (accessed 20 June 2005).
15  Kusugak and Krykorka, *Arctic Stories*, 30.
16  Ibid., 30.
17  Ibid., 32.
18  Ibid., 40.
19  Mormon traditions have long drawn on constructions of Native American culture to bolster Mormon claims of constituting a chosen people within the United States. In 1827, Smith asserted that an angel gave him two golden tablets detailing a history that established Native Americans as the lost tribe of Israel.
20  Orson Scott Card, *Red Prophet: The Tales of Alvin Maker*, Vol. 2 (London: Arrow Books, 1988), 65.
21  Ibid., 125.
22  Ibid., 310.
23  Ibid., 384.
24  Ibid., 393.
25  Pratt, *Imperial Eyes*, 4.
26  Thomas King, *The Truth about Stories: A Native Narrative* (Toronto: House of Anansi Press, 2003), 105–106.

27  Ibid., 106.
28  Pamela Knights, "England's Dark Ages? The North-East in Robert Westall's *The Wind Eye* and Andrew Taylor's *The Coal House*," in *The Presence of the Past in Children's Literature*, ed. Ann Lawson Lucas (Westport, CT: Greenwood, 2003), 168.
29  Stephens, *Language and Ideology*, 218.
30  Ibid., 220.
31  Ibid., 221.
32  Joanna Orwin, *Ihaka and the Prophecy* (Auckland, NZ: Oxford University Press, 1984), 110.
33  Ibid., 134.
34  Ibid., 139.
35  Joseph Bruchac, *Children of the Longhouse* (New York: Penguin, 1996), 148–49.
36  Ibid., 148.
37  See my discussion of Weaver's approach to Native American literatures in chapter 2.
38  The terms "Old Men" and "Young Men" relate to whether players have fathered children rather than to age. Ohkwa'ri plays with the Old Men's team because he acts as a surrogate for Thunder's Voice, an elderly man who can no longer play.
39  Bruchac, *Children of the Longhouse*, 139.
40  Ibid., 112–13.
41  See introduction, xx.
42  Linton, "Ethical Reading and Resistant Texts," 43.
43  Bruchac, *Children of the Longhouse*, n.p.
44  The word *balanda*, used across the Northern Territory to refer to white people, derives from *Hollander*, used by the Macassans to refer to the Dutch.
45  Joan Clark, *The Dream Carvers* (Toronto: Penguin, 1995), 115.
46  Ibid., 177.
47  Ingeborg Marshall, *A History and Ethnography of the Beothuk* (Montreal and Kingston: McGill-Queen's University Press, 1996), 444.
48  Robyn McCallum, *Ideologies of Identity in Adolescent Fiction* (New York and London: Garland, 1999), 56.
49  For a discussion of this trope in Australian children's literature, see Bradford, *Reading Race*, 83: 104–108.
50  Lorraine Orman, *Cross Tides* (Dunedin, NZ: Longacre Press, 2004), 78.
51  Ibid., 196.
52  Ibid., 117.
53  Ibid., 78.
54  Kevin Major, *Blood Red Ochre* (New York: Dell Publishing, 1989), 11.
55  Ibid., 38.
56  Ibid., 41.
57  The term *mamateek* refers to the seasonal dwellings built by Beothuk as they moved around regular routes to hunt game and gather food. The *mamateek* of *Blood Red Ochre* houses Dauoodaset's extended family.
58  Shanawdithit was captured in 1823, with two other Beothuk women, and lived first on Exploits Island and later in St. John's until her death. She was generally known as Nancy.
59  Major, *Blood Red Ochre*, 147.
60  Ken Coates, "The 'Gentle' Occupation: The Settlement of Canada and the Dispossession of the First Nations," in *Indigenous Peoples' Rights in Australia, Canada, and New Zealand*, ed. P. Havemann (Auckland: Oxford University Press, 1999), 141.
61  Felice Holman, *Real* (New York: Atheneum, 1997), 61.

62  Ibid., 172.

63  Ibid., 159.

64  Ashcroft, *Post-Colonial Transformation*, 48.

### Part Two: Place and Postcolonial Significations
### 5: Space, Time, Nation [pp. 123–146]

1  Michel Foucault, "Questions on Geography," in *Power/Knowledge: Selected Interviews and Other Writings 1972–1977* (Brighton, UK: Harvester Press, 1980), 70.

2  Edward W. Soja, *Postmodern Geographies: The Reassertion of Space in Critical Social Theory* (London: Verso, 1989), 6.

3  Ashcroft, *Post-Colonial Transformation*, 125.

4  Anthony Giddens, *The Consequences of Modernity* (Cambridge, UK: Polity Press / Basil Blackwell, 1990), 18.

5  Stephen Slemon, "Unsettling the Empire: Resistance Theory for the Second World," in *The Post-Colonial Studies Reader*, ed. B. Ashcroft, G. Griffiths, and H. Tiffin (London: Routledge, 1995), 104.

6  Doreen Massey, *Space, Place and Gender* (Cambridge, UK: Polity Press, 1994), 6.

7  Elizabeth George Speare, *The Sign of the Beaver* (New York: Dell Publishing, 1983), 116. Attean's pidgin English constructs hierarchical relations between him and Matt.

8  Massey, *Space, Place and Gender*, 6.

9  Speare, *The Sign of the Beaver*, 116.

10  Ibid., 118.

11  Ibid., 134.

12  Ibid., 134.

13  Ibid., 117.

14  Ibid., 117.

15  Ibid., 117.

16  Ibid., 135.

17  Ibid., 135.

18  It should, however, be noted that interracial sexual relations did not carry the same meanings for all colonial societies. In Australia, they were associated very starkly with the dilution of racial purity, whereas in Canada people of mixed race (Métis) constituted such an important frontier group that they were regarded rather as a new force; see Wolfe, *Settler Colonialism and the Transformation of Anthropology*, 163–214. Nevertheless, the struggle of Métis for recognition and rights as citizens has been arduous and protracted; see Bonita Lawrence, *"Real" Indians and Others: Mixed-Blood Urban Native Peoples and Indigenous Nationhood* (Vancouver and Toronto: University of British Columbia Press, 2004), 82–101.

19  Clare Bradford, "Performances of Colour: Narratives of Passing in Contemporary Settler Society Texts," in *Poetry, Performance and Playfulness*, ed. K. Mallan and S. Pearce (Flaxton, QLD: Post Pressed, 2004), 77–84.

20  See David Pearson, *The Politics of Ethnicity in Settler Societies: States of Unease* (Basingstoke, UK: Palgrave, 2001), 120: "In 1975 a national land march, 30 000 strong, highlighted a decade of visible and vocal protest actions highlighting conflicts over land and fishery ownership, the revival of Maori culture and the assertion of rights under the Treaty of Waitangi."

21  Joan de Hamel, *Take the Long Path* (Auckland: Penguin, 1980), 112.

22  The yellow-eyed penguins of the book are native to the Otago peninsula.

23  Michael Arvaarluk Kusugak and Vladyana Krykorka, *Northern Lights: The Soccer Trails* (Toronto: Annick Press, 1993), 12.

24  Ibid., 12.

25  Olive Patricia Dickason, *Canada's First Nations: A History of Founding Peoples from Earliest Times*, 388.

26  Ibid., 388.

27  Kusugak and Krykorka, *Northern Lights*, 18.

28  Ibid., 20.

29  Ibid., 26. The Inuktitut word *taima*, which at the end of a stretch of speech means "that's enough" or "enough," functions here to install cultural difference. (See my discussion of Indigenous textuality, in chapter 2.)

30  The *inuksugaq* (or *inukshuk*) is formed out of heavy rocks arranged in the form of a human. In *Hide and Sneak*, Kusugak explains that "inuksugaqa were built in a long line to corral caribou to a place where they could be hunted," and in order to help people find their way home; see Michael Arvaarluk Kusugak and Vladyana Krykorka, *Hide and Sneak*, 3.

31  Elaine Russell, *A Is for Aunty* (Sydney: ABC Books, 2000), 16.

32  Ibid., 12.

33  Ibid., 25.

34  Ibid., 11.

35  Ibid., 17.

36  Speare, *The Sign of the Beaver*, 117.

37  Ibid., 31.

38  Ibid., 116.

39  For an illuminating account of treaty discourses in texts by Native American and Maori authors, see Chadwick Allen, "Postcolonial Theory and the Discourse of Treaties," *American Quarterly* 52.1 (2000), 59–89.

40  Stephen Slemon, "Post-Colonial Critical Theories," in *New National and Post-Colonial Literatures: An Introduction*, ed. B. King (Oxford, UK: Clarendon Press, 1996), 187.

41  Homi K. Bhabha, "The World and the Home," in *Dangerous Liaisons: Gender, Nation, and Postcolonial Perspectives*, ed. A. McClintock, A. Mufti, and E. Shohat (Minneapolis: University of Minnesota Press, 1997), 445.

42  Pierre Bourdieu, *Outline of a Theory of Practice* (Cambridge, UK: Cambridge University Press, 1977), 78.

43  Ashcroft, *Post-Colonial Transformations*, 160.

44  See Louise Erdrich's glossary in *The Birchbark House* (New York: Hyperion, 1999), 241: "Anishinabe: the original name for the Ojibwa or Chippewa people, a Native American group who originated in and live mainly in the northern North American woodlands." *Anishinabeg* is the plural of *Anishinabe*.

45  The Land Wars of the 1860s represented a struggle for land ownership, but were also about opposing conceptions of the land and how it should be used. See Wendy Larner and Paul Spoonley, "Post-Colonial Politics in Aotearoa/New Zealand," in *Unsettling Settler Societies: Articulations of Gender, Race, Ethnicity and Class*, ed. D. Stasiulis and N. Yuval-Davis (London: Sage Publications, 1995), 43–44.

46  Gavin Bishop, *The House That Jack Built* (Auckland, NZ: Scholastic, 1999), 32–33. Papatuanuku is the Earth Mother.

47  Ibid., 32.

48  Bhabha, "The World and the Home," 445.

49  For a discussion of this text, see Mavis Reimer, "Homing and Unhoming: The Ideological Work of Canadian Children's Literature," in *Home Words: Discourses of Children's Literature in Canada*, ed. Mavis Reimer (Waterloo, ON: Wilfrid Laurier University Press, forthcoming).

50  Janet Lunn, *Shadow in Hawthorn Bay* (Toronto: Lester and Orpen Dennys, 1986), 6.

51  Pierre Bourdieu, *Sociology in Question* (London: Sage Publications, 1993), 87.

52  Ibid., 87.

53  Ibid., 203.

54  In Canadian art history the Group of Seven is group of artists who painted what are regarded as iconic representations of Canadian landscapes during the first three decades of the twentieth century.

55  Erin Manning, "I Am Canadian: Identity, Territory and the Canadian National Landscape," *Theory and Event* 4.4 (2000), 7.

56  Lunn, *Shadow in Hawthorn Bay*, 216.

57  John Stephens and Robyn McCallum, *Retelling Stories, Framing Culture: Traditional Story and Metanarratives in Children's Literature* (New York: Garland, 1998), 11.

58  This is very clear in a sequence in *The House That Jack Built* depicting the marriage of a Maori woman and a Pakeha man, where a Christian clergyman is represented as vanquishing a Maori spirit.

59  Erdrich, *The Birchbark House*, 238.

60  Bourdieu, *Sociology in Question*, 87.

61  Erdrich, *The Birchbark House*, 239.

62  Diana Kidd, *Two Hands Together* (Ringwood, VIC: Penguin, 2000), 99.

63  Ibid., 101.

64  Ibid., 96–97.

65  Ibid., 97. The children dance around a Hills Hoist, a rotary clothesline, invented in Australia, that became an icon of the Australian suburban backyard after the Second World War.

66  Ibid., 96.

67  Ashcroft, *Post-Colonial Transformation*, 197.

68  Ibid., 197.

69  Deborah Bird Rose, "The Year Zero and the North Australian Frontier," in *Tracking Knowledge in North Australian Landscapes: Studies in Indigenous and Settler Ecological Knowledge Systems*, ed. D. Bird Rose and A. Clarke (Casuarina, NT: North Australia Research Unit, ANU, 1997), 33–34.

## 6: Borders, Journeys, and Liminality [pp. 147–168]

1  Paul Carter, *The Road to Botany Bay* (London and Boston: Faber and Faber, 1987), 158.

2  Johannes Fabian, *Time and the Other: How Anthropology Makes Its Object* (New York: Columbia University Press, 1983), 17.

3  David Harvey, *Justice, Nature and the Geography of Difference* (Malden, MA, and Oxford, UK: Blackwell, 1996), 284.

4  In Australia, thousands of Aboriginal children were removed from their families from 1910 to 1970. In the United States, hundreds of Indian boarding schools operated from 1879, when the Carlisle Institute was founded, through to the 1960s. In Canada, the federal government assumed control of the residential schools in 1874, and they continued into the 1960s. It is estimated that around 90,600 people alive today in Canada attended residential schools. The removal of Indigenous children in all three nations was motivated by the desire to assimilate them into white culture by destroying their links with Indigenous cultures. The policies implemented by successive New Zealand governments from the 1860s were somewhat different,

since although Native schools were established for Maori children, providing education intended to assimilate these children and fit them for menial occupations, few such establishments were boarding schools, and by 1953, 60 per cent of Maori children attended public primary schools.

5  Doreen Massey, "Travelling Thoughts," in *Without Guarantees: In Honour of Stuart Hall*, ed. P. King, L. Grossberg, and A. McRobbie (London and New York: Verso, 2000), 231.

6  Ibid., 231.

7  James Houston, *Drifting Snow: An Arctic Search* (Toronto: McClelland and Stewart, 1992), 143.

8  Ibid., 150.

9  Ibid., 149.

10  Chiori Santiago and Judith Lowry, *Home to Medicine Mountain* (San Francisco, CA: Children's Book Press, 1998), 3.

11  Ibid., 4.

12  Ibid., 4.

13  Ibid., 7.

14  Ibid., 7.

15  Richard Terdiman, *Discourse/Counter-Discourse*, 57.

16  Santiago and Lowry, *Home to Medicine Mountain*, 30.

17  Ibid., 32.

18  Ibid., 25.

19  Bill Neidjie, *Story about Feeling* (Broome, WA: Magabala Books, 1989), 170.

20  Daisy Bates is a contradictory figure in Australian history. She lived at a remote camp at Ooldea in South Australia from 1919 until 1936 and firmly believed in the dying race theory, producing the popular book *The Passing of the Aborigines*.

21  Edna Tantjingu Williams, Eileen Wani Wingfield, and Kunyi June-Anne McInerney, *Down the Hole, Up the Tree, Across the Sandhills ... Running from the State and Daisy Bates* (Alice Springs, NT: IAD Press, 2000), 4.

22  Ibid., 38.

23  Deborah Bird Rose, *Dingo Makes Us Human: Life and Land in an Australian Aboriginal Culture* (Cambridge and New York: Cambridge University Press, 2000), 107.

24  Williams, Wingfield, and McInerney, *Down the Hole*, 46.

25  McDonald is non-Aboriginal and Pryor Aboriginal. The protagonist of *Njunjul the Sun* is the same boy as in McDonald and Pryor's *My Girragundji* (1998) and *The Binna Binna Man* (1999).

26  Homi Bhabha, "Introduction: Locations of Culture," *The Location of Culture* (London and New York: Routledge, 1994), 3–4.

27  Ibid., 4.

28  Ashcroft, Griffiths, and Tiffin, *Post-Colonial Studies*, 182.

29  Will is a member of the Sto:loh (or Sto:lo) Nation, an alliance of communities in the Fraser Valley, British Columbia.

30  Lee Maracle, *Will's Garden* (Penticton, BC: Theytus Books, 2002), 39.

31  Ibid., 40.

32  Ibid., 40.

33  Ibid., 80.

34  Ibid., 70.

35  Ibid., 55.

36  Homi Bhabha, "Introduction: Locations of Culture," 7.

37  Ibid., 7.

38  Maracle, *Will's Garden*, 148–49.
39  Joseph Bruchac, *The Heart of a Chief* (New York: Dial, 1998), n.p.
40  Ibid., 109.
41  Ibid., 109.
42  Ibid., 110.
43  Ibid., 111.
44  Ibid., 111.
45  Ibid., 140.
46  See John Fiske, Bob Hodge, and Graeme Turner, *Myths of Oz: Reading Australian Popular Culture* (Sydney, NSW: Allen and Unwin, 1987), 42–53.
45  Ashcroft, *Post-Colonial Transformation*, 76.
46  Ibid., 76.
49  Pat Lowe, *Feeling the Heat* (Camberwell, VIC: Penguin, 2002), 181.
50  Ibid., 181.
51  See Stephens, *Language and Ideology in Children's Literature*, 52–54.
52  For Aboriginal people in remote towns and communities, Aboriginal English is generally a second or third language.
53  Lowe, *Feeling the Heat*, 259.
54  Paula Boock, *Home Run* (Dunedin, NZ: Longacre Press, 1995), 84.
55  Ibid., 85.
56  Ibid., 107.
57  Ibid., 113.
58  Vince Marotta, "The Ambivalence of Borders: The Bicultural and the Multicultural," in *Race, Colour and Identity in Australia and New Zealand*, ed. J. Docker and G. Fishcher (Sydney: University of New South Wales Press, 2000), 178.

## 7: Politics and Place [pp.169–198]

1  Seed, *American Pentimento*, 2.
2  Well-established systems of currency exchange operated among Native Americans; however, these systems were local and not general, and the notion that land might be bought and sold for currency was outside Native American traditions. See Seed, *American Pentimento*, 12–28.
3  Richard H. Bartlett, "Native Title in Australia: Denial, Recognition, and Dispossession," in *Indigenous Peoples' Rights in Australia, Canada, and New Zealand*, ed. P. Havemann (Oxford: Oxford University Press, 1999), 413. Native title legislation in Australia has generally favoured the interests of non-Aboriginal claimants, including sheep and cattle ranchers and mining companies.
4  Augie Fleras and Jean Leonard Elliott, *The "Nations Within": Aboriginal-State Relations in Canada, the United States, and New Zealand* (Toronto: Oxford University Press, 1992), 2.
5  See Fleras and Elliott, *The "Nations Within,"* ix–xii.
6  Paul Havemann, "Indigenous Peoples, the State and the Challenge of Differentiated Citizenship," in *Indigenous Peoples' Rights in Australia, Canada, and New Zealand*, ed. P. Havemann (Oxford, UK: Oxford University Press, 1999), 472.
7  Gary Paulsen, *Canyons* (New York: Dell Publishing, 1990), n.p.
8  Ibid., 5.
9  See chapter 4 for a discussion of three double-stranded narratives, which similarly involve plots where contemporary characters encounter figures living in colonial times.

10  Paulsen, *Canyons*, 152.

11  Ibid., 10.

12  Ibid., 11.

13  Ibid., 32.

14  Ibid., 132.

15  Ibid., 41.

16  See chapter 1 for an explanation of this term.

17  Seed, *American Pentimento*, 161.

18  Paulsen, *Canyons*, 151.

19  Ibid., 153.

20  Perry Nodelman, "Focalisation and Property in Canadian Novels about Meetings Between European and Aboriginal Young People" (Paper delivered at the conference of the Australasian Children's Literature Association for Research, University of Technology, Sydney, 17 July 2004).

21  Martha Brooks, *Bone Dance* (Toronto: Groundwood Books, 1997), 23.

22  Ibid., 50.

23  Ibid., 14-15.

24  Ibid., 79-80.

25  Diana Brydon, "The White Inuit Speaks: Contamination as Literary Strategy," in *Past the Last Post: Theorizing Post-Colonialism and Post-Modernism* (Hemel Hempstead, UK: Harvester Wheatsheaf, 1991), 196.

26  Brooks, *Bone Dance*, 148.

27  Ibid., 149.

28  Seed, *American Pentimento*, 2.

29  Pat Lowe and Jimmy Pike, *Desert Cowboy* (Broome, WA: Magabala Books, 2000), 83.

30  Ibid., 103.

31  Ibid., 103.

32  Deborah Bird Rose, *Dingo Makes Us Human*, 29.

33  In Canada, the Indian Act of 1869 and the acts of legislation that followed defined who was to be accorded Indian status. Children with Indian status were obliged to attend residential schools, whose aim was to assimilate Indian children into white society. The Kalamak Indian Residential School is a fictive setting based on the many Canadian residential schools attended by status-Indian children.

34  Lawrence, *"Real" Indians and Others*, 106.

35  Shirley Sterling, *My Name Is Seepeetza* (Toronto: Groundwood Books, 1992), 12-13.

36  Ibid., 91.

37  Ibid., 91.

38  Ibid., 103.

39  Ibid., 125.

40  See Fleras and Elliott, *The "Nations Within,"* 158-69.

41  Craig Kee Strete, Michelle Netten Chacon, and Francisco X. Mora, *How the Indians Bought the Farm* (New York: Greenwillow Books, 1996), 4.

42  Ibid., 20.

43  Ibid., 29-31.

44  See Allen, *Blood Narrative*, 162-75.

45  Strete, Chacon, and Mora, *How the Indians Bought the Farm*, 4.

46  Jane Jacobs, "Resisting Reconciliation: The Secret Geographies of (Post)Colonial Australia," in *Geographies of Resistance*, ed. S. Pile and M. Keith (London: Routledge, 1997), 208.

47  Allen Say, *Home of the Brave* (New York: Houghton Mifflin, 2002), 18.

48  Ibid., 22.
49  Ibid., 22.
50  Ibid., 28.
51  Ibid., 30.
52  This narrative pattern occurs, for instance, in Mary-Ellen Lang Collura, *Winners* (Toronto: Douglas and McIntyre, 1984); Yvette Edmonds, *Yuit* (Toronto: Napoleon Publishing, 1993); Monica Hughes, *Log Jam* (Toronto: HarperCollins, 1989); and Scott O'Dell, *Black Star, Bright Dawn* (Boston, MA: Houghton Mifflin, 1998).
53  Jean Little, *Willow and Twig* (Toronto: Penguin, 2000), 29.
54  Fleras, "Politicising Indigeneity," 192.
55  Deborah L. Delaronde and Gary Chartrand, *Flour Sack Flora* (Winnipeg, MB: Pemmican Publications, 2001), 4.
56  See my discussion of this text in chapter 2.
57  DePasquale and Wolf, "Home and Native Land."
58  See Sherry Farrell Racette, "Beads, Silk and Quills: The Clothing and Decorative Arts of the Metis," in *Metis Legacy*, ed. L.J. Barkwell, L. Dorion, and D.R. Préfontaine (Winnipeg, MB: Pemmican Publications, 2001), 181–88.
59  The historical note at the end of *Flour Sack Flora* explains that "companies such as Robin Hood Flour and Five Roses Flour sold their products using unbleached cotton cloth as their container. The unbleached cotton sacks were a part of Canadian family life and history"; see Delaronde and Chartrand, *Flour Sack Flora*, 48.
60  The word *kuia* is the Maori term for an elderly woman or grandmother.
61  Patricia Grace and Robyn Kahukiwa, *The Kuia and the Spider* (Auckland: Penguin, 1981), 32.
62  Ibid., 5.
63  The word *trolley* is the New Zealand term for a handmade cart, variously known in other Englishes as a soapbox cart, billy-cart, and go-cart. *Pram* (abbreviated from "perambulator") is the NZ English term for baby carriage.
64  Cynthia Leitich Smith, *Indian Shoes* (New York: HarperCollins, 2002), 8.
65  Ibid., 10.
66  Stuart Hall, "The Local and the Global: Globalization and Ethnicity," in *Dangerous Liaisons: Gender, Nation, and Postcolonial Perspectives,"* ed. A. McClintock, A. Mufti, and E. Shohat (Minneapolis: University of Minnesota Press, 1997), 185.

## 8: Allegories of Place and Race [pp. 199–223]

1  Stephen Slemon, "Monuments of Empire: Allegory/Counter Discourse/Post-Colonial Writing," *Kunapipi* 9.3 (1987), 11.
2  Ashcroft, *Post-Colonial Transformation*, 105.
3  King and Monkman, *A Coyote Columbus Story*, 4.
4  Ibid., 14.
5  Nabokov, *A Forest of Time*, vi.
6  Ibid., 108.
7  Ibid., 109.
8  King and Monkman, *A Coyote Columbus Story*, 22.
9  Ibid., 26.
10  Ibid., 29.
11  Nabokov, *A Forest of Time*, 112.
12  Edouard Glissant, *Caribbean Discourse: Selected Essays* (Charlottesville: University Press of Virginia, 1989), 64.

13  King and Monkman, *A Coyote Columbus Story*, 26.

14  Joan Gordon, "Utopia, Genocide and the Other," in *Edging into the Future: Science Fiction and Contemporary Cultural Transformation*, ed. V. Hollinger and J. Gordon (Philadelphia: University of Pennsylvania Press, 2002), 209.

15  See, for instance, Ronnie D. Lipschutz, "Aliens, Alien Nations, and Alienation in American Political Economy and Popular Culture," in *To Seek Out New Worlds: Exploring Links between Science Fiction and World Politics*, ed. J. Weldes (New York: Palgrave Macmillan, 2003), 79–98; Charles Ramirez Berg, "Immigrants, Aliens, and Extraterrestrials: Science Fiction's Alien 'Other' as (Among *Other* Things) New Hispanic Imagery," *CineAction!* 18 (Fall 1989), 3–17; Vivian Sobchack, "Postmodern Modes of Ethnicity," in *Postmodern After-Images: A Reader in Film, Television and Video*, ed. P. Brooker and W. Brooker (London: Arnold, 1997), 112–28.

16  Andrew Macdonald, Gina Macdonald, and Mary Ann Sheridan, *Shape-Shifting: Images of Native Americans in Recent Popular Fiction* (Westport, CT: Greenwood Press, 2000), 245.

17  Helen Addison-Smith, "E.T. Go Home: Indigeneity, Multiculturalism and 'Homeland' in Contemporry Science Fiction Cinema," *Papers: Explorations into Children's Literature* 15.1 (2005), 27.

18  Margaret Mahy, *Aliens in the Family* (London: Methuen, 1986), 5.

19  See Said, *Orientalism*, 40; Bradford, *Reading Race*, passim.

20  Mahy, *Aliens in the Family*, 7.

21  Ibid., 7.

22  Gillian Rubinstein, *Beyond the Labyrinth* (South Yarra, VIC: Hyland House, 1988), 170.

23  See Frank P. Tomasulo, "The Gospel according to Spielberg in *E.T. the Extra-Terrestrial*," *Quarterly Review of Film and Video* 18.3 (2001): 273–82.

24  Vivian Sobchack, *Screening Space: The American Science Fiction Film*, 2nd ed. (New Brunswick, NJ: Rutgers University Press, 1997), 284–85.

25  Rubinstein, *Beyond the Labyrinth*, 163.

26  Rubinstein, *Beyond the Labyrinth*, 168.

27  Mahy, *Aliens in the Family*, 168.

28  Sobchack, *Screening Space*, 294.

29  Michel Foucault, *This Is Not a Pipe*, trans. and ed. James Harkness (Berkeley: University of California Press, 1982), 44.

30  Sobchack, *Screening Space*, 294.

31  Lipschutz, "Aliens, Alien Nations, and Alienation," 96.

32  Geoffrey Whitehall, "The Problem of the 'World and Beyond': Encountering 'the Other' in Science Fiction," in *To Seek Out New Worlds: Exploring Links Between Science Fiction and World Politics*, ed. J. Weldes (New York: Palgrave Macmillan, 2003), 172.

33  See Darko Suvin, *Metamorphoses of Science Fiction: On the Poetics and History of a Literary Genre* (New Haven, CT: Yale University Press, 1979), 9. A core strategy of defamiliarization in science fiction is the invention of *nova*, "new things," such as aliens, spaceships, cyborgs, and time machines, which both draw attention to themselves for their difference and novelty, and also symbolically refer to concepts and ideologies relating to humanity and human experience.

34  Mary Caraker, *The Faces of Ceti* (Boston, MA: Houghton Mifflin, 1991), 67.

35  Ibid., 192.

36  Brian Caswell, *Deucalion* (St. Lucia: University of Queensland Press, 1995), 146.

37  See chapter 7, where I discuss the cultural and legal practices that characterized British colonialism in regard to land.

38  Caraker, *The Faces of Ceti*, 68.

39  Ibid., 28.

40  Examples abound of such linguistic practices. For instance, the name *Iroquois* derives from the derogatory name "killer people," given to the Hotinonshonni people by their Algonquian enemies. See James Wilson, *The Earth Shall Weep: A History of Native America* (New York: Atlantic Monthly Press, 1999), 101–107.

41  Caraker, *The Faces of Ceti*, 189.

42  Ibid., 168.

43  Ibid., 168.

44  Ibid., 166.

45  Ibid., 121.

46  Monica Hughes, *The Golden Aquarians* (New York: Simon and Schuster, 1995), 1.

47  Ibid., 20.

48  See chapter 7, p. xx. The Mabo Judgment of the Australian High Court in 1992 rejected the doctrine of *terra nullius.*

49  Brian Caswell, *Deucalion* (St. Lucia: University of Queensland Press, 1995), 24.

50  Ibid., 24.

51  See Claire Smith, *Country, Kin and Culture*, 12–18.

52  Caswell, *Deucalion*, 155.

53  Raffaella Baccolini, "'A useful knowledge of the present is rooted in the past': Memory and Historical Reconciliation in Ursula K. le Guin's *The Telling*," in *Dark Horizons: Science Fiction and the Dystopian Imagination*, ed. R. Baccolini and T. Moylan (New York: Routledge, 2003), 115.

54  Victor Kelleher, *Red Heart* (Ringwood, VIC: Penguin, 2001), 119.

55  Ibid., 139.

56  Ibid., 193.

57  Ibid., 221.

58  Ibid., 206.

59  Ibid., 57.

60  Ibid., 57.

61  Jack Lasenby, *Kalik* (Dunedin, NZ: Longacre Press, 2001), 235.

62  I owe this insight to Margaret Aitken, whose reading of Lasenby's *Taur* alerted me to the connections between the Salt Men and colonial imaginings of Maori cultures.

63  Jack Lasenby, *Because We Were the Travellers* (Dunedin, NZ: Longacre Press, 1997), 127.

64  Jack Lasenby, *The Shaman and the Droll* (Dunedin, NZ: Longacre Press, 1999), 25.

65  Peter Hulme, "Introduction: The Cannibal Scene," in *Cannibalism and the Colonial World*, ed. F. Barker, P. Hulme, and M. Iversen (Cambridge, MA: Cambridge University Press, 1998), 3.

66  Powhiri Wharemarama Rika-Heke, "Margin or Centre? 'Let me tell you! In the Land of my Ancestors I am the Centre': Indigenous Writing in Aotearoa," in *English Postcoloniality: Literatures from Around the World*, ed. R. Mohanram and G. Rajan (Westport, CT: Greenwood Press, 1996), 150.

67  See John Pratt, "Assimilation, Equality, and Sovereignty in New Zealand / Aotearoa: Maori and the Social Welfare and Criminal Justice Systems," in *Indigenous Peoples' Rights in Australia, Canada, and New Zealand*, ed. P. Havemann (Auckland: Oxford University Press, 1999), 316–34.

68  Stephen Turner, "A Legacy of Colonialism: The Uncivil Society of Aotearoa / New Zealand," *Cultural Studies* 13.3 (1999), 419.

**Conclusion** [pp. 225–227]

1  Ghassan Hage, *Against Paranoid Nationalism: Searching for Hope in a Shrinking Society* (Annandale, NSW: Pluto Press, 2003), 48.

2  It should be noted, however, that under the conservative government of John Howard in Australia, Indigenous issues are relegated to the background of political thought, so that children's authors swim against the tide when they address such issues.

3  Williams, Wingfield, and McInerney, *Down the Hole*, 42.

# Bibliography and References

## Children's Texts

Armstrong, Jeannette. *Slash*. Penticton, BC: Theytus, 1985.

———. "Threads of Old Memory." In *Breathtracks*, by J. Armstrong, 58–61. Stratford, ON: Williams-Wallace and Theytus Books, 1991.

Arthy, Judith. *The Children of Mirrabooka*. Ringwood, VIC: Penguin, 1997.

Baillie, Allan. *Songman*. Ringwood, VIC: Penguin, 1994.

Berolah, Lorraine, LilyJane Collins, and Noel Cristaudo. *Betty and Bala and the Proper Big Pumpkin*. St. Lucia: University of Queensland Press, 1996.

Bishop, Gavin. *The House That Jack Built*. Auckland and Sydney: Scholastic, 1999.

Boock, Paula. *Home Run*. Dunedin, NZ: Longacre Press, 1995.

Brooks, Martha. *Bone Dance*. Toronto: Douglas and McIntyre, 1997.

Bruchac, Joseph. *The Arrow over the Door*. New York: Dial, 1998.

———. *Children of the Longhouse*. New York: Penguin, 1996.

———. *Eagle Song*. New York: Dial, 1997.

———. *The Heart of a Chief*. New York: Dial, 1998.

———. "The Hungry One." In *Skins: Contemporary Indigenous Writing*, ed. Kateri Akiwenzie-Damm and Josie Douglas, 65–72. Alice Springs, NT: Jukurrpa Books; Wiarton, ON: Kegedonce Press, 2000.

———. *Skeleton Man*. New York: HarperCollins Publishers, 2001.

Bunting, Eve, and John Sandford. *Moonstick: The Seasons of the Sioux*. New York: Joanna Cotler Books, 1997.

Burks, Brian. *Walks Alone*. San Diego, CA: Harcourt Brace, 1998.

Campbell, Maria. *Halfbreed*. Lincoln: University of Nebraska Press, 1973.

Cannon, A.E. *The Shadow Brothers*. New York: Delacorte Press, 1990.

Caraker, Mary. *The Faces of Ceti*. Boston, MA: Houghton Mifflin, 1991.

Card, Orson Scott. *Red Prophet: The Tales of Alvin Maker*. Vol. 2. London: Arrow Books, 1988.

Caswell, Brian. *Deucalion*. St Lucia: University of Queensland Press, 1995.

Cheney, Lynne, and Robin Preiss Glasser. *America: A Patriotic Primer*. New York and London: Simon and Schuster, 2002.

Choyce, Lesley. *Clearcut Danger*. Halifax, NS: Formac Publishing, 1992.

Clark, Joan. *The Dream Carvers*. Toronto, ON: Penguin, 1995.

Collins, Paul. *The Earthborn*. New York: Tor Books, 2003.

———. *Sneila*. Ringwood, VIC: Penguin, 2003.

Collura, Mary-Ellen Lang. *Winners*. Toronto: Douglas and McIntyre, 1984.

Creech, Sharon. *Walk Two Moons*. New York: HarperCollins Publishers, 1994.

Cuthand, Beth, and Mary Longman. *The Little Duck*. Penticton, BC: Theytus, 1999.

Delaronde, Deborah L., and Gary Chartrand. *Flour Sack Flora*. Winnipeg, MB: Pemmican Publications, 2001.

Dorion, Betty. *Melanie Bluelake's Dream*. Regina, SK: Coteau Books, 1995.

Dorris, Michael. *Guests*. New York: Hyperion, 1994.

———. *Morning Girl*. New York: Hyperion, 1992.

———. *Sees Behind Trees*. New York: Hyperion, 1996.

———. *The Window*. New York: Hyperion, 1997.

Dowd, John. *Ring of Tall Trees*. Vancouver, BC: Raincoast Books, 1992.

Doyle, Brian. *Spud Sweetgrass*. Toronto: Groundwood, 1992.

Durrant, Lynda. *The Beaded Moccasins: The Story of Mary Campbell*. New York: Clarion, 1998.

Edmonds, Yvette. *Yuit*. Toronto: Napoleon Publishing, 1993.

Edwards, Yvonne, and Brenda Day. *Going for Kalta: Hunting for Sleepy Lizards at Yalata*. Alice Springs, NT: IAD Press, 1997.

Erdrich, Louise. *The Birchbark House*. New York: Hyperion Books, 1999.

*E.T. the Extra-Terrestrial.* Dir. Steven Spielberg. Universal, 1982.

Goble, Paul. *Adopted by the Eagles: A Plains Indian Story of Friendship and Treachery*. New York: Simon and Schuster, 1994.

———. *Iktomi and the Boulder: A Plains Indian Story*. New York: Orchard Books, 1988.

———. *Iktomi and the Coyote: A Plains Indian Story*. New York: Orchard Books, 1998.

———. *Iktomi Loses His Eyes: A Plains Indian Story*. New York: Orchard Books, 1999.

———. *The Legend of the White Buffalo Woman*. Washington, DC: National Geographic Society, 1998.

Grace, Patricia, and Kerry Gemmill. *The Trolley*. Auckland: Penguin, 1993.

Grace, Patricia, and Robyn Kahukiwa. *The Kuia and the Spider*. Auckland: Penguin, 1981.

Greene, Gracie, Joe Tramacchi, and Lucile Gill. *Tjarany Roughtail*. Broome, WA: Magabala Books, 1992.

Gwynne, Phillip. *Deadly Unna?* Ringwood, VIC: Penguin, 1998.

———. *Nukkin Ya.* Ringwood, VIC: Penguin, 2000.

Hamel, Joan de. *Take the Long Path.* Auckland: Penguin, 1980.

Hamm, Diane Johnston. *Daughter of Suqua.* Morton Grove, IL: Albert Whitman, 1997.

Heiss, Anita. *Who Am I? The Diary of Mary Talence, Sydney 1937.* Lindfield, NSW: Scholastic, 2001.

Hendry, Frances Mary. *Atlantis.* Oxford, UK: Oxford University Press, 1997.

Highway, Tomson, and Brian Deines. *Caríbou Song: Atíhko Níkamon.* Toronto: HarperCollins, 2001.

Holman, Felice. *Real.* New York: Atheneum, 1997.

Hoover, H.M. *Another Heaven, Another Earth.* London: Methuen, 1983.

Houston, James. *Drifting Snow: An Arctic Search.* Toronto: McClelland and Stewart, 1992.

———. *River Runners: A Tale of Hardship and Bravery.* New York and Toronto: Penguin, 1979.

Hudson, Jan. *Sweetgrass.* Edmonton, AB: Tree Frog Press, 1984.

Hughes, Monica. *The Golden Aquarians.* New York: Simon and Schuster, 1995.

———. *The Guardian of Isis.* Toronto: Tundra Books, 1981.

———. *The Isis Pedlar.* Toronto: Tundra Books, 1982.

———. *The Keeper of the Isis Light.* Toronto: Tundra Books, 1980.

———. *Log Jam.* Toronto: HarperCollins, 1989.

Johnston, Basil H. *Indian School Days.* Toronto: Key Porter Books, 1988.

Katz, Welwyn Wilton. *False Face.* Toronto: Groundwood Books/Douglas and McIntyre, 1987.

Keen, Sally M. *Moon of Two Dark Horses.* New York: Penguin, 1995.

Kelleher, Victor. *Red Heart.* Ringwood, VIC: Penguin, 2001.

Kidd, Diana. *The Fat and Juicy Place.* Pymble, NSW: Angus and Robertson, 1992.

———. *Two Hands Together.* Ringwood, VIC: Penguin, 2000.

King, Thomas, and William Kent Monkman. *A Coyote Columbus Story.* Toronto: Douglas and McIntyre, 1992.

Kusugak, Michael Arvaarluk, and Vladyana Krykorka. *Arctic Stories.* Toronto: Annick Press, 1998.

———. *Hide and Sneak.* Toronto: Annick Press, 1992.

———. *Northern Lights: The Soccer Trails.* Toronto: Annick Press, 1993.

Lasenby, Jack. *Because We Were the Travellers.* Dunedin, NZ: Longacre Press, 1997.

———. *Kalik.* Dunedin, NZ: Longacre Press, 2001.

———. *The Shaman and the Droll.* Dunedin, NZ: Longacre Press, 1999.

———. *Taur.* Dunedin, NZ: Longacre Press, 1998.

Lawrence, Louise. *The Crowlings.* London: Collins, 1999.

Laza, Aidan, and Alick Tipoti. *Kuiyku Mabaigal: Waii and Sobai.* Broome, WA: Magabala Books, 1998.

Little, Jean. *Willow and Twig*. Toronto, ON: Penguin, 2000.

Littlechild, George. *This Land Is My Land*. Emeryville, CA: Children's Book Press, 1993.

Lowe, Pat. *Feeling the Heat*. Camberwell, VIC: Penguin, 2002.

———. *The Girl with No Name*. Ringwood, VIC: Penguin, 1994.

Lowe, Pat, and Jimmy Pike. *Desert Cowboy*. Broome, Western Australia: Magabala Books, 2000.

———. *Jilji: Life in the Great Sandy Desert*. Broome, Western Australia: Magabala Books, 1990.

Lucashenko, Melissa. *Killing Darcy*. St. Lucia: University of Queensland Press, 1998.

———. *Too Flash*. Alice Springs, NT: IAD Press, 2002.

Lunn, Janet. *Shadow in Hawthorn Bay*. Toronto: Lester and Orpen Dennys, 1986.

McDonald, Meme, and Boori Monty Pryor. *The Binna Binna Man*. St. Leonards, NSW: Allen and Unwin, 1999.

———. *My Girragundji*. St. Leonards, NSW: Allen and Unwin, 1998.

———. *Njunjul the Sun*. Crows Nest, NSW: Allen and Unwin, 2002.

Mahy, Margaret. *Aliens in the Family*. London, UK: Methuen, 1986.

Major, Kevin. *Blood Red Ochre*. New York: Dell Publishing, 1989.

Maracle, Lee. *Will's Garden*. Penticton, BC: Theytus Books, 2002.

Matcheck, Diane. *The Sacrifice*. New York: Farrar, Straus and Giroux, 1998.

McKinnon, Kingi. *When the Kehua Calls*. Auckland: Scholastic, 2002.

Mikaelson, Ben. *Touching Spirit Bear*. New York: HarperCollins, 2001.

Moloney, James. *Dougy*. St. Lucia: University of Queensland Press, 1993.

———. *Gracey*. St. Lucia: University of Queensland Press, 1994.

Mosionier, Beatrice Culleton. *In Search of April Raintree*. Critical ed. Ed. Cheryl Suzack. Winnipeg, MB: Peguis, 1999.

Murray, Bonnie, and Sheldon Dawson. *Li Minoush*. Trans. Rita Flamand. Winnipeg, MB: Pemmican, 2001.

Neidjie, Bill. *Story about Feeling*. Broome, Western Australia: Magabala, 1989.

O'Dell, Scott. *Black Star, Bright Dawn*. Boston, MA: Houghton Mifflin, 1998.

Orman, Lorraine. *Cross Tides*. Dunedin, NZ: Longacre Press, 2004.

Orwin, Joanna. *Ihaka and the Prophecy*. Auckland: Oxford University Press, 1984.

———. *Owl*. Dunedin, NZ: Longacre Press, 2001.

*Papunya School Book of Country and History*. Crows Nest, NSW: Allen and Unwin, 2001.

Paulsen, Gary. *Canyons*. New York: Dell Publishing, 1990.

*Pocahontas*. Dir. Mike Gabriel and Eric Goldberg. Disney, 1995.

Price, Susan. *The Sterkam Handshake*. London: HarperCollins, 1998.

Qualey, Marsha. *Revolutions of the Heart*. New York: Houghton Mifflin, 1993.

*The Rabbit-Proof Fence*. Dir. Phillip Noyce. Miramax, 2002.

Randall, Bob, and Kunyi June-Anne McInerney. *Tracker Tjuĝingji*. Alice Springs, NT: IAD Press, 2003.

Rubinstein, Gillian. *Beyond the Labyrinth*. South Yarra, VIC: Hyland House, 1988.

Russell, Elaine. *A Is for Aunty*. Sydney, NSW: ABC Books, 2000.

Sadler, Marilyn. *Alistair and the Alien Invasion*. New York: Simon and Schuster, 1994.

Santiago, Chiori, and Judith Lowry. *Home to Medicine Mountain*. San Francisco, CA: Children's Book Press, 1998.

Sargent, Pamela. *Earthseed*. London: HarperCollins, 1983.

Savage, Deborah. *Flight of the Albatross*. New York: Houghton Mifflin, 1989.

Say, Allen. *Home of the Brave*. New York: Houghton Mifflin, 2002.

Scott, Ann Herbert. *Brave as a Mountain Lion*. New York: Clarion Books, 1996.

Silvey, Diane. *Raven's Flight*. Vancouver, BC: Raincoast Books, 2000.

Slapin, Beverly, and Annie Esposito. *10 Little White People: A Counting Rhyme*. Berkeley, CA: Oyata, 1995.

———. *Basic Skills: Caucasion Americans Workbook*. Berkeley, CA: Oyata, 1994.

Slipperjack, Ruby. *Honour the Sun*. Winnipeg, MB: Pemmican, 1987.

Smith, Cynthia Leitich. *Indian Shoes*. New York: HarperCollins, 2002.

———. *Rain Is Not My Indian Name*. New York: HarperCollins, 2001.

Smith, Cynthia Leitich, Cornelius Van Wright, and Ying-Hwa Hu. *Jingle Dancer*. New York: William Morrow, 2000.

Spalding, Andrea. *Finders Keepers*. Vancouver, BC: Beach Holme Publishing, 1995.

Speare, Elizabeth George. *The Sign of the Beaver*. New York: Dell Publishing, 1983.

Sterling, Shirley. *My Name Is Seepeetza*. Toronto: Douglas and McIntyre, 1992.

Strete, Craig Kee. *The World in Grandfather's Hands*. New York: Clarion Books, 1995.

Strete, Craig Kee, Michelle Netten Chacon, and Francisco X. Mora. *How the Indians Bought the Farm*. New York: Greenwillow Books, 1996.

Taylor, William. *Beth and Bruno*. Auckland: Ashton Scholastic, 1992.

Tipene, Tim. *Kura Toa: Warrior School*. Auckland: Reed Publishing, 2004.

Tipene, Tim, and Henry Campbell. *Taming the Taniwha*. Auckland: Reed Publishing, 2001.

Turner, Ann. *The Girl Who Chased away Sorrow: The Diary of Sarah Nita, a Navajo Girl*. New York: Scholastic, 1999.

Utemorrah, Daisy, and Pat Torres. *Do Not Go Around the Edges*. Broome, Western Australia: Magabala Books, 1990.

Vanasse, Deb. *A Distant Enemy*. New York: Lodestar Books/Dutton, 1997.

Waboose, Jan Bourdeau, and Halina Below. *Where Only the Elders Go: Moon Lake Loon Lake*. Manotick, ON: Penumbra Press, 1994.

Wagamese, Richard. *Keeper'n Me*. Toronto: Doubleday, 1994.

Ward, Glenyse. *Unna Ya Fullas*. Broome, Western Australia: Magabala Books, 1991.

———. *Wandering Girl*. Broome, Western Australia: Magabala Books, 1988.

Williams, Edna Tantjingu, Eileen Wani Wingfield, and Kunyi June-Anne McInerney. *Down the Hole, Up the Tree, Across the Sandhills ... Running from the State and Daisy Bates*. Alice Springs, NT: IAD Press, 2000.

Wrightson, Patricia. *Behind the Wind*. London: Hutchinson, 1981.
———. *The Dark Bright Water*. London: Hutchinson, 1979.
———. *The Ice Is Coming*. London: Hutchinson, 1977.

## References

Addison-Smith, Helen. "E.T. Go Home: Indigeneity, Multiculturalism and 'Homeland' in Contemporary Science Fiction." *Papers: Explorations into Children's Literature* 15.1 (2005): 27–35.

Alcoff, Linda. "The Problem of Speaking for Others." *Cultural Critique* 20 (Winter 1991–92): 5–32.

Aldred, Lisa. "Plastic Shamans and Astroturf Sun Dances: New Age Commercialization of Native American Spirituality." *American Indian Quarterly* 24.3 (2000): 329–53.

Allen, Chadwick. *Blood Narrative: Indigenous Identity in American Indian and Maori Literary and Activist Texts*. Durham and London: Duke University Press, 2002.

———. "Postcolonial Theory and the Discourse of Treaties." *American Quarterly* 52.1 (2000): 59–89.

Althusser, Louis. *Essays on Ideology*. London: Verso, 1984.

Anderson, Ian. "Black Bit, White Bit." In *Blacklines: Contemporary Critical Writing by Indigenous Australians*, ed. Michele Grossman, introd. Ian Anderson, Michele Grossman, Marcia Langton, and Aileen Moreton-Robinson, 43–51. Carlton, VIC: Melbourne University Press, 2003.

Althusser, Louis. *Essays on Ideology*. London: Verso, 1984.

Ashcroft, Bill. *Post-Colonial Transformation*. London and New York: Routledge, 2001.

Ashcroft, Bill, Gareth Griffiths, and Helen Tiffin. *The Empire Writes Back: Theory and Practice in Post-Colonial Literatures*. London and New York: Routledge, 1989.

———. *Post-Colonial Studies: The Key Concepts*. London and New York: Routledge, 2000.

Baccolini, Raffaella, "'A useful knowledge of the present is rooted in the past': Memory and Historical Reconciliation in Ursula K. le Guin's *The Telling*." In *Dark Horizons: Science Fiction and the Dystopian Imagination*, ed. Raffaella Baccolini and Tom Moylan, 113–34. New York: Routledge, 2003.

Bainbridge, Joyce, and Brenda Wolodko. "Canadian Picture Books: Shaping and Reflecting National Identity." *Bookbird* 40.2 (2002): 21–27.

Bartlett, Richard H. "Native Title in Australia: Denial, Recognition, and Dispossession." In *Indigenous Peoples' Rights in Australia, Canada, and New Zealand*, ed. Paul Havemann, 408–27. Oxford, UK: Oxford University Press, 1999.

Batty, Nancy, and Robert Markley. "Writing Back: Speculative Fiction and the Politics of Postcolonialism, 2001." *Ariel* 33.1 (2002): 5–14.

Berg, Charles Ramirez. "Immigrants, Aliens, and Extraterrestrials: Science Fiction's Alien 'Other' as (Among *Other* Things) New Hispanic Imagery." *CineAction* 18 (Fall 1989): 3–17.

Bhabha, Homi. "Introduction: Locations of Culture." In *The Location of Culture*, 85–92. London and New York: Routledge, 1994.

———. "Of Mimicry and Man: The Ambivalence of Colonial Discourse." In *The Location of Culture*, by H. Bhabha, 85–92. London and New York: Routledge, 1994.

———. "The Other Question: Stereotype, Discrimination and the Discourse of Colonialism." In *The Location of Culture*, 66–84. London and New York: Routledge, 1994.

———. "The World and the Home." In *Dangerous Liaisons: Gender, Nation, and Postcolonial Perspectives*, ed. Anne McClintock, Aamir Mufti, and Ella Shohat, 445–55. Minneapolis and London: University of Minnesota Press, 1997.

Bird, S. Elizabeth. "Introduction: Constructing the Indian, 1830s–1990s." In *Dressing in Feathers: The Construction of the Indian in American Popular Culture*, ed. S. Elizabeth Bird, 1–12. New York: Westview Press, 1996.

Bourdieu, Pierre. *Outline of a Theory of Practice*. Cambridge and London: Cambridge University Press, 1977.

———. *Sociology in Question*. London: Sage Publications, 1993.

Bradford, Clare. "The End of Empire? Colonial and Postcolonial Journeys in Children's Books." *Children's Literature* 29 (2001): 196–218.

———. "'Oh, How Different!: Authorship, Ownership and Authority in Aboriginal Textuality for Children." *Lion and the Unicorn* 27.2 (2003): 199–217.

———. "Performances of Colour: Narratives of Passing in Settler Society Texts." In *Seriously Playful: Genre, Performance and Text*, ed. K. Mallan and S. Pearce, 77–84. Flaxton, QLD: Post Pressed, 2004.

———. "The Picture Book: Some Postmodern Tensions." *Papers: Explorations into Children's Literature* 4.3 (1993): 10–14.

———. *Reading Race: Aboriginality in Australian Children's Literature*. Carlton South, VIC: Melbourne University Press, 2001.

———. "Transformative Fictions: Postcolonial Encounters in Australian Texts." *Children's Literature Association Quarterly* 28.4 (2003–2004): 195–202.

Bruchac, Joseph. "Storytelling and the Sacred: On the Uses of Native American Stories." In *Through Indian Eyes: The Native Experience in Books for Children*, ed. Beverly Slapin and Doris Seale, 64–69. Berkeley, CA: Oyate, 1998.

Brydon, Diana. "The White Inuit Speaks: Contamination as Literary Strategy." In *Past the Last Post: Theorizing Post-Colonialism and Post-Modernism*, ed. Ian Adam and Helen Tiffin, 191–203. Hemel Hempstead, UK: Harvester Wheatsheaf, 1991.

Burton, Antoinette, ed. *After the Imperial Turn: Thinking With and Through the Nation*. Durham and London: Duke University Press, 2003.

Campbell, Joseph. *The Hero with a Thousand Faces*. 1949. London: Abacus, 1975.

Carter, Paul. *The Road to Botany Bay: An Essay in Spatial History*. London and Boston: Faber and Faber, 1987.

Castle, Kathryn. *Britannia's Children: Reading Colonisation Through Children's Books and Magazines*. Manchester: Manchester University Press, 1996.

Chakravarty, Dipesh. "Postcoloniality and the Artifice of History: Who Speaks for 'Indian' Pasts?" *Representations* 32 (Winter 1992): 1–26.

Claes, Rhonda, and Deborah Clifton. "Institutional Child Abuse: Needs and Expectations for Redress of Victims of Abuse at Native Residential Schools." Law Commission of Canada/Commission du droit du Canada, http://www.lcc.gc.ca/research_project/98child_abuse-en.asp (20 June 2005).

Clifford, James. *Routes: Travel and Translation in the Late Twentieth Century*. Cambridge, MA, and London: Harvard University Press, 1997.

Coates, Ken. "The 'Gentle' Occupation: The Settlement of Canada and the Dispossession of the First Nations." In *Indigenous Peoples' Rights in Australia, Canada, and New Zealand*, ed. Paul Havemann, 141–61. Toronto, ON: Oxford University Press, 1992.

Coombe, Rosemary J. *The Cultural Life of Intellectual Properties: Authorship, Appropriation and the Law*. New York: Routledge, Chapman and Hall, 1998.

Cumming, Peter. "'The Only Dirty Book': The Rape of April Raintree." In *In Search of April Raintree*, by Beatrice Culleton Mosionier, critical ed., Cheryl Suzack, 307–22. Winnipeg, MB: Peguis, 1999.

Curtis, Edward S. Library of Congress. *Edward S. Curtis's The North American Indian: Photographic Images*. Item 3 of 40. *American Memory*. Library of Congress, http://memory.loc.gov/cgi-bin/query/D?curt:3:./temp/~a mmem)_rjoi:: (accessed 3 April 2007).

Deloria, Vine. "Ethnoscience and Indian Realities." In *Spirit and Reason: The Vine Deloria, Jr., Reader*, ed. B. Deloria, K. Foehner, and S. Scinta, 63–71. Golden, CO: Fulcrum Publishing, 1999.

Dening, Greg. *Mr Bligh's Bad Language: Passion, Power and Theatre on the Bounty*. Cambridge and New York: Cambridge University Press, 1992.

DePasquale, Paul, and Doris Wolf. "Home and Native Land: A Study of Canadian Aboriginal Picture Books by Aboriginal Authors." In *Home Words: Discourses of Children's Literature in Canada*, ed. Mavis Reimer. Waterloo, ON: Wilfrid Laurier University Press, forthcoming.

———. "A Select Bibliography of Canadian Picture Books for Children by Aboriginal Writers." *Canadian Children's Literature* 115/116 (2004): 44–59.

Dickason, Olive Patricia. *Canada's First Nations: A History of Founding People from Earliest Times*. Don Mills, ON: Oxford University Press, 2002.

Docker, John, and Gerhard Fischer, eds. *Race, Colour and Identity in Australia and New Zealand*. Sydney, NSW: University of New South Wales Press, 2000.

Dodson, Michael. "The End in the Beginning: Re(de)finding Aboriginality." In *Blacklines: Contemporary Critical Writing by Indigenous Australians*, ed. Michele Grossman, introd. Ian Anderson, Michele Grossman, Marcia

Langton, and Aileen Moreton-Robinson, 25–42. Carlton, VIC: Melbourne University Press, 2003.

Fabian, Johannes. *Time and the Other: How Anthropology Makes Its Object.* New York: Columbia University Press, 1983.

Fee, Margery. "Deploying Identity in the Face of Racism." In *In Search of April Raintree*, critical ed., by Beatrice Culleton Mosionier, ed. Cheryl Suzack, 211–26. Winnipeg, MB: Peguis, 1999.

Fiske, John, Bob Hodge, and Graeme Turner. *Myths of Oz: Reading Australian Popular Culture.* Sydney, NSW: Allen and Unwin, 1987.

Fleras, Augie. "Politicising Indigeneity: Ethno-Politics in White Settler Dominions." In *Indigenous Peoples' Rights in Australia, Canada, and New Zealand*, ed. Paul Havemann, 191–92. Toronto: Oxford University Press, 1992.

Fleras, Augie, and Jean Leonard Elliott. *The "Nations Within": Aboriginal–State Relations in Canada, the United States, and New Zealand.* Toronto: Oxford University Press, 1992.

Foucault, Michel. *Discipline and Punish: The Birth of the Prison.* Trans. Alan Sheridan. Harmondsworth, UK: Penguin, 1979.

———. *Power/Knowledge: Selected Interviews and Other Writings, 1972–1977.* Brighton, UK: Harvest Press, 1980.

———. "Questions on Geography." In *Power/Knowledge: Selected Interviews and Other Writings, 1972–1977*, 63–77. Brighton, UK: Harvester Press, 1980.

———. *This Is Not a Pipe.* Trans. and ed. James Harkness. Berkeley: University of California Press, 1982.

Francis, Daniel. *The Imaginary Indian: The Image of the Indian in Canadian Culture.* Vancouver, BC: Arsenal Pulp Press, 1997.

Gandhi, Leela. *Postcolonial Theory: A Critical Introduction.* St. Leonards, NSW: Allen and Unwin, 1998.

Giddens, Anthony. *The Consequences of Modernity.* Cambridge: Polity Press, 1990.

Glissant, Edouard. *Caribbean Discourse: Selected Essays.* Charlottesville: University Press of Virginia, 1989.

Goble, Paul. *Hau Kola—Hello Friend.* Katonah, NY: Richard C. Owen, 1994.

Gordon, Joan, "Utopia, Genocide and the Other." In *Edging into the Future: Science Fiction and Contemporary Cultural Transformation*, ed. Veronica Hollinger and Joan Gordon, 204–16. Philadelphia: University of Pennsylvania Press, 2002.

Griffiths, Tom, and Libby Robin, eds. *Ecology and Empire: Environmental History of Settler Societies.* Edinburgh: Keele University Press, 1997.

Grossman, Michele, ed. *Blacklines: Contemporary Critical Writing by Indigenous Australians.* Introd. Ian Anderson, Michele Grossman, Marcia Langton, and Aileen Moreton-Robinson. Carlton, VIC: Melbourne University Press, 2003.

Hall, Stuart. "The Local and the Global: Globalization and Ethnicity." In *Dan-*

*gerous Liaisons: Gender, Nation, and Postcolonial Perspectives*, ed. Anne McClintock, Aamir Mufti, and Ella Shohat, 173–87. Minneapolis: University of Minnesota Press, 1997.

Harvey, David. *Justice, Nature and the Geography of Difference*. Massachusetts and Oxford: Blackwell, 1996.

Havemann, Paul, "Indigenous Peoples, the State and the Challenge of Differentiated Citizenship." In *Indigenous Peoples' Rights in Australia, Canada, and New Zealand*, ed. P. Havemann, 468–75. Oxford, UK: Oxford University Press, 1999.

Heiss, Anita M. *Dhuuluu-Yala To Talk Straight: Publishing Indigenous Literature*. Canberra: Aboriginal Studies Press, 2003.

Hokari, Minoru. "Images of Australian Colonialism: Interpretations of the Colonial Landscape by an Aboriginal Historian." *Senri Ethnological Studies* 60 (2002): 153–69.

———. "Localised History: 'Dangerous' Histories from the Gurindji Country." *Locality* (Autumn 2002): 4–7.

———. "Maintaining History: The Gurindji People's 'Truthful Histories.'" *Cultural Survival Quarterly* 26.2 (2002), http://www.culturalsurvival.org/publications/csq.

Hoy, Helen. "'Nothing but the Truth': Discursive Transparency in Beatrice Culleton." In *In Search of April Raintree*, critical ed., by Beatrice Culleton Mosionier, ed. Cheryl Suzack, 273–93. Winnipeg, MB: Peguis, 1999.

Huggan, Graham. *Territorial Disputes: Maps and Mapping Strategies in Contemporary Canadian and Australian Fiction*. Toronto and London: University of Toronto Press, 1994.

Hulme, Peter. "Including America," *Ariel* 26.1 (1995): 117–20.

———. "Introduction: The Cannibal Scene." In *Cannibalism and the Colonial World*, ed. F. Barker, Peter Hulme, and M. Iversen, 1–38. Cambridge, UK: Cambridge University Press, 1998.

Jacobs, Jane. "Resisting Reconciliation: The Secret Geographies of (Post)colonial Australia." In *Geographies of Resistance*, ed. Steve Pile and Michael Keith, 203–18. London: Routledge, 1997.

Janiewski, Dolores. "Gendering, Racializing and Classifying: Settler Colonization in the United States, 1590–1990." In *Unsettling Settler Societies: Articulations of Gender, Race, Ethnicity and Class*, ed. Daiva Stasiulis and Nira Yuval-Davis, 132–60. London: Sage Publications, 1995.

Khorana, Meena, ed. *Critical Perspectives on Postcolonial African Children's and Young Adult Literature*. Westport, CT, and London: Greenwood Press, 1998.

King, Thomas. *The Truth about Stories: A Native Narrative*. Toronto: House of Anansi Press, 2003.

Knights, Pamela. "England's Dark Ages? The North-East in Robert Westall's *The Wind Eye* and Andrew Taylor's *The Coal House*." In *The Presence of the*

*Past in Children's Literature*, ed. Ann Lawson Lucas, 167–75. Westport, CT: Greenwood, 2003.

Lacan, Jacques. *Ecrits: A Selection*. Translated by Bruce Fink with Heloise Fink and Russell Grigg. New York: W.W. Norton, 2002.

Langton, Marcia. *"Well, I heard it on the radio and I saw it on the television …": An Essay for the Australian Film Commission on the Politics and Aesthetics of Filmmaking by and about Aboriginal People and Things*. Woolloomooloo, NSW: Australian Film Commission, 1993.

Larner, Wendy, and Spoonley, Paul. "Post-Colonial Politics in Aotearoa/New Zealand." In *Unsettling Settler Societies: Articulations of Gender, Race, Ethnicity and Class*, ed. Daiva Stasiulis and Nira Yuval-Davis, 39–64. London: Sage Publications, 1995.

LaRocque, Emma. "Preface, or Here Are Our Voices—Who Will Hear?" In *Writing the Circle: Native Women of Western Canada* , ed. Jeanne Perreault and Sylvia Vance, xv–xxx. Edmonton, AB: NeWest Publishers, 1990.

Lawrence, Bonita. *"Real" Indians and Others: Mixed-Blood Urban Native Peoples and Indigenous Nationhood*. Vancouver and Toronto: University of British Columbia Press, 2004.

Levy, Michael M. "Editor's Introduction II: Boys and Science Fiction." *Lion and the Unicorn* 28.2 (2004): ix–xi.

Linton, Patricia. "Ethical Reading and Resistant Texts." In *Post-Colonial Literatures: Expanding the Canon*, ed. Deborah L. Madsen, 29–44. London: Pluto Press, 1999.

Lipschutz, Ronnie D. "Aliens, Alien Nations, and Alienation in American Political Economy and Popular Culture." In *To Seek Out New Worlds: Exploring Links Between Science Fiction and World Politics*, ed. Jutta Weldes, 79–98. New York: Palgrave Macmillan, 2003.

MacCann, Donnarae, ed. "Anti-Racism and Children's Literature." Special issue, *Lion and the Unicorn* 25.3 (2001): 337–52.

———. "Editor's Introduction: Racism and Antiracism: Forty Years of Theories and Debates." *Lion and the Unicorn* 25.3 (2001): 337–52.

Macdonald, Andrew, Gina Macdonald, and Mary Ann Sheridan. *Shape-Shifting: Images of Native Americans in Recent Popular Fiction*. Westport, CT: Greenwood Press, 2000.

Madsen, Deborah L. "Beyond the Commonwealth: Post-Colonialism and American Literature." In *Post-Colonial Literatures: Expanding the Canon*, ed. Deborah L. Madsen. 1–13. London: Pluto Press, 1999.

Manning, Erin. *Ephemeral Territories: Representing Nation, Home, and Identity in Canada*. Minneapolis and London: University of Minnesota Press, 2003.

———. "I Am Canadian: Identity, Territory and the Canadian National Landscape." *Theory and Event* 4.4 (2000): 1–24.

Marshall, Ingeborg. *A History and Ethnography of the Beothuk*. Montreal and Kingston, ON: McGill-Queen's University Press, 1996.

Marotta, Vince, "The Ambivalence of Borders: The Bicultural and the Multi-cultural." In *Race, Colour and Identity in Australia and New Zealand*, ed. J. Docker and G. Fishcher, 177–89. Sydney: University of New South Wales Press, 2000.

Massey, Doreen. *Space, Place and Gender*. Cambridge, UK: Polity Press, 1994.

———. "Travelling Thoughts." In *Without Guarantees: In Honour of Stuart Hall*, ed. P. King, L. Grossberg, and A. McRobbie, 225–32. London and New York: Verso, 2000.

McCallum, Robyn. *Ideologies of Identity in Adolescent Fiction*. New York and London: Garland, 1999.

———. "Very Advanced Texts: Metafictions and Experimental Work." In *Understanding Children's Literature*, ed. Peter Hunt, 138–50. London and New York: Routledge, 1999.McDougall, Russell, and Gillian Whitlock, eds. *Australian/Canadian Literatures in English: Comparative Perspectives*. North Ryde, NSW: Methuen, 1987.

McClintock, Anne. *Imperial Leather: Race, Gender and Sexuality in the Colonial Contest*. New York: Routledge, 1995.

McDougall, Russell, and Gillian Whitlock, eds. *Australian/Canadian Literatures in English: Comparative Perspectives*. North Ryde, NSW: Methuen, 1987.

McGillis, Roderick. "'And the Celt Knew the Indian': Knowingness, Postcolonialism, Children's Literature." In *Voices of the Other: Children's Literature and the Postcolonial Context*, ed. R. McGillis, 223–35. New York: Garland, 1999.

———, ed. *Voices of the Other: Children's Literature and the Postcolonial Context*. New York and London: Garland Publishing, 1999.

———, and Meena Khorana, eds. "Postcolonial/Postindependence Perspective: Children's and Young Adult Literature." Special issue, *Ariel* 28.1 (1997).

McKay, Graham. *The Land Still Speaks*. Canberra: Australian Government Publishing Service, 1996.

McLeod, Neal. "Coming Home Through Stories." In *(Ad)dressing Our Words: Aboriginal Perspectives on Aboriginal Literature*, ed. Armand Garnet Ruffo, 17–36. Penticton, BC: Theytus, 2001.

McNickle, Darcy. *They Came Here First: The Epic of the American Indian*. Philadelphia, PA: J.B. Lippincott, 1949.

Mills, Sara. *Discourses of Difference: An Analysis of Women's Travel Writing and Colonialism*. London and New York: Routledge, 1991.

Moylan, Tom, "'The moment is here ... and it's important': State, Agency, and Dystopia in Kim Stanley Robinson's *Antarctica* and Ursula K. Le Guin's *The Telling*." In *Dark Horizons: Science Fiction and the Dystopian Imagination*, ed. Raffaella Baccolini and Tom Moylan, 135–54. New York: Routledge, 2003.

Mudrooroo. *The Indigenous Literature of Australia: Milli Milli Wangka*. South Melbourne, VIC: Hyland House, 1997.

Muecke, Stephen. Introduction. In *Gularabulu: Stories from the West Kimberley*, by Paddy Roe, ed. Stephen Muecke, i–ix. Fremantle, Western Australia: Fremantle Arts Centre Press, 1983.

———. *Textual Spaces: Aboriginality and Cultural Studies*. Kensington: New South Wales University Press, 1992.

Nabokov, Peter. *A Forest of Time: American Indian Ways of History*. Cambridge and New York: Cambridge University Press, 2002.

New, W.H. "Colonial Literatures." In *New National and Post-Colonial Literatures: An Introduction*, ed. B. King, 102–19. Oxford, UK: Oxford University Press, 1996.

Ngugi wa Thiong'o. *Decolonising the Mind: The Politics of Language in African Literature*. London: James Currey, 1986.

Nodelman, Perry. "At Home on Native Land: A Non-Aboriginal Canadian Scholar Discusses Aboriginality and Property in Canadian Double-Focalized Novels for Young Adults." In *Home Words: Discourses of Children's Literature in Canada*, ed. Mavis Reimer. Waterloo, ON: Wilfrid Laurier University Press, forthcoming.

———. "Focalisation and Property in Canadian Novels about Meetings Between European and Aboriginal Young People." Paper delivered at the biennial conference of the Australasian Children's Literature Association for Research, University of Technology, Sydney, NSW, 16–17 July 2004.

———. "The Other: Orientalism, Colonialism, and Children's Literature." *Children's Literature Association Quarterly* 17.1 (1992): 29–35.

O'Brien, Susie. "The Place of America in an Era of Postcolonial Imperialism." *Ariel* 29.2 (1998): 159–83.

Ono, Kent A., and Derek T. Buescher. "Deciphering Pocahontas: Unpackaging the Commodification of a Native American Woman." *Critical Studies in Media Communication* 18.1 (2001): 23–43.

Pearson, David. *The Politics of Ethnicity in Settler Societies: States of Unease*. Basingstoke, Hampshire, UK: Palgrave, 2001.

Perkins, Hetti. "Seeing and Seaming: Contemporary Aboriginal Art." In *Blacklines: Contemporary Critical Writing by Indigenous Australians*, ed. Michele Grossman, introd. Ian Anderson, Michele Grossman, Marcia Langton, and Aileen Moreton-Robinson, 97–103. Carlton, VIC: Melbourne University Press, 2003.

Pound, Francis. *The Space Between: Pakeha Use of Maori Motifs in Modernist New Zealand Art*. Auckland: Workshop Press, 1994.

Pratt, John. "Assimilation, Equality, and Sovereignty in New Zealand/Aotearoa: Maori and the Social Welfare and Criminal Justice Systems." In *Indigenous Peoples' Rights in Australia, Canada, and New Zealand*, ed. Paul Havemann, 316–34. Auckland: Oxford University Press, 1999.

Pratt, Mary Louise. *Imperial Eyes: Travel Writing and Transculturation*. Routledge: London and New York, 1992.

Racette, Sherry Farrell. "Beads, Silk and Quills: The Clothing and Decorative Arts of the Metis." In *Metis Legacy*, ed. Lawrence J. Barkwell, Leah Dorion, and Darren R. Préfontaine, 181–88. Winnipeg, MB: Pemmican Publications, 2001.

Reese, Debbie. "'Mom, Look! It's George, and He's a TV Indian!'" *Horn Book Magazine* 74 (1998): 636–43.

Reimer, Mavis. "Homing and Unhoming: The Ideological Work of Canadian Children's Literature." In *Home Words: Discourses of Children's Literature in Canada*, ed. Mavis Reimer. Waterloo, ON: Wilfrid Laurier University Press, forthcoming.

Richards, Jeffrey, ed. *Imperialism and Juvenile Literature*. Manchester, UK: Manchester University Press, 1989.

Rice, Julian. *Black Elk's Story: Distinguishing Its Lakota Purpose*. Albuquerque: University of New Mexico Press, 1991.

Rika-Heke, Powhiri Wharemarama, "Margin or Centre? 'Let me tell you! In the Land of my Ancestors I am the Centre': Indigenous Writing in Aotearoa." In *English Postcoloniality: Literatures from Around the World*, ed. R. Mohanram and G. Rajan, 147–64. Westport, CT, and London: Greenwood Press, 1996.

Ritchie, James. *Becoming Bicultural*. Wellington, NZ: Huia Publishers, 1992.

Root, Deborah. "'White Indians': Appropriation and the Politics of Display." In *Borrowed Power: Essays on Cultural Appropriation*, ed. Bruce Ziff and Pratima V. Rao, 225–33. New Brunswick, NJ: Rutgers University Press, 1997.

Rorty, Richard. *Contingency, Irony, and Solidarity*. Cambridge and New York: Cambridge University Press, 1989.

Rosaldo, Renato. *Culture and Truth: The Remaking of Social Analysis*. Boston, MA: Beacon Press, 1993.

Rose, Deborah Bird. *Dingo Makes Us Human: Life and Land in an Australian Aboriginal Culture*. Cambridge and New York: Cambridge University Press, 2000.

———. "The Year Zero and the North Australian Frontier." In *Tracking Knowledge in North Australian Landscapes: Studies in Indigenous and Settler Ecological Knowledge Systems*, ed. Deborah Bird Rose and Anne Clarke, 19–35. Casuarina, NT: North Australian Research Unit, ANU, 1997.

Rose, Deborah Bird, and Anne Clarke, eds. *Tracking Knowledge in North Australian Landscapes: Studies in Indigenous and Settler Ecological Knowledge Systems*. Casuarina, NT: North Australian Research Unit, ANU, 1997.

Russell, Lynette, ed. *Colonial Frontiers: Indigenous–European Encounters in Settler Societies*. Manchester and New York: Manchester University Press, 2001.

Said, Edward. *Orientalism: Western Conceptions of the Orient*. New York: Pantheon Books, 1978.

Saxby, Maurice. *The Proof of the Puddin': Australian Children's Literature, 1970–1990*. Sydney, NSW: Ashton Scholastic, 1993.

Seale, Doris. "Parting Words: The Works of Paul Goble." *MultiCultural Review* 10 (March 2001): 119–20.

Seed, Patricia. *American Pentimento: The Invention of Indians and the Pursuit of Riches*. Minneapolis: University of Minnesota Press, 2001.

Sharkey, Betsy. "Beyond Teepees and Totem Poles." Rev. of *Pocahontas*. *New York Times*, 11 June 1995: sec. 2.1, 22.

Slemon, Stephen. "Monuments of Empire: Allegory/Counter-Discourse/Post-Colonial Writing." *Kunapipi* 9.3 (1987): 1–16.

———. "Post-Colonial Critical Theories." In *New National and Post-Colonial Literatures: An Introduction*, ed. B. King, 178–97. Oxford, UK: Clarendon Press, 1996.

———. "Unsettling the Empire: Resistance Theory for the Second World." In *The Post-Colonial Studies Reader*, ed. Bill Ashcroft, Gareth Griffiths, and Helen Tiffin, 104–10. London: Routledge, 1995.

Smith, Claire. *Country, Kin and Culture: Survival of an Australian Aboriginal Community*. Kent Town, SA: Wakefield Press, 2004.

Smith, Cynthia Leitich. "A Different Drum: Native American Writing." *Horn Book Magazine* 78 (2002): 409–12.

Smith, Linda Tuhiwai. *Decolonizing Methodologies: Research and Indigenous Peoples*. Dunedin, NZ: University of Otago Press, 1999.

Sobchack, Vivian, "Postmodern Modes of Ethnicity." In *Postmodern After-Images: A Reader in Film, Television and Video*, ed. Peter Brooker and Will Brooker, 112–28. London, UK: Arnold, 1997.

———. *Screening Space: The American Science Fiction Film*. 2nd ed. New Brunswick, NJ: Rutgers University Press, 1997.

Societas Internationalis Limnologiae (SIL). "Ethnologue: Languages of the World." http://www.ethnologue.com (accessed 3 April 2007).

Soja, Edward W. *Postmodern Geographies: The Reassertion of Space in Critical Social Theory*. London and New York: Verso, 1989.

Spivak, Gayatri Chakravorty. "Can the Subaltern Speak?" In *Colonial Discourse and Postcolonial Theory: A Reader*, ed. P. Williams and L. Chrisman, 66–111. Hemel Hempstead, UK: Harvester Wheatsheaf, 1985.

Stasiulis, Daiva, and Nira Yuval-Davis, eds. *Unsettling Settler Societies: Articulations of Gender, Race, Ethnicity and Class*. London: Sage Publications, 1995.

Stephens, John. "Gender, Genre and Children's Literature." *Signal* 79 (1996): 17–30.

———. *Language and Ideology in Children's Fiction*. London and New York: Longman, 1992.

Stephens, John, and Robyn McCallum. *Retelling Stories, Framing Culture: Traditional Story and Metanarratives in Children's Literature*. New York: Garland Publishing, 1998.

Stewart, Michelle Pagni. "Judging Authors by the Color of Their Skin? Quality Native American Children's Literature." *Melus* 27.2 (2002): 179–96.

Stott, Jon C. *Native Americans in Children's Literature.* Phoenix, AZ: Oryx Press. 1995.

Strong, Pauline Turner. "Animated Indians: Critique and Contradiction in Commodified Children's Culture." *Cultural Anthropology* 11.3 (1996): 405–24.

Suvin, Darko. *Metamorphoses of Science Fiction: On the Poetics and History of a Literary Genre.* New Haven, CT: Yale University Press, 1979.

Terdiman, Richard. *Discourse/Counter-Discourse: The Theory and Practice of Symbolic Resistance in Nineteenth-Century France.* Ithaca and London: Cornell University Press, 1985.

Thompson, Melissa Kay. "A Sea of Good Intentions: Native Americans in Books for Children." *Lion and the Unicorn* 25.3 (2001): 353–74.

Tomasulo, Frank P. "The Gospel According to Speilberg in *E.T." The Extra-Terrestrial." Quarterly Review of Film and Video* 18.3 (2001): 273–82.

Torres, Pat. "Interested in Writing about Indigenous Australians?" *Australian Author* 26.3 (1994): 24–25, 30.

Trites, Roberta Seelinger. "Manifold Narratives: Metafiction and Ideology in Picture Books." *Children's Literature in Education* 25.4 (1994): 225–42.

Turner, Stephen. "A Legacy of Colonialism: The Uncivil Society of Aotearoa/New Zealand." *Cultural Studies* 13.3 (1999): 408–22.

Viswanathan, Gauri. *Masks of Conquest: Literary Study and British Rule in India.* New York: Columbia University Press, 1989.

Weaver, Jace. *That the People Might Live: Native American Literatures and Native American Community.* New York and Oxford: Oxford University Press, 1997.

Whitehall, Geoffrey. "The Problem of the 'World and Beyond': Encountering 'The Other' in Science Fiction." In *To Seek Out New Worlds: Exploring Links between Science Fiction and World Politics,* ed. Jutta Weldes, 169–93. New York: Palgrave Macmillan, 2003.

Whitlock, Gillian. "A 'White-Souled State': Across the South with Lady Barker." In *Text, Theory, Space: Land, Literature and History in South Africa and Australia,* ed. Kate Darian-Smith, L. Gunner, and S. Nuttall, 65–80. London and New York: Routledge, 1996.

Wilson, James. *The Earth Shall Weep: A History of Native America.* New York: Atlantic Monthly Press, 1999.

Wolfe, Patrick. *Settler Colonialism and the Transformation of Anthropology.* London and New York: Cassell, 1999.

Womack, Craig S. *Red on Red: Native American Literary Separatism.* Minneapolis: University of Minnesota Press, 1999.

Wrightson, Patricia. "Ever Since My Accident: Aboriginal Folklore and Australian Fantasy." *Horn Book* 56.6 (1980): 609–17.

Wyss, Hilary E. "Captivity and Conversion." *American Indian Quarterly* 23.3–4 (1999): 63–82.

Young-Ing, Greg. "Aboriginal Text in Context." In *(Ad)dressing Our Words: Aboriginal Perspectives on Aboriginal Literatures*, ed. Armand Garnet Ruffo, 233–42. Penticton, BC: Theytus, 2001.

Ziff, Bruce, and Pratima V. Rao, eds. *Borrowed Power: Essays on Cultural Appropriation*. New Brunswick, NJ: Rutgers University Press, 1997.

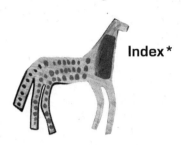

# Index*